Superpowering India

SUPERPOWERING INDIA

Capt.(IN) Komal Malik

Dr. Bimal Chandra Kumar

PRASHANT PUBLISHING HOUSE
DELHI-110094

Published by :
Prashant Publishing House
C-34, 28 Foota Road, Gali-3,
West Karwal Nagar, Delhi-110094
Phone : 011-22963970, Mob. : 9810396373
e-mail.: prashantpublishinghouse@gmail.com

Superpowering India

First Published 2016

ISBN 978-93-80565-69-9

PRINTED IN INDIA
Published by Mr. R.K. Jha M/s Prashant Publishing House and Published at H.S. Offset House Press, Delhi.

Contents

	Preface	*(vii)*
1.	India as an Emerging Superpower	1
2.	Rising Military Super Power of India	44
3.	India: Making of Superpower	81
4.	Challenges of Foreign Policy and Super Power in India	96
5.	India: the Emerging Asian Super Power	147
6.	Globalization of Indian Economic Power	156
7.	India's Superpower Delusions	188
8.	Management of Security Chellenges for Super Power	209
9.	Modi Make India a Global Superpower	263
10.	India: The Next Solar Superpower	282
	Bibliography	293
	Index	295

Preface

India is a natural super power kept under leash by colonial control exercised through native leaders. Superpowering India, in nine chapters filled with massive unassailable data, rips open the veneer of socialism to show that the ugliest phase of capitalism is continuing in India for benefit of the elite, in violation of even the inappropriate Indian constitution. In rationality, morality, ethical and religious value systems, Superpowering India treads the path avoided by authorities on welfare economics in the last one hundred years.

A potential superpower is a state or a political and economic entity that is speculated to be, or is in the process of becoming, a superpower at some point during the 21st century. Presently, only the United States fulfills the criteria to be considered a superpower. India become a super power in modern world. Predictions about potential superpower have been made in the past, but they have not been perfect. States most commonly mentioned as being potential superpowers are China, India, the European Union, Russia and Brazil. Collectively, these potential superpowers (and the United States) comprise 68.0% of global nominal GDP, 62.4% of global GDP (PPP), more than one third of the total land area and more than 50% of the world's population. Many have compared India's pattern of growth to its neighbor, China.

The countries have much in common—physical borders, immense populations, similar challenges, ancient civilizations, and quickly-rising economies. India also measures itself against China, coveting its economic power and international standing, including its permanent seat on the United Nations Security Council. The independent India and the leaders who shaped its destiny in the second half of the twentieth century have drawn much on India rich heritage to foster relations with and have fruitfully intervened in the international affairs of the modern world.

The Indian Armed Forces, India's main defence organisation, consists of two main branches: the core Military of India and the Indian Paramilitary Forces. The Military of India maintains thethird largest active duty force in the world after China and the United States, while theIndian Paramilitary Forces, over a million strong, is the second largest paramilitary force in the world. Combined, the total armed forces of India are 2,414,700 strong, the world's third largestdefence force.

India's neighbours occupy much of its attention in its overall foreign policy dilemmas. Except Bhutan and Maldives, India is facing security challenges from all its neighbours. Most of these challenges are traditional in nature; however non-traditional challenges such as environmental issue are also prominently emerging in their security discourse. The foreign policy strategy of India is fundamentally aimed to protect its core national interests; safeguarding territorial integrity and sovereignty, and economic prosperity. Ensuring these interests has been the principal foreign policy agenda for successive governments post-independence. Though the tools and approach used to achieve the desired foreign policy objectives have varied.

The book has taken in its ambit all aspects, segments and organs of the state to establish conclusively that delinquencies of high constitutional authorities with debilitated military have been effective instrument of torture for control over the country.

—*Editor*

1

India as an Emerging Superpower

The Republic of India is considered as one of the possible emerging superpowers of the world.This potential is attributed to several indicators, the primary ones being its demographic trends and a rapidly expanding economy and by GDP India became world's fastest growing economy in 2015 with 7.3% GDP rate. country must overcome many of the economic, social, and political problems before it can be considered a superpower. It is also not yet influential on the international stage as compared to the United States or the former Soviet Union.

POINTS AGAINST THE RISE OF INDIA AS A SUPERPOWER

Political obstacles

Cost of democratic republicanism

Democratic republicanism has its value, more so in a multi-ethnic country like India. However, the applicability of the "theoretical" virtues of republicanism on a country like India is sometimes questioned. Some thinkers consider India's diverse democracy to levy a huge tax on its economy. The Indian government has to consider many interest groups before decision making. However, it should be noted that India is relatively a much younger republic when compared to other major democracies. Moreover, it is predicted that in the long run, India being a democracy will provide it an edge over non-democratic competitors like China.

Insurgency

India has had significant successes with quelling many insurgencies, most prominently the Punjab insurgency (Khalistan) and the surrender of large sections of insurgent outfits like the United Liberation Front of Asom in 1992 and National Liberation Front of Tripura in 2000-2001. However the Indian government has acknowledged that there has been a dramatic increase in support for the Maoists(Naxalite) insurgency in the last decade. Maoist rebels have increased their influence over the last 10 years, especially in regions near Nepal, particularly by targeting and gaining support from poor villages in India. The boom in support appears to have been also boosted by the successes of the nearly 10-year-old Maoist rebellion in Nepal. The maoist insurgency exploits the poor by forced conscription. India's government has recently taken a new stance on the Maoist insurgency, pulling the affected states together to coordinate their response. It says it will combine improved policing with socio-economic measures to defuse grievances that fuel the Maoist cause.

Disputes

India's growth is impeded by disputes with its neighboring China and Pakistan (over historical border and ideological issues) and disputes with Bangladesh (over water availability and the Farakka Dam). Hence, India's neighbors such as China and Pakistan remain distrustful towards India. It is also occasionally burdened with instability issues within some localised-regions of the subcontinent. In an effort to reduce political tension and increase economic cooperation, in recent years, India has improved its relations with its neighbors.

Lack of international representation

India is not a permanent member of the UNSC, although currently it is one of the four-nations group actively seeking a permanent seat in the council. Thus India lacks the ability to extend its influence or ideas on international events in the way superpowers do.

Economic obstacles

Poverty

As of 2011, approximately 21.9% of India's population lived below poverty line. Poverty also begets child labour. Various reforms, including mass employment schemes have been undertaken by the government to tackle this problem, and India has been quite successful in reducing its share of poverty. The number of people living on $1 a day is expected to fall in South Asia from 41.5 per cent in 1990 to 16.4 per cent until 2015. However, the issue of poverty in India is not fully resolved. There is consensus among economists that overall poverty in India has declined, the extent of poverty reduction is often debated. The economic reforms of the early 1990s were followed by rates of high economic growth. Its effect on poverty remain controversial, and the official numbers published by the Government of India, showing a reduction of poverty from 36% (1993–94) to 26% (1999 – 00), to 22% (2004–05), have been challenged both for allegedly showing too little and too much poverty reduction.

While there is a consensus on the fact that liberalization has led to a reduction of income poverty, the picture is not so clear if one considers other non-pecuniary dimensions (such as health, education, crime and access to infrastructure). With the rapid economic growth that India is experiencing, it is likely that a significant fraction of the rural population will continue to migrate toward cities, making the issue of urban poverty more significant in the long run.

Economist Pravin Visaria has defended the validity of many of the statistics that demonstrated the reduction in overall poverty in India. He insisted that the 1999-2000 survey was well designed and supervised, and he further defended that just because the numbers did not appear to fit preconceived notions about poverty in India, they should not be dismissed outright. Nicholas Stern, vice president of the World Bank, has published defenses of the poverty reduction statistics. He argues that increasing globalization and investment opportunities have contributed significantly to the reduction of poverty in the country. India, has shown one of the clearest co-relation trends of globalization with the accelerated rise in per-capita income.

Infrastructure

The social infrastructure in India such as roads, power grid, water, communications infrastructure, housing and education are often below standards, and not catching up with the tune of its economic progress. Continued poor infrastructure might serve as a bottleneck to further economic development. The 2012 India blackouts, which affected millions, was a result of such problems. The government is, however, improving the infrastructure, such as expanding the freeway and highway system and bringing it up to global standards. As of 2005, India only had 4,885 km of central-divided expressways, while the U.S. and China have 90,000 km and 41,000 km of expressways, respectively.

Disorganization

India's continual economic prosperity is also hindered by bad governance and ubiquitous red tape ('Bureaucratic Raj'). Retrogressive government regulations affect many areas. For example, in some states, black outs and power rationing are common due to underinvestment, differing state and local regulations, etc.

Inflation and overheating

Despite India's growth spurt of 8% p.a. in recent years, its sustainable pace is still much lower than China's, which puts its economy more at risk of overheating and rising inflation. The Reserve Bank of India (RBI) has acknowledged the risk of overheating and has been tightening monetary policy steadily. It is debatable whether this alone will be sufficient to ease inflationary pressures.

The economy is running near or above capacity, and the RBI has noted that production must rise at a pace sufficient to match overall GDP growth if further inflationary pressures are to be avoided. The Indian government has said that much of the rise in inflation recently can be attributed to short-term supply constraints, such as a shortage of key foodstuffs thanks to an erratic summer monsoon.

Energy dependence and costs

India heavily depends on foreign oil - a phenomenon likely to continue until non-fossil/renewable energy technology becomes economically viable in the country. To avert an energy crisis, India is desperately seeking alternate means of energy. India can sustain its growth to higher trajectories only by the co-operation of other countries. As for now, India is energetically expensive since India has to import over 70% of its energy, thus making costs of comforts - like personal car or even air conditioning - extremely high. It is however, steadily combating its energy issues.

Unemployment

Unless India finds a quick way to generate jobs, its population of unemployed youths could be a reason of unstability. India's growth in the services sector and Information Technology sector has not been matched by growth in manufacturing which can provide more jobs.Some claim that this sector may lose importance in the future. India is leveraging on new sectors like the KPO (Knowledge Process Outsourcing).

Health

India's health scenario is dismal with diseases and malnutrition constantly affecting the poorest quarter of the populace.Mortality is still relatively high and the bane of AIDS is spreading quickly. According to a report of United Nations Development Programme, India has the highest population living with AIDS/HIV and its economy might suffer a setback if it does not check the problem of the virus' spread.

It is estimated that India's economic growth will decline by 0.86 percentage annually if the AIDS problem is not properly dealt with. To improve the situation, a number of projects such as the building of hospital chains (like the Apollo Hospitals, amongst others) has laid the foundation for a health system that matches global standards. However, these hospitals are sometimes used by foreigners as a cheap yet effective source of health services and much remains to be done for India's very poor.

Low literacy

As per the 2001 India census, India's national literacy is only 65.2 percent. Literacy drive is spreading slowly to other states. India's youth (age 15 to 24) literacy rate was 76.4% between 2000 and 2004. At current rates India will take no less than 20 years for a literacy of 95%. Literacy in India is not homogeneous, some states in India have more impressive literacy rates than others. Kerala, a south-Indian state widely recognized as the most well-educated state in India, recorded an impressive 90.92% literacy rate in 2001. On the other hand, the north-Indian state of Bihar lags behind with 47.53%. India's adult literacy rates (61.3% in 2002), is just a little better compared to other nations in South Asia except Sri Lanka's 92%, with Nepal next at 44%, Pakistan at 41.5% and Bangladesh the lowest at 41.1%.

Climate and environmental problems

The majority of India lies in the tropical climate zone, which may have a negative impact on its agricultural and overall economic development. The climate thesis of economic development was first argued by Adam Smith and recently by David Landes in his *The Wealth and Poverty of Nations*.

Tropical areas generally average enough rainfall, but the timing is often irregular and unpredictable. The rain drops are large and the rate of fall often torrential. One answer to irregular moisture is storage and irrigation, but this is countered in these regions by incredibly high rates of evaporation. In the Agra region of India, for example, rainfall exceeds the needs of local agriculture for only two months in the year, and the excess held in the soil in those wet months dries up in only three weeks.Tropical zones are also more prone to endemic water-borne and parasitic diseases such as cholera and malaria.

As a result of climate change, the Gangotri Glacier, among others, is receding. Also, of the 3 million premature deaths in the world that occur each year due to outdoor and indoor air pollution, the highest number are assessed to occur in India.

Social issues

Communal violence

India has a diverse mix of various religions and races. The majority are Hindus by religion, followed by Muslims, Sikhs, Christians, Jains,Buddhists, Bahaii and many more. Though most religions in India have been practising religious tolerance in their histories, the partition and subsequent terrorism had created some degree of uneasiness among some. The uneducated masses of these various groups sometimes get at odds with one another. However, in recent years, relations between the different religious groups have considerably changed for better. For instance, a real chunk of India's celebrities - sporting legends, film stars, industrialists, artists, politicians, scientists, head-of-state, etc. - have come from various non-majority roots, representing the emerging face of new diverse India.

Social divide

The problem of India's social divide is often linked to its millennia-old caste system. In an attempt to eliminate the caste system, the Indian government has introduced special quotas for low-caste Indians in educational institutions and jobs. The measure is with the motive of helping lower-caste Indians to pursue higher education and thereby elevate their standard of life. However, the system is often criticised about its effectiveness as so called creamy layer (rich among the lower caste) get non-needed advantage & leave other lower caste groups poor only. There also have been cases of reverse-discrimination and persecution of upper castes by lower castes.

FACTORS IN FAVOUR

Geographic factors

Location

India, the 7th largest nation by area, lies at the north-central region of Indian Ocean - a zone with unprecedented potential for growth in the scale of transoceanic commerce, with many Eurasian and increasingly Afro-Asian sea-trade routes passing through or close to Indianterritorial waters. The subcontinent's land and water resources, though strained, is yet sustaining its massive population. According to George Curzon, 1st Marquess Curzon of Kedleston of the British Empire:

The central position of India, its magnificent resources, its teeming multitude of men, its great trading harbors, its reserve of military strength, supplying an army always in a high state of efficiency and capable of being hurled at a moment's notice upon any point either of Asia or Africa—all these are assets of precious value.

On the West, India must exercise a predominant influence over the destinies of Persia and Afghanistan; on the north, it can veto any rival in Tibet; on the north-east . . . it can exert great pressure upon China, and it is one of the guardians of the autonomous existence of Siam. Possession of India gave the British Empire its global reach.

Possible Future Advantage of Location

Energy

In the future, the world is expected to exit the "fossil fuel age", and perhaps the "nuclear energy age", and enter the *"renewable-energy age"* or even further into the *"fusion power age"*, if and whenever these technologies become economically sustainable. Being a region in thesunny tropical belt, the Indian subcontinent could greatly benefit from a renewable energy trend, as it has the ideal combination of both - high solar insolation and a big consumer base density.

For example, considering the costs of energy consumed for temperature control (a major factor influencing a region's energy intensity) and the fact that - cooling load requirements, unlike heating, are roughly in phase with the sun's intensity, cooling from the excessive solar radiation could make great energetic (and hence economic) sense in the subcontinent, whenever the required technology becomes competitively cheaper. India also has 25% of the world's thorium resources.

Demographic factors

High population

India has the world's second largest population. The PGR for the country is 1.25. A very large number of India's population, consisting of 50% of the whole, are below the age group of 24. This provides the nation with a large workforce for many decades, helping in its growth.The government is training a 400 million-workforce, which is larger than the population of theUnited States and Brazil combined.

Young population

Due to its high birth rate India has a young population compared to most aging nations. It has approximately 65% of its population below the age of 35. In addition, declining fertility is beginning to reduce the youth dependency rate which may produce a demographic dividend. In the coming decades, while some of the powerful nations will witness a decrease in workforce numbers, India is expected to have an increase. For example, whileEurope is well past its demographic window, the United States entered its own in 1970 (lasting until 2015), China entered its own in 1990 (and will last until 2025), India would not enter its own window until 2010 (and it will last until 2050). Regionally, South Asia is supposed to maintain the youngest demographic profile after Africa and the Middle East, with the window extending up to the 2070s.

Global diaspora

More than 35 million Indians live across the globe. Under fair opportunities, they have become socio-economically successful.

Foreign language skills

The importance of the English language in the 21st century is a topic of debate, nonetheless the growing pool of non-native English speakers makes it the best contender for "Global language" status. Incidentally, India has the world's largest Englishspeaking/ understanding population. It claims one of the largest workforce of engineers, doctors and other key professionals, all comfortable with English. It has the 2nd largest population of "fluent English" speakers, second only to the United States, with estimates ranging from 150 to 250 million speakers, and is expected to have the largest in coming decades. Indians are also learningDutch, Italian, Japanese, Korean, Mandarin Chinese, Russian, and Spanish.

Political factors

The BRICS leaders in 2014. Left to right:Putin, Modi, Rousseff, Xi and Zuma.

Democratic republicanism

India is the world's largest democratic republic, more than three times bigger than the next largest (the United States). It has so far been successful politically, especially considering its functionality despite its difficult ethnic composition. The fact that India is a democracyhas improved its relations with other democratic nations and significantly improved its ties with the majority of the nations in the developed world.

Candidacy for Security Council

India has been pressing for permanent membership of the United Nations Security Council (as part of the G4 nations) but with a clause that it won't exercise its veto for the next 15 years. It has received backing from France, Russia, and the United Kingdom.However, China and the United States have not been supportive of the bid. With improvedIndia–United States relations, the United States is expected by some to reconsider its stand.

As of 2016,India is said to have receive support from all the five permanent members of United Nations Security Council for its candidacy.

Foreign relations

India has developed relationships with the world powers like the European Union, Japan,Russia, and the United States. It also developed relationships with the African Union (particularly South Africa), the Arab World,Southeast Asia, Israel and South American nations (particularly Brazil). In order to make the environment favourable for economic growth, India is investing on its relations with China. It has significantly boosted its image among Western nations and signed a civilian nuclear deal with the United States in March 2006. It is also working for better relationships with Pakistan.

Role in international politics

Historically, India was one of the founding members of Non-Aligned Movement, and had good relationships with Soviet Union and other parts of western world. It played regional roles in South Asian affairs, e.g. its use of the Indian Peace Keeping Force in the Bangladesh Liberation War and in Sri Lanka.

It took a leading initiative to improve relations between African and Asian countries. India is an active member of the Commonwealth and the WTO.

The evolving economic integration politics in the West and in Asia is influencing the Indian mood to slowly swing in favour of integration with global economy. Currently, India's political moves are being influenced by economic imperatives.

New Delhi is also being observed to slowly, cautiously, and often hesitantly, step into the unchartered role of becoming one of the two major seats of political power in Asia, the other being at Beijing. Some enlightened thinkers from the subcontinent have also envisioned, over the long run, of a South Asian version of free trade zone and even a Union, where the South Asian nations relinquish all past animosities and move to make economic growth a pan subcontinental phenomenon.

Multipolarity

A new and highly controversial geopolitical strategy, being debated in the West, is whether India should be trusted/helped to become an economically strong democratic citizen of the world and be used to balance the powerful but non-democratic forces, to insure a more stable world. Generally speaking it is discussed in the context of adopting a policy of offshore balancing on the part of the United States. A new American strategy towards India has been indicated in George W. Bush's recent visit to the subcontinent.

Economic growth

India's current economic growth (as the world's fastest-growing major economy as of 2015) has improved its standing on the world's political stage, even though it is still a developing country, but one that is showing strong development. Many nations are moving to forge better relationships with India.

Economic factors

Booming economy

The economy of India is currently the world's third largest in terms of real GDP (PPP) after the USA and the People's Republic of China.

The World Bank estimates India to overtake China as the fastest-growing major economy in the world in 2015 Its record growth was in the third quarter of 2003, when it grew higher than any other emerging economy at 10.4%.Interestingly, estimates by the IMF show that in 2011, India became the third largest economy in the world, overtaking the Japanese economy and the Seventh largest economy by GDP (Nominal). India is expected to grow at 7.5% in 2015.

Primary sector

India, growing at 9% per year, is the world's second largest producer of food next to China. Food processing accounts for USD 69.4 billion as gross income.

Secondary sector

India is still relatively a small player in manufacturing when compared to many world leaders. Some new trends suggest an improvement in future, since the manufacturing sector is growing at 11-12%.

Tertiary and quaternary sector

India currently has an expanding IT industry which is considered one of the best in the world. Some have begun to describe India as a*technology superpower*. It is considered the World's Office and is leading in the Services Industry. This is mainly due to the availability of a large pool of highly skilled, low cost, English speaking workforce.

Science and technology

India is trying to develop more high skilled, English speaking people to fit in the futureknowledge economy. India is becoming one of the world's leading producers of computer software and with mushrooming R&D centres it is experiencing a steady revolution in science and technology. A typical example of India's rising scientific endeavours is that it was the 3rd nation to found a National Space Agency called ISRO, after the USSR and the U.S.

It was the third Asian nation to send satellites into space after China and Japan in 1970, starting with Aryabhata in 1975. In January 2007, India became the fourth nation to completeatmospheric reentry In October 2008, India launched its first unmanned lunar probe,Chandrayaan 1, which operated until August 2009.

On 14 November 2008, the Moon Impact Probe separated from the Chandrayaan orbiter at 20:06 and was deliberately made to strike the Moon near the south pole, making India the fourth country to reach the Moon's surface. Among its many achievements was the discovery of the widespread presence of water molecules in lunar soil. On 24 September 2014 India became the fourth nation to have a satellite orbiting Mars.

India is the first Asian nation to achieve this and the first to do so in its first try. India and the United States have increased mutual cooperation in space-travel related technologies, such as increasing the interoperability between Indian and US systems, and prospects for a commercial space launch agreement with India that would allow US satellites to be launched on Indian vehicles. India is among the world leaders in remote sensing, a technology coming to great use, among others, to Indian fishermen & farmers. India is also trying to join international R&D projects - e.g. it has recently joined the European Galileo GPS Project and the ITER for fusion energy club. Some Indian educational and research institutions like IIT, NIT, BITS Pilani, IIM, IISc, TIFR and AIIMS are among the world's best.

Energy

To reduce the energy crisis, India is presently constructing ~ 9 civilian nuclear power reactors and several hydro-power stations. On 25 January 2007, Russian president Vladimir Putin offered to build 4 more reactors on a visit to India and India is expected to clinch this deal of strategical importance. Recently it also made a civilian nuclear energy deal with the US and EU. In recent years, India joined China to launch a vigorous campaign to acquire oil fields around the world and now has stake in several oil fields (in the Middle East and Russia).

Mass transit system

India is in the process of developing modern mass rapid transit systems to replace its existing system which is seen as inadequate to cater to present and future urban requirements. A modern metro rail system is already in place in the cities of Delhi, Mumbai, Chennai andKolkata. Work is in progress or would be commencing shortly for developing similar mass transit system in cities of NOIDA, Hyderabad, Bangalore, Indore, Ahmedabad and Kochi. Indoreis leading the track by implementing world class GPS enabled, low floor buses in a Rapid Transport System. With growth in economy and technology, India is welcoming modernisation. The Indian rail network traverses the length and breadth of the country, covering a total length of 63,140 km (39,200 miles). It is one of the largest and busiest rail networks in the world, transporting over 9 billion passengers and over 350 million tonnes of freight annually. Its operations covers twenty-seven states and three Union territories and also links the neighbouring countries of Nepal, Bangladesh and Pakistan. However, other public transport systems, such as buses are often not up to the standards followed in developed countries. India is heading to wards high-speed rail in the country.

Tourism

India, with its diverse and fascinating history, arts, music, culture, spiritual & social models has witnessed the growth of a booming tourism industry. India is a historic place with a diverse history of over five millennia. About 3.9 million tourists travelled to India in 2005, each spending approximately $1,470 per person, higher than that of France (the leading tourist destination in the world). Foreign visitors in 2005 spent more than US $15.4 billion annually in India. Many travellers find the cultural diversity an enriching experience, despite the hassles inefficiency, pollution and overcrowding. Monuments like the Taj Mahal are among the many attractions of this land. As of 2006, Conde Nast Traveller ranked India the 4th most preferred travel destination. The Planning Commission expects 5.8 million tourists travelling to India by 2010. The World Travel and Tourism Council believes India's tourism industry will grow at 10% per annum in the next decade, making it lead the world in terms of growth. Tourism contributes 6% of India's GDP and employed 40 million people, making it an important factor in India's economic growth.

Medical services

"First World medical services at Third World prices" - Indian Metros have emerged as the leading destination of medical tourism. Last year, an estimated 150,000 foreigners visited India for medical procedures, and the number is increasing at the rate of about 15 percent a year.

Military factors

Soldiers from the Grenadier Regiment during 2015 Moscow Victory Day Parade.

Total strength

The Indian Armed Forces, India's main defence organisation, consists of two main branches: the core Military of India and the Indian Paramilitary Forces. The Military of India maintains thethird largest active duty force in the world after China and the United States, while theIndian Paramilitary Forces, over a million strong, is the second largest paramilitary force in the world. Combined, the total armed forces of India are 2,414,700 strong, the world's third largestdefence force.

Army

The Army of India, as the Indian army was called under

British rule before 1947, played a crucial role in checking the advance of Imperial Japan into South Asia during World War II. It also played a leading role in the liberation of Bangladesh in 1971. Today, the Indian Army is the world's third largest army after United States Army.

Air force

The Indian Air Force is the fourth largest air force in the world. India recently inducted its second indigenously manufactured combat aircraft. India is also developing the fifth generation stealth aircraft.

Navy

The Indian Navy is the world's fifth largest navy. It is considered to have blue-watercapabilities with sophisticated missile-capable warships, aircraft carrier, minesweepers, advanced submarines and the latest aircraft in its inventory, along with a significant use of state of the art technology that is indigenously manufactured. It operates two aircraft carriers and also plans to induct the INS Vikrant by 2018 followed by a larger INS Vishal.

Integrated Guided Missile Development Program (IGMDP)

India started the IGMDP to be a self-reliant nation in missile development. The IGMDP program includes five missiles like the Prithvi and Agni of ballistic missiles, surface to air missiles Trishul and Akash and also the anti tank Nag missile. Prithvi and Agni missiles are inducted into the armed forces and form the basis of Indian nuclear second strike capability. Trishul missile is declared a technology demonstrator. The Akash (Sky) is in service with the Indian Army and the Indian Air Force. While Nag and Helina missiles are undergoing user trials. Recently, a new weapons system, the beyond visual range air-to-air Astra missile was added to the project. Also India has fielded many modern missiles like the anti ballistic missiles like theAAD and PAD along with submarine launched ballistic missiles for its Arihant class of nuclear ballistic submarines. The expertise in developing these missiles has helped Indian scientists to contribute to joint weapon development programs like the Brahmos and Barak-II. India is also developing long range cruise missiles similar to the Tomahawk class of missiles called Nirbhay. There are reports of India developing an intercontinental ballistic missile beyond the range of ten thousand kilometers. India is self-reliant in missile technology.

Nuclear weapons

India has possessed nuclear weapons since 1974, when it did the Pokharan I nuclear tests, and the means to deliver them over long distances. However, India is not a signatory to theNuclear Non-Proliferation Treaty (on grounds of security concerns and that India condemns the NPT as discriminatory).

Arms imports

India is currently one of the world's largest arms importers, spending an estimated US$16.97 billion in 2004. India has made military technology deals with the Russian Federation, the U.S., Israel and the EU.

Current major roles

The Indian Armed Forces plays a crucial role in anti-terrorist activities and maintaining law and order in the disputed Kashmir region. India has also participated in several United Nations peace-keeping missions, currently being the largest contributor to UN peace keeping force and is the largest contributor to the United Nations Democratic Fund, to which the USA, the world's only current superpower, contributes nothing.

Cultural factors

History

India is one of two ancient civilizations, dating back to at least 5000 years, which have stood the test of time and survived against all odds. Indians invented the numbering system (introduced into the West by Arabic mathematicians, Arabic numerals), the concept of zero, basic algebra, etc. India has a long history of cultural intercourse with many regions of the world, especially within Asia, where its cultural influence has spread through the philosophy of religions like Buddhism, Hinduism, Sikhism, etc. - particularly in East and Southeast Asia. Many religions with origins outside the Indian continent - Islam, Christianity, Judaism, Zoroastrianism, Bahá'í Faith - have found followers in India. Indian culture has spread to foreign lands through wandering traders, philosophers, migration and less through conquest. According to Chinese ambassador to the United States, Hu Shih:

India conquered and dominated China culturally for 20 centuries without ever having to send a single soldier across her border. - Hu Shih

Past experience of having powerful states

The Maurya, Gupta, Mughal, Vijayanagara and Chola empires provide the necessary confidence that a powerful state can be established despite having diversity.

Cinema

India's film industry produces more feature films than any other. In a year, it sold 3.6 billion tickets, more than any other film industry in the world (In comparison, Hollywood sold 2.6 billion tickets). The cinemas play a major role in spreading Indian culture worldwide. Indian cinema transcended its boundaries from the days of film Awara, a great hit in Russia. Bollywood films are seen in central and west Asia. Indian films have also found audience in eastern societies. India's film industry is now becoming increasingly popular in Western society, with Bollywood festivals occurring numerous cities and Bollywood dance groups performing in New Years Eve celebrations, treatment which other non-English film industries generally do not receive.

Unity in diversity of world view

India has a multi-ethnic, multi-lingual and multi-religious society living together. The subcontinent's long and diverse history has given it a unique eclectic culture. It is often associated with spirituality. Thanks to its history of both indigenous and foreign influences - like the ancient Indian religions (Buddhism, Hinduism, Jainism and Sikhism and the ancient Middle East Asian schools of thought (Abrahamic - Islam, Christianity, Judaism etc.) - the current Indian civilizational psyche is evolving into a complex mix of them - sometimes a superposition of religious philosophies with acceptance of the conflicting cosmologies, sometimes striking a middle ground, and sometimes taking the practical attitude - popular with the young - of "filtering the common best, and leaving the rest", thus leading to the creation of many syncretic mix of faiths (such as Sai Baba of Shirdi). Since Independence, India has regained its more progressive schools of thought, like -democracy, secularism, rule of law, esteem for human rights, rational deductive reasoning, development of Science and Technology, etc. - are making slow but steady inroads into the collective modern Indian psyche. India's diversity forces it to evolve strong foundations oftolerance and pluralism, or face breakup. The Indian public is now also accepting modern western influences in their society and media - and what is emerging is a confluence of its past local culture with the new western culture ("Social Globalisation"). For some futuristicsocial thinkers, the miscegenation of diverse ancient culture with modernity, spirituality with science/technology, Eastern with Western world-view is potentially making India a social laboratory for the evolution of futuristic global-unity consciousness.

INDIA AND THE BALANCE OF POWER

After disappointing itself for decades, India is now on the verge of becoming a great power. The world started to take notice of India's rise when New Delhi signed a nuclear pact with President George W. Bush in July 2005, but that breakthrough is only one dimension of the dramatic transformation of Indian foreign policy that has taken place since the end of the Cold War. After more than a half century of false starts and unrealized potential, India is now emerging as the swing state in the global balance of power. In the coming years, it will have an opportunity to shape outcomes on the most critical issues of the twenty-first century: the construction of Asian stability, the political modernization of the greater Middle East, and the management of globalization.

Although India's economic growth, its new foreign policy has been less noted. Unlike their U.S. counterparts, Indian leaders do not announce new foreign policy doctrines. Nonetheless, in recent years, they have worked relentlessly to elevate India's regional and international standing and to increase its power. New Delhi has made concerted efforts to reshape its immediate neighborhood, find a modus vivendi with China and Pakistan (its two regional rivals), and reclaim its standing in the "near abroad": parts of Africa, the Persian Gulf, Central and Southeast Asia, and the Indian Ocean region. At the same time, it has expanded relations with the existing great powers — especially the United States.

India is arriving on the world stage as the first large, economically powerful, culturally vibrant, multiethnic, multireligious democracy outside of the geographic West. As it rises, India has the potential to become a leading member of the "political West" and to play a key role in the great political struggles of the next decades. Whether it will, and how soon, depends above all on the readiness of the Western powers to engage India on its own terms.

Three Strategic Circles

India's grand strategy divides the world into three concentric circles. In the first, which encompasses the immediate neighborhood, India has sought primacy and a veto over the actions of outside powers. In the second, which encompasses the so-called extended neighborhood stretching across Asia and the Indian Ocean littoral, India has sought to balance the influence of other powers and prevent them from undercutting its interests. In the third, which includes the entire global stage, India has tried to take its place as one of the great powers, a key player in international peace and security.

Three things have historically prevented India from realizing these grand strategic goals. First, the partition of the South Asian subcontinent along religious lines (first into India and Pakistan, in 1947, then into India, Pakistan, and Bangladesh, in 1971) left India with a persistent conflict with Pakistan and an internal Hindu-Muslim divide. It also physically separated India from historically linked states such as Afghanistan, Iran, and the nations of Southeast Asia. The creation of an avowedly Islamic state in Pakistan caused especially profound problems for India's engagement with the Middle East. Such tensions intertwined with regional and global great-power rivalries to severely constrict India's room for maneuver in all three concentric circles.

The second obstacle was the Indian socialist system, which caused a steady relative economic decline and a consequent loss of influence in the years after independence. The state-socialist model led India to shun commercial engagement with the outside world. As a result, India was disconnected from its natural markets and culturally akin areas in the extended neighborhood.

Finally, the Cold War, the onset of which quickly followed India's independence, pushed India into the arms of the Soviet Union in response to Washington's support for Pakistan and China — and thus put the country on the losing side of the great political contest of the second half of the twentieth century. Despite being the largest democracy in the world, India ended up siding with the opposite camp on most global issues.

The last decade of the twentieth century liberated India from at least two of these constraints; state socialism gave way to economic liberalization and openness to globalization, and the Cold War ended. Suddenly, New Delhi was free to reinvent its foreign policy — positioning itself to face the rise of China, shifting its strategic approach to its other neighbours, and beginning to work closely with the world's existing great powers.

Varieties Of Influence

India's recent embrace of openness and globalization has had an especially dramatic effect on the country's role in the region. As the nations of the subcontinent jettison their old socialist agendas, India is well positioned to promote economic integration. Although the pace has been relatively slow, the process has begun to gain traction. The planned implementation of the South Asian Free Trade Agreement this summer signals the coming reintegration of the subcontinent's markets, which constituted a single economic space until 1947.

At the same time, optimism on the economic front must be tempered by an awareness of the problematic political developments in India's smaller neighbours. The struggle for democracy and social justice in Nepal, interminable political violence and the rise of Islamic extremism in Bangladesh, and the simmering civil war in Sri Lanka underscore the potential dangers of failing states on the subcontinent. There are also the uncertain futures of Pakistan and Afghanistan: defeating religious extremism and creating modern and moderate states in both countries is of paramount importance to India. A successful Indian strategy for promoting peace and prosperity within the region would require preventing internal conflicts from undermining regional security, as well as resolving India's own conflicts with its neighbours.

In the past, great-power rivalries, as well as India's own tensions with Pakistan and China, have complicated New Delhi's effort to maintain order in the region. Today, all of the great powers, including the United States and China, support the Indian objective of promoting regional economic integration. The Bush administration has also started to defer to Indian leadership on regional security issues. Given the new convergence of U.S. and Indian interests in promoting democracy and countering extremism and terrorism, New Delhi no longer suspects Washington of trying to undercut its influence in the region. As a result, it is more prepared than ever to work with the United States and other Western powers to pursue regional goals.

Meanwhile, the external environment has never been as conducive as it is today to the resolution of the Indo-Pakistani conflict over Kashmir. The conflict has become less and less relevant to India's relations with the great powers, which has meant a corresponding willingness on New Delhi's part to work toward a solution. Of particular importance has been the steady evolution of the U.S. position on Kashmir since the late 1990s.

The support extended by President Bill Clinton to India in its limited war with Pakistan in 1999 removed the perception that Washington would inevitably align with Islamabad in regional conflicts. But India remained distrustful of the Clinton administration's hyperactive, prescriptive approach to Kashmir. It has been more comfortable with the low-key methods of the Bush administration, which has avoided injecting itself directly into the conflict. The Bush administration has also publicly held Pakistan responsible for cross-border terrorism and has extracted the first-ever assurances from Pakistan to put an end to the attacks. New Delhi does not entirely believe these promises, but it has nonetheless come to trust Washington as a source of positive of influence on Islamabad.

These developments have opened the way for a peace process between the two governments. With the growing awareness that the normalization of relations with Pakistan would end a debilitating conflict and help India's regional and global standing, New Delhi has begun to negotiate seriously for the first time in decades. Although the pace of talks has not satisfied Pakistan, the two sides have agreed on a range of confidence-building measures. Indian Prime Minister Manmohan Singh has rejected the idea of giving up territory, but he has often called for innovative solutions that would improve living conditions and for common institutions that would connect Kashmiris across the Line of Control. Singh has made clear that the Indian leadership is ready to risk political capital on finding a diplomatic solution to Kashmir.

India's recent effort to resolve its long-standing border dispute with China has been just as bold. New Delhi decided in 2003 to seek a settlement with Beijing on a political basis, rather than on the basis of legal or historical claims. As a result, during Chinese Premier Wen Jiabao's visit to New Delhi in April 2005, India and China agreed on a set of principles to guide the final settlement. The two governments are now exploring the contours of mutually satisfactory territorial compromises.

India's search for practical solutions to the disputes over Kashmir and its border with China suggests that the country has finally begun to overcome the obsession with territoriality that has consumed it since its formation. Ironically, the nuclearization of India and Pakistan in 1998 may have helped in this regard: although nuclearization initially sharpened New Delhi's conflicts with both Islamabad and Beijing, it also allowed India to approach its territorial problems with greater self-assurance and pragmatism.

India Unbound

Progress on the resolution of either of these conflicts, especially the one over Kashmir, would liberate India's political and diplomatic energies so that the country could play a larger role in the world. It would also finally release India's armed forces from the constraining mission of territorial defense, allowing them to get more involved in peace and stability operations around the Indian Ocean. Even with all the tensions on the subcontinent, the armies of India, Pakistan, and Bangladesh have been among the biggest contributors to UN peacekeeping operations. The normalization of Indo-Pakistani relations would further free up some of the best armed forces in the world for the promotion of the collective good in the greater Middle East, Africa, and Asia.

Even as the Kashmir and China questions have remained unsettled, India's profile in its extended neighborhood has grown considerably since the early 1990s. India's outward economic orientation has allowed it to reestablish trade and investment linkages with much of its near abroad. New Delhi is negotiating a slew of free- and preferential-trade agreements with individual countries as well as multilateral bodies including the Association of Southeast Asian Nations (ASEAN), the Gulf Cooperation Council (GCC), and the Southern African Development Community. Just as China has become the motor of economic growth in East Asia, a rising India could become the engine of economic integration in the Indian Ocean region.

After decades of being marginalized from regional institutions in different parts of Asia, India is also now a preferred political partner for ASEAN, the East Asian Summit, the GCC, the Shanghai Cooperation Organization, and the African Union. Moreover, it has emerged as a major aid donor; having been an aid recipient for so long, India is now actively leveraging its own external assistance to promote trade as well as political objectives. For example, India has given $650 million in aid to Afghanistan since the fall of the Taliban. Meanwhile, the search for oil has encouraged Indian energy companies to tail their Western and Chinese counterparts throughout the world, from Central Asia and Siberia and to western Africa and Venezuela.

On the security side, India has been actively engaged in defense diplomacy. Thanks to the strength of its armed forces, India is well positioned to assist in stabilizing the Indian Ocean region. It helps that there has been a convergence of U.S. and Indian political interests: countering terrorism, pacifying Islamic radicalism, promoting democracy, and ensuring the security of sea-lanes, to name a few. The Indian navy in particular has been at the cutting edge of India's engagement with the region — as was evident from its ability to deploy quickly to areas hit by the tsunami at the end of 2004. The Indian navy today is also ready to participate in multinational military operations.

Axes And Allies

The end of the Cold War freed India to pursue engagement with all the great powers — but especially the United States. At the start of the 1990s, finding that its relations with the United States, China, Japan, and Europe were all underdeveloped, India moved quickly to repair the situation. Discarding old socialist shibboleths, it began to search for markets for its products and capital to fuel its long-constrained domestic growth. Economic partnerships were easy to construct, and increasing trade flows provided a new basis for stability in India's relations with other major powers. India's emergence as an outsourcing destination and its new prowess in information technology also give it a niche in the world economy — along with the confidence that it can benefit from economic globalization.

Barely 15 years after the collapse of the Soviet Union, India's omnidirectional engagement with the great powers has paid off handsomely. Never before has India had such expansive relations with all the major powers at the same time — a result not only of India's increasing weight in the global economy and its growing power potential, but also of New Delhi's savvy and persistent diplomacy.

The evolution of Sino-Indian ties since the 1990s has been especially important and intriguing. Many see violent conflict between the two rising Asian powers as inevitable. But thanks to New Delhi's policy of actively engaging China since the late 1980s, the tensions that characterized relations between them from the late 1950s through the 1970s have become receding memories. Bilateral trade has boomed, growing from less than $200 million in the early 1990s to nearly $20 billion in 2005. In fact, China is set to overtake the European Union and the United States as India's largest trading partner within a few years. The 3,500-kilometer Sino-Indian border, over which the two countries fought a war in 1962, is now tranquil. And during Wen's visit to India in April 2005, India and China announced a "strategic partnership" — even though just seven years earlier New Delhi had cited concerns over China as a reason for performing nuclear tests, prompting a vicious reaction from Beijing.

India has also cooperated with China in order to neutralize it in conflicts with Pakistan and other smaller neighbours. In the past, China tended to be a free rider on regional security issues, proclaiming noninterference in the internal affairs of other nations while opportunistically befriending regimes in pursuit of its long-term strategic interests. This allowed India's subcontinental neighbours to play the China card against New Delhi when they wanted to resist India's attempts to nudge them toward conflict resolution. But now, Beijing has increasingly avoided taking sides in India's disputes, even as its economic and security profile in the region has grown.

China is not the only Asian power that India is aiming to engage and befriend. Japan has also emerged as an important partner for India, especially since Japanese Prime Minister Junichiro Koizumi has transformed Japanese politics in the last few years. During a visit to New Delhi just a couple of weeks after Wen's in April 2005, Koizumi announced Japan's own "strategic partnership" with India. (This came despite Japan's harsh reaction to India's nuclear test in 1998, which prompted Japanese sanctions and an effort by Tokyo to censure India in the United Nations and other multilateral forums.) Amid growing fears of a rising China and the incipient U.S.-Indian alliance, Japan has elevated India to a key player in its long-term plans for Asian security.

Recognizing the need to diversify its Asian economic portfolio, Tokyo has also, for political reasons, begun to direct some of its foreign investment to India (which has overtaken China as the largest recipient of Japanese development assistance). Since the start of the Bush administration, Japan has also shown increasing interest in expanding military cooperation with India, especially in the maritime domain. India, too, has recognized that it shares with Japan an interest in energy security and in maintaining a stable balance of power in Asia. Japan actively supported India's participation in the inaugural East Asian Summit, in December 2005, despite China's reluctance to include New Delhi. Neither India nor Japan wants to base their political relationship exclusively on a potential threat from China, but both know that deepening their own security cooperation will open up new strategic options and that greater coordination between Asian democracies could limit China's impact.

India's relations with Europe have been limited by the fact that New Delhi is fairly unimpressed with Europe's role in global politics. It senses that Europe and India have traded places in terms of their attitudes toward the United States: while Europe seethes with resentment of U.S. policies, India is giving up on habitually being the first, and most trenchant, critic of Washington. As pessimism overtakes Europe, growing Indian optimism allows New Delhi to support unpopular U.S. policies.

Indians consistently give both the United States and the Bush administration very favorable marks; according to a recent Pew Global Attitudes poll, for example, the percentage of Indians with a positive view of the United States rose from 54 percent in 2002 to 71 percent in 2005. And whereas a declining Europe has tended to be skeptical of India's rise, the Bush administration has been fully sympathetic to India's great-power aspirations.

Still, India does have growing economic and political ties with some European powers. Although many smaller European countries have been critical of the U.S.-Indian nuclear deal, the continent's two nuclear powers, France and the United Kingdom, have been supportive. Paris, in particular, bet long ago (well before Washington did, in fact) that a rising India would provide a good market for high-tech goods; with this in mind, it shielded New Delhi from the ire of the G-8 (the group of eight highly industrialized nations) after India tested nuclear weapons in May 1998.

In the last several years, the United Kingdom has also started to seize economic opportunities in India and has been generally accommodating of New Delhi's regional and global aspirations. In the wake of the Soviet Union's collapse, India also worked to maintain a relationship with Russia. The two states resolved residual issues relating to their old semi-barter rupee-ruble trading arrangements, recast their 1971 peace and friendship treaty, and maintained military cooperation. When President Vladimir Putin succeeded Boris Yeltsin, in 2000, India's waiting game paid off. A newly assertive Moscow was determined to revive and expand its strategic cooperation with India. New Delhi's only problems with Moscow today are the weakening bilateral trade relationship and the risk of Russia's doing too much to strengthen China's military capabilities.

Charm Offensive

At the end of the Cold War, the prospect of India's building a new political relationship with the United States seemed remote. Washington had long favored Pakistan and China in the region, India had in turn aligned itself with the Soviet Union, and a number of global issues seemed to pit the two countries against each other. Yet after the Cold War, India set about wooing the United States. For most of the Clinton administration, this sweet-talking fell on deaf ears, in part because Clinton officials were so focused on the Kashmir dispute and nonproliferation. Clinton, driven by the unshakable assumption that Kashmir was one of the world's most dangerous "nuclear flashpoints" and so needed to be defused, emphasized "preventive diplomacy" and was determined to "cap, roll back, and eventually eliminate" India's nuclear capabilities. Of course, Clinton's approach ran headlong into India's core national security concerns — territorial integrity and preserving its nuclear option. Pressed by Washington to circumscribe its strategic capabilities, New Delhi reacted by testing nuclear weapons.

But even as it faced U.S. sanctions, New Delhi also began to proclaim that India was a natural ally of the United States. Although the Clinton administration was not interested in an alliance, the nuclear tests forced the United States to engage India seriously for the first time in five decades. That engagement did not resolve the nuclear differences, but it did bring Clinton to India in March 200o

— the first American presidential visit to India in 22 years. Clinton's personal charm, his genuine empathy for India, and his unexpected support of India in the 1999 war with Pakistan succeeded in improving the atmospherics of the relations and in putting New Delhi on Washington's radar screen in a new way.

It took Bush, however, to transform the strategic context of U.S.-Indian relations. Convinced that India's influence will stretch far beyond its immediate neighborhood, Bush has reconceived the framework of U.S. engagement with New Delhi. He has removed many of the sanctions, opened the door for high-tech cooperation, lent political support to India's own war on terrorism, ended the historical U.S. tilt toward Pakistan on Kashmir, and repositioned the United States in the Sino-Indian equation by drawing closer to New Delhi.

India has responded to these sweeping changes by backing the Bush administration on missile defense, the International Criminal Court, and finding alternative approaches to confronting global warming. It lent active support to Operation Enduring Freedom in Afghanistan by protecting U.S. assets in transit through the Strait of Malacca in 2002, agreed to work with the United States on multinational military operations outside of the UN framework, and, in 2005 and 2006, voted twice with Washington against Iran — an erstwhile Indian ally — at the International Atomic Energy Agency. India also came close to sending a division of troops to Iraq in the summer of 2003 before pulling back at the last moment. Every one of these actions marked a big departure in Indian foreign policy. And although disappointed by India's decision to stay out of Iraq, the Bush administration recognized that India was in the midst of a historic transformation of its foreign policy — and kept faith that India's own strategic interests would continue to lead it toward deeper political cooperation with Washington. New Delhi's persistence in reaching out to Washington since 1991 has been driven by the belief that only by fundamentally changing its relationship with the world's sole superpower could it achieve its larger strategic objectives: improving its global position and gaining leverage in its relations with other great powers.

But India's ability to engage everyone at the same time might soon come to an end. As U.S.-Chinese tensions grow and Washington looks for ways to manage China's influence, questions about India's attitude toward the new power politics will arise: Can India choose to remain "nonaligned" between the United States and China, or does India's current grand strategy show a clear bias toward the United States?

The nuclear pact unveiled by Bush and Singh in July 2005 — and consolidated when Bush went to New Delhi in March 2006 — was an effort by Washington to influence the ultimate answer to that question. Bush offered to modify U.S. nonproliferation laws (subject to approval by Congress, of course) and revise the global nuclear order to facilitate full cooperation with India on civilian nuclear energy. New Delhi, in return, has promised to separate its civilian and military nuclear programs, place its civilian nuclear plants under international safeguards, and abide by a range of nonproliferation obligations. India's interest in such a deal has been apparent for a long time. Having failed to test weapons before the Nuclear Nonproliferation Treaty was drafted, in 1968, India was trapped in an uncomfortable position vis-à-vis the nuclear order: it was not willing to give up the nuclear option, but it could not be formally accommodated by the nonproliferation regime as a nuclear weapons state.

India's motives for wanting a change in the nuclear regime are thus obvious. But for the Bush administration, the deal is less about nuclear issues than it is about creating the basis for a true alliance between the United States and India — about encouraging India to work in the United States' favor as the global balance of power shifts. Ironically, it was the lack of a history of mutual trust and cooperation — stemming in part from past nuclear disputes — that convinced the Bush administration that a nuclear deal was necessary.

An Impossible Ally?

Many critics argue that the Bush administration's hopes for an alliance are misplaced. They insist that the traditionally nonaligned India will never be a true ally of the United States. But such critics misunderstand India's nonalignment, as well as the nature of its realpolitik over the past 60 years. Contrary to a belief that is especially pervasive in India itself, New Delhi has not had difficulty entering into alliances when its interests so demanded. Its relationship with the Soviet Union, built around a 1971 peace and friendship treaty, had many features of an alliance (notwithstanding India's claim that such ties were consistent with nonalignment); the compact was in many ways a classic response to the alignment of Washington, Beijing, and Islamabad. India has also had treaty-based security relationships with two of its smaller neighbours, Bhutan and Nepal, that date back to 1949-50 — protectorate arrangements that were a reaction to China's entry into Tibet.

In fact, there is no contradiction between India's alleged preference for "moralpolitik" (in opposition to pure power politics, or Machtpolitik) and the Bush administration's expectation of an alliance with India. New Delhi is increasingly replacing the idea of "autonomy," so dear to Indian traditionalists, with the notion of India's becoming a "responsible power." (Autonomy is thought appropriate for weak states trying to protect themselves from great-power competition but not for a rising force such as India.) As India starts to recognize that its political choices have global consequences, it will become less averse to choosing sides on specific issues. Alliance formation and balancing are tools in the kits of all great powers — and so they are likely to be in India's as well.

That India is capable of forming alliances does not, however, mean that it will necessarily form a long-term one with the United States. Whether it does will depend on the extent of the countries' shared interests and their political capacity to act on them together. The Bush administration expects that such shared interests — for example, in balancing China and countering radical Islam in the Middle East — will provide the basis for long-term strategic cooperation. This outcome is broadly credible, but it is by no means inevitable, especially given the United States' seeming inability to build partnerships based on equality. When it comes to facing a rising China, India's tendency to engage in regional balancing with Beijing has not come to an end with the proclamation of a strategic partnership between the two nations. Indeed, preventing China from gaining excessive influence in India's immediate neighborhood and competing with Beijing in Southeast Asia are still among the more enduring elements of India's foreign policy. Despite Western concerns about the military regime in Myanmar, New Delhi has vigorously worked to prevent Yangon from falling completely under Beijing's influence, and India's military ties with the Southeast Asian nations are expanding rapidly. In 2005, when Pakistan pushed for giving China observer status in the South Asian Association for Regional Cooperation, India acted quickly to bring Japan, South Korea, and the United States in as well.

Given India's deep-seated reluctance to play second fiddle to China in Asia and the Indian Ocean region — and the relative comfort of working with a distant superpower — there is a structural reason for New Delhi to favor greater security cooperation with Washington.

In the Middle East, too, India has a common interest with the United States in preventing the rise of radical Islam, which poses an existential threat to India. Given its large Muslim population — at nearly 150 million, the third largest in the world — and the ongoing tensions stemming from the subcontinent's partition, India has in the past acted on its own to avert the spread of radical Islam. When Washington aligned with conservative Islamic forces in the Middle East during the Cold War, India's preference was for secular nationalist forces in the region. When the United States acted ambivalently toward the Taliban in the mid-1990s, India worked with Russia, Iran, and the Central Asian states to counter the Taliban by supporting the Northern Alliance. Now, although some in India are concerned that alignment with the United States might make India a prime target for Islamist extremists, there is no way India can compromise with radical Islam, which threatens its very unity.

But shared interests do not automatically produce alliances. The inequality of power between the two countries, the absence of a habit of political cooperation between them, and the remaining bureaucratic resistance to deeper engagement in both capitals will continue to limit the pace and the scope of strategic cooperation between India and the United States. Still, there is no denying that India will have more in common with the United States than with the other great powers for the foreseeable future.

While New Delhi has acknowledged that U.S. support is necessary for India's rise to be successful, Washington has recognized India's potentially critical role in managing emerging challenges to global order and security.

As a major beneficiary of accelerating globalization, India could play a crucial role in ensuring that other developing countries manage their transitions as successfully as it has, that is, by taking advantage of opportunities while working to reduce the pain of disruption.

Given the pace of its expansion and the scale of its economy, India will also become an important force in ensuring that the unfolding global redistribution of economic power occurs in an orderly fashion. Meanwhile, India could become a key player in the effort to modernize the politics of the Middle East. If nothing else, India's success in ensuring the rights and the integration of its own Muslim minority and in reaching peace with Pakistan would have a powerful demonstration effect.

To secure a long-term partnership with India, Washington must build on the argument of "Indian exceptionalism" that it has advanced in defense of the recent nuclear pact, devising a range of India-specific policies to deepen cooperation. India is unlikely, however, to become a mere subsidiary partner of the United States, ready to sign on to every U.S. adventure and misadventure around the world. It will never become another U.S. ally in the mold of the United Kingdom or Japan. But nor will it be an Asian France, seeking tactical independence within the framework of a formal alliance.

Given the magnitude of the global security challenges today, the United States needs more than meek allies. It should instead be looking to win capable and compatible partners. A rising India may be difficult at times, but it will act broadly to defend and promote the many interests it shares with Washington. Assisting India's rise, then, is in the United States' own long-term interest.

GLOBAL RESPONSE TO THE DEAL

The U.S. attempt to incorporate India into the global nuclear order is another example of how international regimes are merely reflections of global power realities. The global nuclear nonproliferation regime cannot have any credibility with India outside it, and it is now in the strategic interests of the United States to bring India into the fold. After years of isolating India, the time has come for the international community, led by the United States, to make some adjustments. A rethink of the global nuclear order is, therefore, in the offing.

At a time when the nuclear nonproliferation regime seems to be crumbling under the weight of its own contradictions, India can rightfully claim that it was one of the first states to draw the attention of the world community to the challenges facing this regime.

India has always been dissatisfied with the global nonproliferation and arms control regime, because it constrained its autonomy to make foreign policy decisions as dictated by national interests. India argued that an inequitable regime that gave only a few countries the permanent right to nuclear weapons and denied others this right was inherently unstable.

The U.S.-India pact is recognition by the United States of the rising global profile of India and an attempt to carve out a strategic partnership with a nation with which it shares not only a range of significant interests but also a whole range of political and cultural values. More significantly, there is a sense in India that, with this agreement, the world has finally reconciled itself to India's status as a nuclear power and a major global player.

The U.S.-India nuclear agreement has been viewed by most in the Indian strategic community as part of an emerging Indo-U.S. strategic partnership. With the United States making it clear that the nuclear pact was unique to India and would not be repeated with Pakistan, one of the major Indian complaints against the United States, that it tries to equate India and Pakistan, also seems to have been redressed. The long-standing distrust of the United States and a reflexive anti-Americanism that thrived in India has now been relegated to a small group of left-wing political parties whose views on foreign policy are increasingly out of the mainstream.

Though irritants remain in U.S.-India bilateral relationship, the most significant of which is going to India's ties with Iran in the near term, Indian foreign policy seems to have reconciled itself to the dominance of the international system by the United States. It is trying to chart a course whereby it can draw on the advantages for its own interests from the current global power configuration. Even if the deal falls through, it is clear that Indian foreign policy interests will continue to converge with those of the United States on a whole range of issues, making the two states important partners of each other in the future.

With the exception of China, other major global powers such as Britain, France, Germany, and Russia seem to have come on board with regard to the U.S.-India nuclear deal, because they are eager to sell nuclear fuel, reactors, and equipment to India. As India continues to settle its problems with NSG, these states hope to participate and contribute to its programme for peaceful uses of nuclear energy.

All of these states expect India to work towards the implementation of the Indo-U.S. nuclear accord. In fact, as late as 2004, despite otherwise excellent Indo-Russian bilateral relations, Moscow had categorically ruled out providing enriched uranium to India for the Tarapur nuclear power plant, citing NSG rules. It had also refused India's request for an additional two 1,000MW reactors for the Koodankulam nuclear power project. But with the nuclear pact on the horizon, Russia has now committed itself to the guaranteed lifetime supply of low enriched uranium for the Koodankulam project as well as to sell four more nuclear reactors to India. Russia also decided to proceed with the lease of two Akula-class nuclear propelled submarines, which was blocked because of Russia's unwillingness to annoy its NSG partners. The French government was one of the first to recognize the need for changing international rules to allow civilian nuclear cooperation with India and is also now awaiting the completion of the implementation of the U.S.-India nuclear deal.

China, on its part, has made its displeasure with the nuclear pact clear by asking India to sign the NPT and dismantle its nuclear weapons. The official Xinhua news agency of China commented that the U.S.-India nuclear agreement "will set a bad example for other countries."

These actions are in keeping with China's long-standing policy of preventing India from joining the ranks of major global powers and keeping it contained to the confines of South Asia. Since the U.S.-India deal is recognition of India's raising global profile, China, not surprisingly, is not very happy with the outcome. China has already decided to sell Pakistan six to eight nuclear reactors at the cost of $10 billion. It is a not so subtle message to the United States that if Washington decides to play favourites, China also retains the same right.

China's actions also conveyed to India that even as India tries hard to break out of the straitjacket of being a South Asian power by forging a strategic partnership with the United States, China will do its utmost to contain India by building up its neighbouring adversaries. India is trying its best to assuage Chinese concerns by repeatedly emphasizing the nonadversarial nature of the U.S.-India partnership vis-à-vis China. During the visit of Chinese president Hu Jintao to India in November 2006, the two states agreed to cooperate in civilian nuclear energy. Though India would have preferred an explicit endorsement of the U.S.-India nuclear pact and a promise to support it at the NSG, the agreement is viewed as a significant change in the Chinese approach towards India.

The global response to the U.S.-India nuclear pact has been remarkably positive given its revolutionary nature though China's role in the NSG, and the IAEA Board of Governors remains a big unknown in the future trajectory of the deal.

THE DIFFERENCE BETWEEN THE INDIAN AND THE US PERCEPTION

The biggest problem with the nuclear deal is the differences between the Indian and the US perception of what the deal means and what it aims to achieve. The following two lists show how both India and the US come from very different, possibly irreconcilable vantage points: The US wants to

- Bring India into the NPT framework
- Increased trade: the balance of trade deficit
- Use India as a counterweight to China's rise (Asian balance of power)
- Get Indian support for increased democratisation of the middle East
- Get Indian support in the anti Iran campaign.

The US will also get access to the Indian nuclear market which will help revive the US nuclear industry which has been dormant since the three miles accident in 1979. 'The US will also use the Indian human resource and India's scientific reactors and recycle them back to India.' Prasad in this article also believes that the US feels that sanctions did not work as India continued with the fast breeder reactor programme. The deal is a way of controlling, regulating and harnessing India.

India on the other hand wants:

- Recognition as a responsible nuclear weapons state
- Access to fissile material and latest nuclear technology
- US support with regard to Pakistan and the China-Pakistan nexus (Asian balance of power)
- Maintain its sovereignty in all aspects of domestic and foreign policy formulation.

The meetings between the US administration and the Indian government did not centre only on the actual deal, such as the one between Cheney and M K Narayan on the 22nd of July 2007. This points to the fact that the nuclear deal is part of a much larger agreement framework. The Indian press has been speculating about a security partnership, which possibly contravenes the sovereignty issue listed above.

Current Standing

On 3rd August 2007, the US and India unveiled the much awaited text of their agreed nuclear deal. The details of the 123 Agreement however revealed the extent of India's compromise with US laws in exchange for nuclear energy for civilian purposes. Both sides had reached a historic milestone in finalizing terms of the nuclear deal on 20th July 2007, marking the culmination of their two years of negotiation. Talks began in Washington on 17th July and were supposed to have lasted only 2 days but were extended for another day after failing to finalize some technical aspects of the operational deal. The agreement is to be valid for 40 years ad will stay in force for 2 additional periods of 10 years each. Each side can end the deal with 6 months notice at the end of 40 years or any subsequent 10 year period. Either side can terminate the deal mid term by giving a year's notice. Now India and US have to woo the Nuclear Suppliers Group to change their guidelines and to reach an agreement with IAEA on their safeguards. If these difficult obstacles are overcome, then President Bush has to ensure that Congress rule in favour of the deal before any implementation can be carried out.

Terms of Negotiation

The US has agreed in principle to provide nuclear technology and fuel to India for civilian use. In December 2006 the US Congress had approved a landmark ruling, the Hyde Act, which allowed US export of civilian nuclear fuel and technology for the first time in 30 years. India gets to have a civilian and military nuclear programme without being a signatory to the NPT agreement, this ending the 'nuclear apartheid' against India.

The detail revealed by the 123 Agreement on the 3rd of July includes the following points:

- The agreement will not to hinder or interfere with India's nuclear program for military purposes.
- US will help India negotiate with the IAEA for an India-specific fuel supply agreement.
- Washington will support New Delhi develop strategic reserves of nuclear fuel to guard against future disruption of supply.
- In case of disruption, the US and India will jointly convene a group of friendly supplier countries to include nations like Russia, France and the UK to pursue such measures to restore fuel supply.

- Both the countries agree to facilitate nuclear trade between themselves in the interest of respective industries and consumers.
- India and the US agree to transfer nuclear material, non-nuclear material, equipment and components.
- Any special fissionable material transferred under the agreement shall be low enriched uranium.
- Low enriched uranium can be transferred for use as fuel in reactor experiments and in reactors for conversion or fabrication.
- The ambit of the deal includes research, development, design, construction, operation, maintenance and use of nuclear reactors, reactor experiments and decommissioning.
- India can develop strategic reserve of nuclear fuel to guard against any disruption of supply over the lifetime of its reactors.
- Agreement provides for consultations on the circumstances, including changed security environment, before termination of the nuclear cooperation.
- Provision for one-year notice period before termination of the agreement.
- The US to engage Nuclear Suppliers Group to help India obtain full access to the international fuel market, including reliable, uninterrupted and continual access to fuel supplies from firms in several nations.
- The US will have the right to seek return of nuclear fuel and technology.
- In case of return, Washington will compensate New Delhi promptly for the "fair market value thereof" and the costs incurred as a consequence of such removal.
- Both the countries to set up a Joint Committee for implementation of the civil nuclear agreement and development of further cooperation in this field.
- The agreement grants prior consent to reprocess spent fuel.

- Sensitive nuclear technology, nuclear facilities and major critical components can be transferred after amendment to the agreement.
- India will establish a new national facility dedicated to reprocessing safeguarded nuclear material under IAEA safeguards.
- Nuclear material and equipment transferred to India by the US would be subject to safeguards in perpetuity.

The Issues

During the past 2 years, the deal was heavily scrutinized by all quarters. As a result many issues, both major and trivial, concerning aspects of the deal were raised. One source of agitation for critics of the deal has been its financing. There has been no mention yet of any details of proposed financing for the project. The government has also failed to address the concerns of reactor safety and waste disposal.

The greatest cause of concern however to Indian policy-makers is the effect this deal would have on the country's existing regime. Problems which remain are the fact that the agreement is governed by US law and the right of return of all materials. Article 2.1 makes it clear that Hyde act and other US laws, not international law will prevail: 'Each party shall implement this agreement in accordance with its respective applicable treaties, national laws, regulations and licence requirements concerning the use of nuclear energy for peaceful purposes.'

National security remains a priority of the Indian government and to commit to a moratorium on conducting further nuclear tests is seen as a compromise of their national sovereignty and national security. Since it is unlikely that the US will make an exception for India, New Delhi could face another round of sanctions should they conduct further testing in accordance with US laws. Although there was no clear mention of consequences of an Indian nuclear test, the agreement does indicate that either party could choose to terminate the deal prior to its expiration resulting from either party's serious concern about a changed security environment or as a response to similar actions by other states which could impact national security.

Critics argue that directly or otherwise, this clause effectively ends India's nuclear testing possibilities if it wants to avoid the termination of the pact. Opposition party, the BJP, led by senior leader Yashwant Sinha, has illustrated the main flaw of the agreement.

According to him, the text of the agreement does state that issues not covered in it will be subject to national laws. This, he adds, refers to the Hyde Act, which was passed in December of 2006.

The Act provides the US President with the discretionary powers to terminate the civil nuclear cooperation if India conducts a nuclear test. In fact the US can scrap the agreement at will (article 14(2) in an unequal deal as India's international safeguards are in perpetuity: 'The party seeking termination has the right to cease further cooperation under this agreement if it determines that a mutually acceptable resolution of outstanding issues has not been possible or cannot be achieved through consultations.' This puts India at the mercy of the supplier who holds all the leverage. Mr. Sinha concludes that the fundamental flaw lies in the fact that the US has provided unenforceable commitments in lieu of enforceable commitments from India. In addition to this, many in India saw the condition that US will continue to support their country's sourcing for fuel even after the deal is concluded as a continuous support from the Americans. However, the agreement provided a clause that allows the party seeking termination of the deal to cease further cooperation under the agreement if it deems that a mutually acceptable resolution of outstanding issues cannot be achieved.

The expectation of India to join in international efforts to sanction and contain Iran's search for uranium enrichment technology is also a difficult diplomatic and economic decision for New Delhi to make.

Although not mentioned explicitly, Nicholas Burns and others from the US team have clearly stated that they are 'counselling India' not to engage with Iran. India did join the UN Security Council's resolutions to constrain Iran's nuclear quest, but the country is still dependent on the Iranians for oil and gas.

However the reality of an Iran-Pakistan-India oil pipeline could be affected by the US anti-Iran policy. In relation to the requirement of reaching an agreement with the IAEA in perpetuity, India has been reluctant unless it is assured access to nuclear materials in perpetuity. However, India's attempts at negotiating this clause with the IAEA seem to be futile as the IAEA is a regulatory and not policy-making body.

The obligation of the US President to annually certify that India is conforming to the needs of the US legislation is viewed by many as an intrusion to its sovereignty.

This again is specified under the Hyde act. Furthermore with the issue of continuity of the American leadership comes the question of consistency of its policy towards India. Adding to that, the subjectivity of such assessment built upon individual judgement, makes the uncertainty of the outcome even more obvious. Nevertheless, such concerns may be exaggerated. As President Bush has already proven through alternate language by agreeing to an "annual assessment" rather than a "certification", the US government can innovatively work their way around such small obstacles.

Although Manmohan Singh's administration heralded the deal as a negotiation victory for New Delhi, this was a rather premature analysis. Upon closer evaluation, terms of the agreement show that the US has very cleverly hidden key clauses in it that places India in an unfavourable position.

The general sense of satisfaction in India surrounding the text of the 123 is derived from the agreement to petty details that New Delhi had been pushing for.

The major component of the deal that has been much of the cause of a triumphant mood in New Delhi is regarding the reprocessing of spent fuel.

Quoted in the Asian Age, A.N Prasad, a former director of the Bhabha Atominc Reseach Centre had said that 'India's three stage nuclear programme, which is geared towards harnessing thorium, is a prized jewel that cannot be sacrificed at the altar of politics.'

As mentioned earlier, New Delhi had been pushing for an allowance for transfer of reprocessing or enrichment technology.

Initial concerns from Washington were that this would allow India to divert nuclear material to its military program.

However, under the condition that India's reprocessing facility be placed under special IAEA safeguards, the allowance has been made in the 123 for her to reprocess spent fuel. However Prasad makes the point that setting up a dedicated reprocessing plant will not make matters any better for the fast breed reactor.

Given the reality of the agreement on the ground and the different priorities of both governments it has to be remembered in New Delhi that this is not a two way deal: 'India is not selling something of critical interest to America in return for nuclear fuel or nuclear technology.

India is a buyer. It is a one way transaction'. This of course makes the situation an unequal one, one which is heavily contested both by the opposition and the government supporting left parties.

2

Rising Military Super Power of India

China has taken serious note of India's growing military power over the last decade. India, which has traditionally talked of the power of argument began to talk of the argument of power. In fact, the 1998 nuclear tests themselves were indicative of the fact that India had begun to realize the role of hard power in securing its national interests and also in making her voice heard in international politics.

India's growing military profile is especially evident in the maritime domain. The Indian navy has emerged as the net security provider in the Indian Ocean over the last decade. In 2004, it unveiled its first-ever naval doctrine that defined India's legitimate areas of interest stretching from the Persian Gulf to the Malacca Straits.

It released its updated version in 2009, incorporating the rapid changes in the geo-strategic environment involving India. India's defense ties with the US have developed at a frenetic pace, which has played the central role in India's military modernization. For example, recent defense contracts signed with the US include US$ 1.1 billion for C-130J Super Hercules transport planes and US$2.4 billion for 10 Globemasters airlifters. In January 2009, the Indian Navy signed an agreement with the U. S. to buy eight P-8I planes worth nearly US$2.1 billion, so as to replace the aging long range aerial reconnaissance fleet of eight Russian-made Tu-142s and five IL-38 planes.

The tests of its China-centric Agni series missile systems and the development of a Ballistic Missile Defense system. India's future military plans are even more ambitious, which further complicates China's strategic calculations. For example, the Indian Ministry of Defense in late 2011 announced its biggest expansion package to date, a US$13 billion military modernization plan. Under this plan within next five years, the Indian army is set to deploy 90,000 more soldiers and raise four new divisions along India's border with China, the largest such mobilization since the Sino-Indian border clashes of 1962.

CHANGING GEARS A SOFT POWER APPROACH?

India's neighbours occupy much of its attention in its overall foreign policy dilemmas. Except Bhutan and Maldives, India is facing security challenges from all its neighbours. Most of these challenges are traditional in nature; however non-traditional challenges such as environmental issue are also prominently emerging in their security discourse. The foreign policy strategy of India is fundamentally aimed to protect its core national interests; safeguarding territorial integrity and sovereignty, and economic prosperity. Ensuring these interests has been the principal foreign policy agenda for successive governments post-independence. Though the tools and approach used to achieve the desired foreign policy objectives have varied.

For instance, Nehru attempted to demonstrate India's leadership at regional as well global level by projecting Gandhian ideals of non-violence and socialistic values of peaceful co-existence despite India's feeble position in the community of nations. This could also be seen as India's soft-power projection in the region. Unfortunately, this neither changed India's image in its neighbourhood nor did it help to secure a permanent membership in the UNSC.

Realizing the fact that ethics and values serve little in foreign policy in a rapidly changing global security environment, Indira Gandhi brazenly adopted a pragmatic approach towards the neighbours. The liberation of Bangladesh in 1970 through direct Indian military intervention and subsequent creation of a nation in South Asia demonstrated India's ability to exercise hard-power in its foreign policy options. Since then, military power has been an indispensible component of India's foreign policy even though it incurs huge drain on its overall GDP. Alas, India's national security challenges such as cross-border terrorism and illegal migration have not been culminated despite piling up of weapons and building arsenal, thus making hard power options futile in persuading its neighbours to act cooperatively.

The end of cold war, which heralded the rise of multipolar world order, dramatically altered India's foreign policy priorities followed by rapid liberalization. Inspired by Joseph Nye's idea of 'Soft-Power', India began to embrace its neighbours with soft-power skills which involved striking a common cord with neighbours on religion, culture, ethnicity and linguistic basis. This realisation was reflected in the famous Gujral Doctrine, the first official Neighbourhood Policy, which sets out five principles to guide India's foreign policy towards its immediate neighbours.

The most convincing reason for this shift from hard-power to soft-power approach was the growing Chinese influence in its neighbourhood. Yet, the lack of a comprehensive neighbourhood policy strategy and dearth of broad understanding of security challenges blurred India's prospect to become an effective regional power. The big question now is how soft power works in India's neighbourhood policy? Sri Lanka can be a best case to examine this question due to two specific reasons: India's hard power approach towards Sri Lanka in the past had been unsuccessful and counter-productive and the new approach is focused on soft power resources.

INDIA'S SOFT POWER PROJECTION: THE SRI LANKAN MODEL

Sri Lanka is a telling tale for India's power projection in the region especially in terms of 'soft-power' after the failure of its 'hard-power' approach in the past. Indo-Sri Lankan relations have dramatically changed in the last few years and embody the change in India's foreign policy perfectly. The change has been even more visible ever since, the United Progressive Alliance (UPA), the

Congress-led coalition formed the government in 2004. It pursued a neo-liberal foreign policy of projecting India's image as a benign power and not a revanchist regional power. It is indeed a palpable shift from a military approach and diplomatic interventions of the previous regime to a soft-approach that emphasises inter-governmental cooperation, economic collaboration and the projection of its ability to lead. To lead here is to define a common goal and to initiate necessary actions to realize it.

Most Indian foreign policy makers today feel that any hard power approach vis-à-vis its neighbours in addressing political crises is counter-productive and are convinced that soft power approach will best serve its ends. This realization came after an unsuccessful peacekeeping humanitarian intervention in Sri Lanka in 1989 which is allegedly seen to be the cause for Rajiv Gandhi's assassination by LTTE. Since then India has been reluctant to use hard power and as a result, India offered complete support to Sri Lanka's political cause of eliminating the LTTE.

Alongside, Sri Lanka also witnessed a tectonic shift in its foreign policy since President Mahindra Rajapaksa assumed office in 2005. His government adopted a realpolitik approach in their foreign policy, shifting away from the traditional Indo-centric approach. For instance, Sri Lanka exploited the strategic value of China's role in South Asia and sought military and economic aid during the war. It also received considerable military equipments from Pakistan and Iran. The idea behind these tactics of forging closer partnership with other regional big players was obvious: to balance India's possible political interference in its internal affairs after the war. In retrospect, it seems that Sri Lanka had deepened its relationship with China just because of mere anticipation of possible Indian military intervention during the war due to India's domestic political pressure even though it supported Sri Lanka's military campaign against LTTE.

Nevertheless, the Pokhran nuclear test in 1998 and similar tests by Pakistan seemed to have restrained India from exercising any hard-power options in its foreign policy strategy towards its neighbours because any such move would encourage arms race and increase external powers' interference in the region. In order to maintain its image as a responsible power of the region, India adopted a comprehensive foreign policy strategy including soft-power tools such as public diplomacy.

Alas, India's soft power approach in Sri Lanka, especially after the war, seems not to be yielding the results it was expected to. Despite the fact that Indian culture, religion-mainly Buddhism, Bollywood and Kollywood movies are quiet popular in Sri Lanka,. There is a simultaneous drift away from Indian influences. These soft power elements have polarized the Sri Lankan society and aggravated friction between Tamils and Sinhalese. For instance, Tamil movies are popular among Tamils whereas Hindi movies are more appealing to the Sinhalese which in effect creates social schism instead of winning their hearts and minds. Likewise, India's effort to review Buddhist religious connection as part of its soft power strategy might irk Hindu religious groups in India.

On the one hand, Chinese culture, goods, and even language are becoming more and more popular among the Sinhalese youth. The reason for this lie in greater employment prospects for the youth amongst Chinese companies which are establishing their bases in Sri Lanka. On the other hand, India's soft-power elements such as yoga, traditional classic dances and other cultural artefacts are more appealing to Tamils because of their ethno-cultural linkages. In fact, the number of students who register for Hindi language course at Indian culture centre have been decreasing in the last few years. However, it is too early to conclude that India's soft-power does not work largely due to the China factor rather what it does imply is that India's soft-power tools are less attractive than Chinese in the new socio-political environment that has emerged after the war.

If India's soft power approach remains concentrated at winning the hearts and minds of one particular group that is the Sinhalese, it will lose the support of the other group like the Tamils in both Sri Lanka as well as in India. Thus while choosing policy options vis-à-vis Sri Lanka on hard issues India must calculate the domestic, regional and global consequences. If India wants to play a responsible role both at regional and global level, it must clearly articulate its vital interest at different levels and keep the interest of its neighbours into consideration as well.

The Sri Lankan case therefore reveals certain interesting factors about India's power projection in the region. First, its shows that India is caught in a policy dilemma while exercising power options vis-à-vis its neighbours. This dilemma is further reinforced by lack of political will from Indian side and dearth of political vision on the regional level. Second, it reveals that India's soft power elements are less attractive as compared to other available sources in its neighbourhood. Third, the domestic consequences of soft-power particularly in the bordering states of India's neighbourhood are hardly taken into account. India needs to learn how to stage-manage the emotions and feelings of masses while making foreign policy decisions, especially with regards to its neighbours. The Sri Lankan case further demonstrates that India should think regionally while drafting foreign policy towards neighbours because of the shared socio-political identity and ethnicity with the neighbours.

Conclusions

More importantly, can India offer a regional leadership role? Shashi Tharoor, the former Minister of State for External Affairs underscores India's soft power while contemplating its potential leadership role. Soft power is an emerging notion in India's foreign policy discourse but not given enough importance. Tharoor makes very interesting distinction between soft and hard power by stating that hard power is exercised; soft power is evoked. He argues that "India is fast becoming super power – not just through trade and politics but through "soft Power", its ability to share its culture with the world through food, music, technology and movies… in the long run it's not the size of the army that matters as much as a country's ability to influence the world's hearts and minds". It is time for India to invest on soft power resources and realize its leadership potentials to shape the political and economic destiny of the region.

In sum, India needs to learn from its past experience which suggests that the use of hard power vis-à-vis neighbours is counter-productive in the long-term. Moreover, the concept of soft power needs to be refined within the larger South Asian regional context. The Western definition of soft power does not seem to fit this more heterogeneous region, which is fraught with all sorts of conflicts despites cultural similarities and civilizational linkages. In the South Asian context, power should be understood as an 'ability to accommodate others concern' rather than ability to influence'. While embarking into any regional leadership role India has to bear in mind that the political stability and economic prosperity of neighbours are indispensable for its national security and stability.

INDIA'S POLY/MULTI-ALIGNED DIPLOMACY

The India that China defeated in 1962 was guided by a foreign policy doctrine called *non-alignment* vis-à-vis the superpower rivalry, and it remained the cornerstone of India's international diplomacy for more than four decades. However, this foreign policy paradigm underwent a U-turn when it metamorphosed into *poly/multi-alignment* under the new leadership in New Delhi in 1998. The new foreign policy outlook broadly had two components, namely, *improving relations with the US* and its *Look East Policy-II*.

The turnaround in India-US relations from being "estranged democracies" during the Cold War to "engaged democracies" in the 2000s has played a central role in bringing out a shift in China's India posture over the last decade. The anti-China element in the dramatically improving Indo-US relations was not very difficult to discern. Chinese scholar Jing-Dong Yuan notes that the warming of US-Indian relations took place at a time when China-US relations were undergoing serious setbacks in the late 1990s. In 1999, NATO bombed the Chinese embassy in the former Yugoslavia (the only embassy that it targeted); in May of that year, the Cox Report charged Chinese nationals with nuclear espionage and accused China of proliferation activities. hostile attitude toward the PRC further exacerbated tensions in early 2001. Also, the revised Nuclear Posture Review (NPR) included China as a nuclear target.

Meanwhile, in a diametrically opposite turn of events, India-US relations suddenly displayed signs of dramatic improvement. US President Bill Clinton visited India in March 2000 (the first presidential visit since Carter's visit in 1978). The US' National Security Strategy Report of 2002 released by the White House redefined India-US relations, stating that because of "India's potential to become one of the great democratic powers of the twenty-first century," the United States would "invest time and resources [for] building strong bilateral relations with India," and "work hard to transform our relationship accordingly." Consequently, the years 2002-03 witnessed a series of high-level meetings and substantial cooperation between the two democracies. Yet another contrast was the U.S.'s approval of Israel's sale of the Phalcon airborne warning and control systems to India in 2003 after the blockage of a similar sale to China in 2000.

Another Chinese security analyst Du Youkang argues that the US strategy of maintaining the balance of power in South Asia during the Cold War has gone beyond the balance of power and has tilted toward India. He cites the Clinton administration's pro-India attitude during the Kargil conflict, and his subsequent official tour to South Asia, where he spent six days in India compared to five hours in Pakistan. The growing strategic ties between the two countries provides a dangerous historical precedent for Beijing. During the Cold War, China perceived India-USSR relations in terms of an anti-China alliance in South Asia. So the strategic partnership between India and the US in the 2000s is, from China's perspective, the revival of the same anti-China alliance – the only difference being that the US has replaced the Soviet Union. Zhang Guihong compared the US-India Western Pacific.

The other pedestal of India's multi-aligned diplomacy included its *Look East Policy-II*. India's Look East Policy-I was officially initiated in 1992. Like most of the previous Indian policies it was reactionary and an outcome of ad hoc-ism. The main driver behind this policy was the economic doldrums of early 1990s, and India saw Southeast Asia as a springboard to join unfolding globalization. However, India displayed an uncharacteristic proactiveness in projecting the Look East policy in its second incarnation in the first-ever India ASEAN summit in Phnom Penh, Cambodia in 2002. India added a politico-security dimension to this policy. It developed security ties with the ASEAN group. From ASEAN's perspective, developing such ties with India (apart from the US presence in the region) provided them a sense of strategic reassurance given their territorial disputes in the South China Sea with a rapidly growing, authoritarian China.

An important highlight of India's Look East Policy-II, from China's viewpoint, has been a transformational improvement in India-Japan relations. Although the ice between their relations was broken with the visit of Prime Minister Mori Yoshiro to India in August 2000, their relations broadened and deepened in the second phase. The April 2005 joint statement issued during Koizumi Junichiro's visit to India introduced a "strategic" dimension to the partnership.

The establishment of the Strategic and Global Partnership between India and Japan in December 2006 elevated relations to a new level. In 2006 Japan became only the second country with which India had a bilateral annual summit apart from Russia. When then Prime Minister Shinzo Abe visited India in August 2007, the joint statement sought to provide a roadmap for new dimensions to the strategic and global partnership. The October 2008 joint statement during Prime Minister Manmohan Singh's visit to Japan mentioned the advancement of the strategic and global partnership, making Japan the only country

Partnership Agreement (CEPA) which came into force in August of the same year. In late December 2011 India's External Affairs minister visited Japan in October 2011 for the Fifth round of the India-Japan Strategic Dialogue. Japanese PM Yoshihiko Noda visited India for the sixth annual meeting of the leaders of India and Japan. It was the success of India's Look East Policy-II (and not Look East Policy I) that made China remark that India's Look East Policy is "look to encircle China."

India Emerging as an Economic Giant

India and China had similar per capita income by 1974. However, China surged well ahead of India thanks to its deep economic engagement with the US after the Policy of Reform and Open Up (*gaige kaifang*) by Deng Xiaoping in 1978. While China's Open Door policy was a well-thought-out initiative, India, following its legacy of taking radical initiatives only while in crisis, embarked upon its own version of Open Door policy in

1991. The much-needed reforms removed obstacles to economic freedom, and India began to play catch-up, steadily re-integrating into the global economy. A Goldman Sachs report from 2007 found another watermark in India's economic history since 1991 when it pointed out that since 2003 India has been one of the fastest growing major economies, leading to rapid increases in per capita income, demand, and integration with the global economy.

The story of India's economic success has captivated Chinese attention over the last decade. Among Chinese scholars a new discourse has begun over India's economic success story, especially in the IT and consensus that China is a great success in exports, inside China, focusing on China's lag in information technology, Chinese researchers ask why India has become so competitive in the international software market when India has many unattractive features."

Chinese scholars now debate an "Indian Model" as an alternative to the "Chinese model" for developing countries. The Indian model, as understood by Chinese scholars, is characterized by avoiding its weaknesses and exploiting its strengths. For example, India leapfrogged from the primary sector (agriculture) to the tertiary sector (services) by exploiting its inherent advantages in the IT sector which includes a vast, young English-speaking population, the entrepreneurial genius of its private sector, computer literacy, a sound banking sector, and a culture that respects the rule of law.

Chinese analysts have especially taken notice of what they call "India New Economy" which is acting like an engine to the Indian Model. Ma Jiali argues that although India is a baby elephant in the manufacturing industry, it is a "doughty tiger" in the information sector. Another set of scholars attributed India's success in this sector to its diaspora. It opined, "India's IT success is also attributed to the large cohort of educated overseas Indians who have good connections and invested heavily in their home country in recent years as a result of favourable government policies. The dynamism brought by the overseas Indians was comparable to the boost brought by the overseas Chinese since the 1978 economic reform in China."

INDIA'S GROWING SOFT POWER

The drivers triggering a shift in China's India posture can be placed under the rubric of India's *hard power*. However, India's (re)rising *soft power* has also contributed to this shift in China's outlook a country's ability to alter the behavior of others through attraction rather than sticks or carrots.

India has been a democracy right since its birth as a modern nation-state in 1947. However, its sluggish economic growth and weak military profile that led to its defeat in 1962 seriously tarnished this aspect of India's soft power.

With the rising India story, its democracy as an important component of its soft power has again come into the global limelight. India has more than 1 billion people. It is linguistically, culturally, racially, and religiously diverse, and it is growing economically at an enviable pace under democratic governmental institutions (except for the emergency period of 1975-77 when civil liberties were undermined). Its culture values peaceful coexistence, nonviolence, and religious tolerance. All of these factors, combined with the largest pool of English speakers outside the US, has increased India's power of attraction without need for coercion or persuasion, a fact not lost on an envious, hard power-minded China.

The country to which India has projected most of its soft power is the US, through the export of highly skilled manpower, consisting mainly of software developers, engineers, and doctors. China has been keeping a close watch on the rising influence of the Indian community in the United States, especially over the last decade.

In order to improve its own soft power in the United States, China has sent far more students to the United States than India. As per the Institute of International Education's annual report in the academic year 2009-10, out of 690,932 international students in the United States nearly 128,000 of them, or more than 18 percent, were from China while India sent only 107,897 students in the same academic year. However, with Oct 2011, educational exchanges between India and the US would rise much faster in the future.

MODERNISING THE INDIAN INFANTRY

Why has it taken the Army so long to conceive an upgrade package for the oldest, most potent and intensely employed fighting arm, the Infantry, even after the so-called revolution in military affairs?

The foot soldier, the original and most versatile weapon system that is always taken for granted, has emerged from the dubious shock and awe strategy of recent campaigns as its ultimate arbiter. India has paid dearly for the neglect of its infantry in terms of cost, casualties and over-stretch of battle. But the Infantry has never let us down. Kargil was its finest hour. Gen VP Malik, the Army Chief of the time, wryly noted: "We will fight with what we have."

So when for the first time an international conference of Army and defence industry was launched last week to put the forgotten soldier centre-stage, some misgivings were natural. While Army Chief Gen JJ Singh outlined his vision for the soldier system of the future, the conspicuous and total absence of Government - MoD - robbed the conference of any sanctity. In sharp contrast, for a MoD-sponsored defence finance seminar earlier in the month, Government officials and ministers were stepping over each other at Vigyan Bhavan.

Free India's Army came into being in 1947 and within weeks, the Infantry soldiers landed in Srinagar to save J&K from being gobbled up by Pakistani tribal raiders. Since then, the Infantry has not ceased fighting proxy wars there and later, elsewhere too. A former Army Chief, Gen SR Choudhury, who was not from the Infantry, described the Infantry as the Army and vice versa. Field Marshal Montgomery said: An army is considered only as good as its Infantry.

The experience of four wars, several border skirmishes, two out-of-area missions, the ceaseless campaign to counter cross-border terrorism in Kashmir, numerous other insurgencies in the North-East, internal stability operations elsewhere in the country and UN peace keeping operations make the Indian Infantry the most battle-hardened and combat rich force in the world. The simple and uncomplaining infantryman has given so much to so many for so little. The modernisation of the infantry was first attempted - halfheartedly - in the mid-1980s by the Perspective Planning branch of the Army Headquarters. The bias for mechanised warfare, zealously pursued by Gen Sundarji, was so pronounced that the Infantry modernisation plan was skipped altogether. Guns, tanks, APCs were the weapons in demand. The Infantry was ignored. Had a modest upgrade package been undertaken at that time, infantry would have been more combat contemporary and effective.

Instead, till recently, some soldiers were still using World War II equipment and clothing. Shameful as it was, soldiers had to buy rucksacks and other accoutrements from the market. DRDO is still to come out with a light bulletproof vest. The Army failed to accurately visualize the nature of combat it would fight in the future. Pakistan-sponsored insurgency in Punjab did not alert the nation and the Army to the proxy war brewing in J&K. We defaulted on both counts - anticipating low intensity conflict and cross border terrorism and preparing the Infantry for it.

Despite the sustained counter-insurgency and counter-terrorism campaign in J&K and the North-East since the 1990s, the Army was sluggish in investing in the infantry. The first Gulf War reintroduced the fiction that wars could be won from the air. The air campaigns in Bosnia and Kosovo temporarily turned fiction into reality. But 9/11 broke the myth of supremacy of air power. Operation Enduring Freedom in Afghanistan lasted 76 days; 65 of these were air operations.

The 11-day land offensive secured a temporary and incomplete victory against the Taliban. Operation Iraqi Freedom on the other hand, fought for 20 days was bereft of any preparatory air campaign though a secret air war preceded it. Unhappily for the US/NATO-led coalition forces, despite their pyrrhic military victories, low intensity wars in Afghanistan and Iraq are continuing in full blaze. The recent 34-day war in Lebanon and the ongoing campaign in Gaza demonstrate the limits of Israel's military power. Used to decisive victories in less than 10 days, Israeli Defence Forces (IDF) were badgered by Hassan Nasrallah's jihadi militia. Reliance on air power, tanks and guns in Lebanon as substitute for ground troops - infantry - was motivated by casualty aversion. We too have to be sensitive to casualties.

The wars in Lebanon, Iraq and Afghanistan spurred by the growing cult of Osama bin Laden and Hassan Nasrallah require a redefinition of the concept of power and military success. Success would necessarily be an inclusive military victory encompassing post-conflict stability and reconstruction. For this we need Infantry. The Indian Army should not get overly seduced by high-sounding warfare like 'netcentric' that the West is being diverted into. This is not to suggest we ignore the strides in high-tech warfare. But as a former US NATO Commander noted recently: "This netcentric stuff is great but our men in Baghdad are being blown up with their Humvees by IEDs." He suggested that we address the battle we are fighting before switching to the one we will fight in the future.

India's supreme operational challenge is and will be the maintenance of internal security. Just last month, Prime Minister Manmohan Singh stated this ground reality. The Infantry is at the heart of counterinsurgency and counter-terrorism operations and may well get sucked into anti-Naxal operations as well. Keeping the Army operationally ready for both conventional and unconventional missions is imperative but the emphasis has to be on the business of the day: CI and CT.

The Indian Infantry is belatedly embarking on a modernisation programme to enhance its combat skills through increased lethality, communications, surveillance, mobility and suvivability. These force multipliers will enable the soldier to fight all-weather, 24x7 and on any terrain in the right battle-configuration albeit with the accent on LIC.

The GSQR for the Future-Infantry-Soldier-As a System (F-INSAS) must empower not encumber the soldier. DRDO must compete with domestic and international industry. DRDO has one more chance to make amends for its omissions and commissions. F-INSAS must strike the right balance between the surge of technology and sensibility of the soldier keeping the battle of the future in mind. Defence Minister AK Antony should accord F-INSAS the highest strategic priority.

2020: DEFENDING INDIAN FORCE

The Flashpoint. NATO's Allied Force saw induction of more than 400 planes into the Balkan skies. Phase-I witnessed cruise missiles, F-117 Nighthawks, B-2 bombers, F-15/16 Eagles, F-16 Falcons and B-52 bombers which rolled in from as the diverse directions and places as Adriatic Sea, Missouri, Italy and England. With that Kosovo moved to a new level of misery.

The largest air attacks since WWII commenced on a country which does not threaten the global equilibrium nor its neighbours. And none know the precise exit strategy nor the endgame. However, this much is clear that the resultant giagantic refugee problem will heavily eat into the NATO manpower and resources for a long time to come.

Of late, unfortunately, the American foreign policy has been driven by ultimatums. Whenever, a disagreement occurs, the lone super power needs to deliver on such threats. But the air attacks without ground troops support cannot always win. So Osama bin Laden remains where he was. Saddam continues to visit his mistresses. And now NATO's credibility is up for grabs. The Balkans is likely to be the graveyard of air-attacks-alone theory. For history argues that a determined infantry cannot be evicted by massive air attacks. The Kosovo spillover will not only impact on the health of the EU, but also put a question mark on the American global dominance.

However, Americans are likely to continue with such ill-advised actions on a variety of flashpoints worldwide in a desperate attempt to disallow emerging new power equations. This will further tie down in knots the NATO credibility. Let's try to visualise how India can re-organise internally to meet the new challenges arising out of the deteriorating international scenario.

The Indian Faultline. This faultline can be traced back to the Mauryan empire's unwise decision of renouncing war. Like corporate graphs, the military power graph of a nation either gradually creeps upwards or if not in use, the law of gravity pulls it downwards! Thus unwittingly, in subsequent centuries the neglect of the military component resulted in unprecedented foreign invasions. Incomprehension of the dynamics of military power by the subsequent rulers and the attempts to absorb, appease and amalgamate the invading armies put the foreign rulers at the seat of power in Delhi with ease. This is akin to allowing an adversary in a soccer match to dominate your half of the field. Obviously goals will be scored.

The other aspect of the Indian Faultline rests on the fact that majority of the Indian rulers employed the military power ruthlessly internally to pacify the outlying provinces (instead of attempting economic development) while refusing to correctly posture it to meet the threats from invasion. This short sighted approach continued on India's attaining independence.

Many elders (product of a similar mindset) tend to defend the actions of Indian political leadership of 1947 on singular ground of inexperience. One tends to disagree because all it needed was to review the historical evidence of foreign subjugation and the leadership would automatically have deduced the reasons. And initiated corrective measures. This small exercise really did not require a very high caliber in leadership either.

On one hand, the international stability appears to be in a tail spin. Because the lone super power is determined to rise and shine at every flashpoint despite the time tested principle of never jump into somebody else's civil war. On the other hand, India is finally waking up to the fact that the world does not feed on morals! India needs to re-look and re-fashion its internal factors to meet the prevailing new external lawlessness.

The Have-Nots. Indians over the centuries have done to the Untouchables, what the Americans did to the Blacks. Suppression. The Blacks even today cannot easily rise in the American society because of one simple fear that they will return the favour in ample measures.

Fortunately for India, the Untouchables retain their levels of tolerance like the rest of the Indians. Therefore, rapid education and economic development of the backward/rural areas needs to be implemented on a war footing. Time lost in this respect will be directly proportionate to heightened levels of social disharmony which India can ill-afford as an emerging power.

Unity-in-Diversity. The Indian tragedy is that this slogan since 1947 has only harped on the aspect concerning *diversity*, encouraging divisive tendencies from Kashmir to Kanyakumari! For aspirations towards building a modem nation-state, the buzz word has to be integration and not disintegration. Give spin to integration by merging the MoD with Service Headquarters and right down the line to the Theatre Command. More efficiency at a much lesser cost with availability of a larger fire power. A unique functional role model of unity in diversity for India is its military. Be it the Sikhs, Rajputs, Jats or the Madras Regiments, the cultural diversity is adequately maintained at the lower end of the spectrum. Uniformity through training is achieved at the higher end of the spectrum.

The social scientist and the economist must sit together with the military analyst to understand, innovate and devise methods to integrate the society accordingly. The military role model respects and encourages secularism and yet manages to effectively knit the diversity in a rare unity. Overall national uniformity in approach is vital for the national health and cannot be disputed. Nor should it be erroneously mistaken as militerization of the Indian mind. Internal harmony will also reduce consumption of military power within. Such surplus of military component then readily will be available to face the external threats. To develop national uniformity in approach, the following elementary steps are recommended.

- Post-independence military actions, battles and wars must be taught to students from the ninth standard onwards. This literature is not only secular but can galvanize the young through acts of courage, compassion and bravery exemplified by the Indian soldier, sailor and the airman. It will also be of immense help to create a larger vision of a diverse India in the young mind. Further, to hone the skills of civilian instructors in the teaching of post independence history in military science departments in colleges, officers from the three services should be put on deputation for two years under study leave provisions.
- On scrutiny, the only all India services are the Army, Navy and the Air Force. Indian Administrative Service or Indian

Police Service merely adorn an all India nomenclature. For example an IAS officer from Bihar cadre normally ends up spending his professional tenure between Bihar and Delhi. This needs to be modified like the military. Officers of the civil services like IAS, IPS, etc. should be posted through out the country to increase their vision and interaction with diverse regions and communities. This will provide a fillip to integration.

- A major boost to uniformity in approach can be achieved by lateral induction of the military in civil services. Officers of the Armed Forces imbibe in them the best man and material management techniques that the country can offer. If they are laterally inducted into central and state administrative and police structures with their seniority intact, they will perform miracles in providing a responsive and a responsible administration. Similarly jawans can be absorbed in the state and central police forces. Training costs come down, efficiency goes up, shortages of manpower ends, and the military remains young. Besides, this simple measure bestows honour and recognition of the soldier's contribution to the nation. Above all this will act as a force-multiplier in national integration.

Internal Reforms. Analysing the Indian genius and skills, one factor stands out. It works the best in a free atmosphere. Scores of Indian fast food joints are now ahead of those owned by multinationals. Infact, for the first time, the latter are forced to cut down their retail prices and cater to the Indian palate. Modern banking facilities at a lesser cost provided by HDFC Ltd. Bank is ahead of the foreign banks. Zee TV revenues score over a foreign channel. Therefore, accelerated pace of internal reforms to free and unleash the Indian enterprenuial energy in the next five years is a must-must. Simultaneously lowering the over-whelming government structures by 35% in the next five years is mandatory for India to gain momentum. The system is not only clogged but eats up revenue in far excess of what it can collect. And hardly delivers. However, the social net for the next twenty years needs to remain intact till the have-nots are brought into the main stream through education. Here, I emphasize on the spread of education in the rural areas because this not only creates new skills and competence but helps check the explosion in population. In actualities, India can afford to export vast amount of brains and yet have an internal surplus! The government needs to exploit this factor.

Defending India. To defend India, we have everything going for us except a vision and a will to ruthlessly implement it. Indians must remember that despite building up of sufficient alliances in our region and out-of-the-region, we must not become complacent and neglect the growth of military power in future. Education of the masses, encouraging the free enterprise, developing the economy of the outlying provinces through an efficient administrative machinery on a war footing (and thus freeing the military power from enormous internal consumption), disallowing demographic changes in the border areas from outside in particular, and giving thrust to national integration while retaining diversity at the lower end of the spectrum are the areas that need to be conceptually worked upon. Simply, put to defend India, the India First generation must take over from the fading elders of India Last generation.-

THE DEBATE OVER INDIAN MILITARY MODERNIZATION

Pakistani leaders view their conventional armed forces as the corner- stone of their strategic deterrent capability and believe, in the words of then President Pervez Musharraf, that 'the conventional balance in South Asia is extremely important to maintain peace in the region.'

Unsurprisingly, a number of Pakistani analysts have sounded warnings about the Indian military's growing quantitative and qualitative advantages. In particular, it has been suggested that the recent furry of overseas weapons acquisitions from countries like Russia and Israel are specifically designed to enhance the Indian military's reconnaissance, precision-strike, and command and control capabilities, which are cornerstones of the so-called Revolution in Military Affairs (RMA). Pakistani security scholars have suggested that the primary consequence of this growing conventional military disparity will be a reduction in Pakistan's conventional deterrence capability and a subsequent decrease in strategic stability in South Asia. This concern would appear to be empirically grounded since a number of scholars have found that sudden shifts in the conventional military balance between pairs of states —particularly enduring rivals – increases the prospect of conflict breaking out. Even more worryingly, informed observers such as the former head of the Pakistan Air Force's Strategic Command, the country's previous ambassadors to the United States and the United Nations, as well as retired senior officers from the Strategic Plans Division (SPD) – the agency responsible for managing Pakistan's nuclear weapons stockpile –have all suggested that Islamabad's inability to keep pace with New Delhi's military build up has increased the pressure to expand Pakistan's nuclear arsenal to include low-yield warheads and short-range missiles such as the 60km Nasr. These comments by non-governmental analysts and retired personnel have been echoed by serving officials. In 2009, the spokesman for Pakistan's Foreign Office warned that 'there are acquisitions of sophisticated weaponry by our neighbor which will disturb the conventional balance between our two countries and hence, lower the nuclear threshold.'

This message was repeated in 2011 by the Director of Arms Control and Disarmament Affairs for the Strategic Plans Division, which administers Pakistan's tactical and strategic nuclear weapons.

Of course, anyone with even a passing familiarity with the politics of South Asia would recognize the incentives that the Pakistani government and government-linked scholars have to exaggerate the impact of Indian military acquisitions. However, fears that India's military modernization is reducing Pakistan's conventional deterrent extends beyond the sub-continent. For example, former Assistant Secretary of Defense Peter Lavoy, contends that 'India's military modernization program has led to a growing disparity between the Indian and Pakistani conventional military capabilities,' the result of which 'will be either a regional arms race ... and/or a lowering of the nuclear threshold ...' Long-time South Asia watcher Rodney Jones is far more certain of the impact, having argued for nearly a decade that the growing conventional force imbalance between India and Pakistan 'has destabilizing effects on their nuclear relationship.' Specifically, Jones believes that India is outstripping Pakistan in 'revolutionary' military assets such as high-performance aircraft, wide-area communications, reconnaissance, and battleûeld awareness. This view has been echoed by nuclear strategist Paul Bracken who argues that 'India has invested heavily in satellites, advanced radars, signals intelligence, and reconnaissance' assets to cultivate new military capabilities. As India develops transformative military capabilities, observers fear that 'this conventional asymmetry increases the danger of the nuclear arms race – it feeds India's hubris and Pakistan's sense of failure.' Indeed, a number of researchers at Washington DC think tanks, including the Carnegie Endowment, the Congressional Research Service, the Council on Foreign Relations, and the Hudson Institute appear to share the beliefs of the Stimson Center's Michael Krepon that Pakistan's recent embrace of the utility of tactical nuclear weapons and broader Pakistani efforts to enhance the quality and quantity of their nuclear arsenal is a result of 'India's growing conventional capabilities and its more proactive military plans.'

Although a number of observers appear to take the 'fact' that India's sizeable and growing conventional military capability is posing a significant threat to Pakistan's conventional deterrent as a given, there are a few dissenting voices. Some Indian analysts have argued that the significant amount of money Pakistan is spending on its own military modernization program – assisted by China and the United States – is actually eroding India's 'slender conventional edge.' In this vein, several retired Indian generals have recently argued that their military lacks conventional superiority over Pakistan as well as the ability to achieve a quick and decisive result against its neighbor.

Despite the dramatic increases in defense spending, Indian analysts contend that the military — in particular the Army — faces numerous capability shortfalls that would hinder military operations against Pakistan. The large number of obsolete tanks, armored vehicles, and artillery pieces, not to mention critical shortages of ammunition and air-defense assets, raise serious questions whether India can undertake large-scale military operations at all, let alone whether ongoing defense modernization really is sharply shifting the conventional balance in its favor. In this vein, Arun Sahgal and Vinod Anand have damningly written that India's military modernization is primarily designed to address the obsolescence of existing platforms 'rather than part of a well thought out force transformation strategy that takes into account the changing nature of war.' As a result, 'despite spending huge sums on force modernization and induction of weapons systems, there is limited or marginal accretion to overall capabilities.'

The most visible manifestation of the 'hollowing out' of the Indian Army occurred in the aftermath of the 2008 Mumbai attacks, when then Army chief General Deepak Kapoor reportedly was forced to admit to the country's political leadership that the Army 'was not ready for war' with Pakistan in retaliation for the terrorist attacks. This view from within India has been bolstered by Stephen Cohen and Sunil Dasgupta, who recently noted the 'puzzling inability of the Indian state to generate sufficient military power to alter its strategic position vis-à- vis Pakistan,' and 'the astounding lack of political direction in Indian efforts at military modernization.'

The scholars, analysts, and government officials surveyed in this section present two starkly different views of the state of conventional deterrence in South Asia. From one perspective, India's increasing defense spending is rapidly undermining the cornerstone of Pakistan's strategic deterrent and pushing Islamabad towards an increased reliance on nuclear weapons. The alternate point of view presents an Indian military with crippling deficiencies, one that is struggling to maintain capabilities despite sharp increases in defense spending, and one that may even be losing ground to Pakistan in several key areas. Does Pakistan retain the ability to deter India through conventional means alone? Is that ability under threat –justifying a turn to nuclear solutions –or should we have confidence in conventional deterrence in South Asia? It is to these questions that we turn in the subsequent sections.

Conventional Deterrence Theory

Conventional deterrence is a subset of deterrence that seeks to prevent the outbreak of conflict during a crisis by maintaining the ability to deny an opponent their goals on the battleûeld through the use of conventional forces. This is substantially different from deterrence by punishment which seeks to avoid conflict by threatening to retaliate against a target the aggressor holds dear –often, but not always, their civilian population.

The foundation of conventional deterrence theory was laid by John Mearsheimer, who advanced the clear-cut thesis that war is most likely to break out during a crisis when an aggressor believes a quick victory is possible.

In contrast, deterrence will hold when a potential attacker judges that the costs of such actions will be high and their chance of success low. Importantly, he argues that policymakers are likely to be deterred from launching military action –even when it has a high probability of ultimate success –if they believe that the forthcoming conflict will be protracted in nature, and thus victory can only be achieved at a substantial cost. In other words, if an aggressor believes that attrition is the only strategy available to them, they will desist.

With the probability of success and cost equally important to policymakers –and cost emerging as a function of the speed with which battleûeld objectives can be achieved –the question of whether battleûeld success can be achieved at a reasonable cost turns on perceptions about the speed with which a decision can be obtained. Mearsheimer's original analysis examined the robustness of conventional deterrence against a range of limited and maximal military strategies irrespective of the presence of nuclear weapons. However, such a discussion of total war without consideration of the two sides' nuclear arsenals lacks plausibility for the present study. Indeed a number of scholars have argued that the presence of nuclear weapons in South Asia means total war is no longer a possibility. Instead, attention will focus solely on the robustness of conventional deterrence in the presence of two limited aims strategies that might be plausibly pursued under the nuclear umbrella.

On land, the limited aims strategy seeks to capture a specific section of enemy territory and then shift to a defensive posture to repel the expected counterattack. Presented with a fait accompli, the defender has the choice between either acquiescing or initiating an unattractive war of attrition to regain the lost territory. The success of the attacker's gambit turns on its ability to achieve strategic surprise and swiftly overcome the limited forces arrayed to defend the objective. If the defender knows an attack is coming, the attacker can still achieve tactical surprise by selecting the specific point of attack, but the range and scope of objectives that can be pursued is constrained. Against a defender who has the ability to quickly react to the initial thrust, the lack of strategic surprise may doom the limited aims strategy.

A second limited aims strategy not originally discussed by Mearsheimer is the use of air or missile strikes against a state to achieve limited political or military objectives. The robustness of deterrence against airstrikes hinges on an assessment of the ability to rapidly achieve the objective at a minimal cost and without escalating the conflict. The idea that airpower employed against a state's industrial base, military infrastructure, or government apparatus could punish or coerce the target state is hardly a new idea.

However, the contemporary efficacy of this strategy is facilitated by the dissemination of advanced sensor systems, long-range guided munitions and stealth technologies.

Thus, from Mearsheimer's framework, the two judgments policy- makers will assess with respect to deterrence against limited aims strategies are the prospects of achieving strategic surprise on the ground and the ability to rapidly strike targets from the air without triggering an escalation of the conflict.

NUCLEAR POWER GROWTH IN INDIA

India now envisages to increase the contribution of nuclear power to overall electricity generation capacity from 2.8% to 9% within 25 years. By 2020, India's installed nuclear power generation capacity will increase to 20,000 MW (2.0×10 Watts, which is 20 GW). As of 2009, India stands 9th in the world in terms of number of operational nuclear power reactors. Indigenous atomic reactors include TAPS-3, and -4, both of which are 540 MW reactors. India's US$717 million fast breeder reactor project is expected to be operational by 2012-13.

The Indian nuclear power industry is expected to undergo a significant expansion in the coming years, in part due to the passing of theU.S.-India Civil Nuclear Agreement. This agreement will allow India to carry out trade of nuclear fuel and technologies with other countries and significantly enhance its power generation capacity. When the agreement goes through, India is expected to generate an additional 25,000 MW of nuclear power by 2020, bringing total estimated nuclear power generation to 45,000 MW.

India has already been using imported enriched uranium for light-water reactors that are currently under IAEA safeguards, but it has developed other aspects of the nuclear fuel cycle to support its reactors. Development of select technologies has been strongly affected by limited imports. Use of heavy water reactors has been particularly attractive for the nation because it allows Uranium to be burnt with little to no enrichment capabilities. India has also done a great amount of work in the development of a thorium centred fuel cycle. While uranium deposits in the nation are limited there are much greater reserves of thorium and it could provide hundreds of times the energy with the same mass of fuel. The fact that thorium can theoretically be utilised in heavy water reactors has tied the development of the two. A prototype reactor that would burn Uranium-Plutonium fuel while irradiating a thorium blanket is under construction at Kalpakkam by BHAVINI - another public sector enterprise like NPCIL

Uranium used for the weapons programme has been separated from the power programme, using uranium from indigenous reserves. This domestic reserve of 80,000 to 112,000 tons of uranium (approx 1% of global uranium reserves) is large enough to supply all of India's commercial and military reactors as well as supply all the needs of India's nuclear weapons arsenal. Currently, India's nuclear power reactors consume, at most, 478 tonnes of uranium per year. Even if India were quadruple its nuclear power output (and reactor base) to 20 GW by 2020, nuclear power generation would only consume 2000 tonnes of uranium per annum. Based on India's known commercially viable reserves of 80,000 to 112,000 tons of uranium, this represents a 40–50 years uranium supply for India's nuclear power reactors (note with reprocessing and breeder reactor technology, this supply could be stretched out many times over). Furthermore, the uranium requirements of India's Nuclear Arsenal are only a fifteenth (1/15) of that required for power generation (approx. 32 tonnes), meaning that India's domestic fissile material supply is more than enough to meet all needs for it strategic nuclear arsenal. Therefore, India has sufficient uranium resources to meet its strategic and power requirements for the foreseeable future.

Indian President A.P.J.Abdul Kalam, stated while he was in office, that "energy independence is India's first and highest priority. India has to go for nuclear power generation in a big way using thorium-based reactors. Thorium, a non fissile material is available in abundance in our country." India has vast thorium reserves and quite limited uranium reserves.

NUCLEAR POWER PLANTS

Anti-nuclear Protests

Following the March 2011 Fukushima nuclear disaster in Japan, populations around proposed Indian NPP sites have launched protests that had found resonance around the country. There have been mass protests against the French-backed 9900 MW Jaitapur Nuclear Power Project in Maharashtra and the 2000 MW Koodankulam Nuclear Power Plant in Tamil Nadu. The Government of West Bengalrefused permission to a proposed 6000 MW facility near the town of Haripur that intended to host 6 Russian reactors. But that now is disputed: it's possible for Bengal to have its first nuclear power plant at Haripur despite resistance. A Public-interest litigation (PIL) has also been filed against the government's civil nuclear programme at the Supreme Court. The PIL specifically asks for the "staying of all proposed nuclear power plants till satisfactory safety measures and cost-benefit analyses are completed by independent agencies". But the

Supreme Court said it was not an expert in the nuclear field to issue a direction to the government on the nuclear liability issue.

Indian Nuclear Power

- India has a flourishing and largely indigenous nuclear power program and expects to have 14,600 MWe nuclear capacity on line by 2020. It aims to supply 25% of electricity from nuclear power by 2050.
- Because India is outside the Nuclear Non-Proliferation Treaty due to its weapons program, it was for 34 years largely excluded from trade in nuclear plant or materials, which has hampered its development of civil nuclear energy until 2009.
- Due to these trade bans and lack of indigenous uranium, India has uniquely been developing a nuclear fuel cycle to exploit its reserves of thorium.
- Now, foreign technology and fuel are expected to boost India's nuclear power plans considerably. All plants will have high indigenous engineering content.
- India has a vision of becoming a world leader in nuclear technology due to its expertise in fast reactors and thorium fuel cycle.

India's primary energy consumption more than doubled between 1990 and 2011 to nearly 25,000 PJ. India's dependence on imported energy resources and the inconsistent reform of the energy sector are challenges to satisfying rising demand.

Electricity demand in India is increasing rapidly, and the 1052 billion kilowatt hours gross produced in 2011 was more than triple the 1990 output, though still represented only some 750 kWh per capita for the year. With huge transmission losses – 222 TWh in 2011, this resulted in only about 774 billion kWh consumption. Gross generation comprised 836 TWh from fossil fuels, 33 TWh from nuclear, 131 TWh from hydro and 53 TWh from other renewables. Coal provides 68% of the electricity at present, but reserves are limited. Gas provides 15%, hydro 12%. The per capita electricity consumption figure is expected to double by 2020, with 6.3% annual growth, and reach 5000-6000 kWh by 2050, requiring about 8000 TWh/yr then. There is an acute demand for more and more reliable power supplies. One-third of the population is not connected to any grid.

At mid-2012, 203 GWe was on line with 20.5 GWe having been added in 12 months. In September 2012 it had 211 GWe. The government's 12th five-year plan for 2012-17 is targeting the addition of 94 GWe over the period, costing $247 billion. Three quarters of this would be coal- or lignite-fired, and only 3.4 GWe nuclear, including two imported 1000 MWe units planned at one site and two indigenous 700 MWe units at another. By 2032 total installed capacity of 700 GWe is planned to meet 7-9% GDP growth, and this was to include 63 GWe nuclear. The OECD's International Energy Agency predicts that India will need some $1600 billion investment in power generation, transmission and distribution to 2035. India has five electricity grids – Northern, Eastern, North-Eastern, Southern and Western. All of them are interconnected to some extent, except the Southern grid. All are run by the state-owned Power Grid Corporation of India Ltd (PGCI), which operates more than 95,000 circuit km of transmission lines. In July 2012 the Northern grid failed with 35,669 MWe load in the early morning, and the following day it plus parts of two other grids failed again so that over 600 million people in 22 states were without power for up to a day.

A KPMG report in 2007 said that India needed to spend US$ 120-150 billion on power infrastructure over the next five years, including transmission and distribution (T&D). It said that T&D losses were some 30-40%, worth more than $6 billion per year. A 2012 report costs the losses as $12.6 billion per year. A 2012 report costs the losses as $12.6 billion per year. A 2010 estimate shows big differences among states, with some very high, and a national average of 27% T&D loss, well above the target 15% set in 2001 when the average figure was 34%. Installed transmission capacity is only about 13% of generation capacity.

Nuclear power supplied 20 billion kWh (3.7%) of India's electricity in 2011 from 4.4 GWe (of 180 GWe total) capacity and after a dip in 2008-09 this is increasing as imported uranium becomes available and new plants come on line. Some 350 reactor-years of operation had been achieved by the end of 2011. India's fuel situation, with shortage of fossil fuels, is driving the nuclear investment for electricity, and 25% nuclear contribution is the ambition for 2050, when 1094 GWe of base-load capacity is expected to be required. Almost as much investment in the grid system as in power plants is necessary.

The target since about 2004 has been for nuclear power to provide 20 GWe by 2020, but in 2007 the Prime Minister referred to this as "modest" and capable of being "doubled with the opening up of international cooperation."

However, it is evident that even the 20 GWe target would require substantial uranium imports. In June 2009 NPCIL said it aimed for 60 GWe nuclear by 2032, including 40 GWe of PWR capacity and 7 GWe of new PHWR capacity, all fuelled by imported uranium.

This 2032 target was reiterated late in 2010 and increased to 63 GWe in 2011. But in December 2011 parliament was told that more realistic targets were 14,600 MWe by 2020-21 and 27,500 MWe by 2032, relative to present 4780 MWe and 10,080 MWe when reactors under construction were on line in 2017.*

* "the XII Plan proposals are being finalized which envisage start of work on eight indigenous 700 MW Pressurised Heavy Water Reactors (PHWRs), two 500 MW Fast Breeder Reactors (FBRs), one 300 MW Advanced Heavy Water Reactor (AHWR) and eight Light Water Reactors of 1000 MW or higher capacity with foreign technical cooperation. These nuclear power reactors are expected to be completed progressively in the XIII and XIV Plans."

The 16 PHWRS and LWRs are expected to cost $40 billion. The eight 700 MWe PHWRs would be built at Kaiga in Karnataka, Gorakhpur in Haryana's Fatehabad District, Banswada in Rajasthan, and Chutka(in Madhya Pradesh.

After liability legislation started to deter foreign reactor vendors, early in 2102 the government said it wanted to see coal production increase by 150 Mt/yr (from 440 Mt/yr) to support 60 GWe new coal-fired capacity to be built by 2015. This would involve Rs 56 billion new investment in rail infrastructure.

Longer term, the Atomic Energy Commission however envisages some 500 GWe nuclear on line by 2060, and has since speculated that the amount might be higher still: 600-700 GWe by 2050, providing half of all electricity. Another projection is for nuclear share to rise to 9% by 2037.

INDIAN NUCLEAR POWER INDUSTRY DEVELOPMENT

Nuclear power for civil use is well established in India. Its civil nuclear strategy has been directed towards complete independence in the nuclear fuel cycle, necessary because it is excluded from the 1970 Nuclear Non-Proliferation Treaty (NPT) due to it acquiring nuclear weapons capability after 1970. (Those five countries doing so before 1970 were accorded the status of Nuclear Weapons States under the NPT.)

As a result, India's nuclear power program has proceeded largely without fuel or technological assistance from other countries. Its power reactors to the mid-1990s had some of the world's lowest capacity factors, reflecting the technical difficulties of the country's isolation, but rose impressively from 60% in 1995 to 85% in 2001-02. Then in 2008-10 the load factors dropped due to shortage of uranium fuel.

India's nuclear energy self-sufficiency extended from uranium exploration and mining through fuel fabrication, heavy water production, reactor design and construction, to reprocessing and waste management. It has a small fast breeder reactor and is building a much larger one. It is also developing technology to utilise its abundant resources of thorium as a nuclear fuel.

The Atomic Energy Establishment was set up at Trombay, near Mumbai, in 1957 and renamed as Bhabha Atomic Research Centre (BARC) ten years later. Plans for building the first Pressurised Heavy Water Reactor (PHWR) were finalised in 1964, and this prototype – Rajasthan 1, which had Canada's Douglas Point reactor as a reference unit, was built as a collaborative venture between Atomic Energy of Canada Ltd (AECL) and NPCIL. It started up in 1972 and was duplicated Subsequent indigenous PHWR development has been based on these units, though several stages of evolution can be identified: PHWRs with dousing and single containment at Rajasthan 1-2, PHWRs with suppression pool and partial double containment at Madras, and later standardized PHWRs from Narora onwards having double containment, suppression pool, and calandria filled with heavy water, housed in a water-filled calandria vault.

The Indian Atomic Energy Commission (AEC) is the main policy body. The Nuclear Power Corporation of India Ltd (NPCIL) is responsible for design, construction, commissioning and operation of thermal nuclear power plants. At the start of 2010 it said it had enough cash on hand for 10,000 MWe of new plant. Its funding model is 70% equity and 30% debt financing. However, it is aiming to involve other public sector and private corporations in future nuclear power expansion, notably National Thermal Power Corporation (NTPC) – see subsection below. NTPC is very much larger than NPCIL and sees itself as the main power producer. NTPC is largely government-owned. The 1962 Atomic Energy Act prohibits private control of nuclear power generation, though it allows minority investment. As of late 2010 the government had no intention of changing this to allow greater private equity in nuclear plants.

Nuclear reactors deployed in India

The two Tarapur150 MWe Boiling Water Reactors (BWRs) built by GE on a turnkey contract before the advent of the Nuclear Non-Proliferation Treaty were originally 200 MWe. They were down-rated due to recurrent problems but have run well since. They have been using imported enriched uranium and are under International Atomic Energy Agency (IAEA) safeguards. However, late in 2004 Russia deferred to the Nuclear Suppliers' Group and declined to supply further uranium for them. They underwent six months refurbishment over 2005-06, and in March 2006 Russia agreed to resume fuel supply. In December 2008 a $700 million contract with Rosatom was announced for continued uranium supply to them.

The two small Canadian (Candu) PHWRs at Rajasthan nuclear power plant started up in 1972 & 1980, and are also under safeguards. Rajasthan 1 was down-rated early in its life and has operated very little since 2002 due to ongoing problems and has been shut down since 2004 as the government considers its future. Rajasthan 2 was restarted in September 2009 after major refurbishment, and running on imported uranium at full rated power.

The 220 MWe PHWRs(202 MWe net) were indigenously designed and constructed by NPCIL, based on a Canadian design. The only accident to an Indian nuclear plant was due to a turbine hall fire in 1993 at Narora, which resulted in a 17-hour total station blackout. There was no core damage or radiological impact and it was rated 3 on the INES scale – a 'serious incident'.

The Madras(MAPS) reactors were refurbished in 2002-03 and 2004-05 and their capacity restored to 220 MWe gross (from 170). Much of the core of each reactor was replaced, and the lifespans extended to 2033/36. Kakrapar unit 1 was fully refurbished and upgraded in 2009-10, after 16 years operation, as was Narora 2, with cooling channel (calandria tube) replacement. Following the Fukushima accident in March 2011, four NPCIL taskforces evaluated the situation in India and in an interim report in July made recommendations for safety improvements of the Tarapur BWRs and each PHWR type. The report of a high-level committee appointed by the Atomic Energy Regulatory Board (AERB) was submitted at the end of August 2011, saying that the Tarapur and Madras plants needed some supplementary provisions to cope with major disasters. The two Tarapur BWRs have already been upgraded to ensure continuous cooling of the reactor during prolonged station blackouts and to provide nitrogen injection to containment structures, but further work is recommended. Madras needs enhanced flood defences in case of tsunamis higher than that in 2004. The prototype fast breeder reactor (PFR) under construction next door at Kalpakkam has defences which are already sufficiently high, following some flooding of the site in 2004.

The Tarapur 3&4 reactors of 540 MWe gross (490 MWe net) were developed indigenously from the 220 MWe (gross) model PHWR and were built by NPCIL. The first – Tarapur 4 – was connected to the grid in June 2005 and started commercial operation in September. Tarapur 4's criticality came five years after pouring first concrete and seven months ahead of schedule. Its twin – unit 3 – was about a year behind it and was connected to the grid in June 2006 with commercial operation in August, five months ahead of schedule. Tarapur 3 & 4 cost about $1200/kW, and are competitive with imported coal. Future indigenous PHWR reactors will be 700 MWe gross (640 MWe net). The first four are being built at Kakrapar and Rajasthan. They are due on line by 2017 after 60 months construction from first concrete to criticality. Cost is quoted at about Rs 12,000 crore (120 billion rupees) each, or $1700/kW. Up to 40% of the fuel they use will be slightly enriched uranium (SEU) – about 1.1% U-235, to achieve higher fuel burn-up – about 21,000 MWd/t instead of one third of this. Initially this fuel will be imported as SEU.

Kudankulam 1&2: Russia's Atomstroyexport is supplying the country's first large nuclear power plant, comprising two VVER-1000 (V-412) reactors, under a Russian-financed US$ 3 billion contract. A long-term credit facility covers about half the cost of the plant. The AES-92 units at Kudankulam in Tamil Nadu state have been built by NPCIL and also commissioned and operated by NPCIL under IAEA safeguards. The turbines are made by Leningrad Metal Works. Unlike other Atomstroyexport projects such as in Iran, there have been only about 80 Russian supervisory staff on the job. Construction started in March 2002.

Russia is supplying all the enriched fuel through the life of the plant, though India will reprocess it and keep the plutonium*. The first unit was due to start supplying power in March 2008 and go into commercial operation late in 2008, but this schedule has slipped by five years. In the latter part of 2011 and into 2012 completion and fuel loading was delayed by public protests, but in March 2012 the state government approved the plant's commissioning and said it would deal with any obstruction. Fuel loading was in September, and unit 1 started up in mid-July 2013, with unit 2 expected to do so early in 2014. Unit 1 was connected to the grid in October 2013 and is expected in commercial operation at full power early in 2014, with unit 2 following in October 2014. Each is 917 MWe net.

While the first core load of fuel was delivered early in 2008 there have been delays in supply of some equipment and documentation. Control system documentation was delivered late, and when reviewed by NPCIL it showed up the need for significant refining and even reworking some aspects. The design basis flood level is 5.44m, and the turbine hall floor is 8.1m above mean sea level. The 2004 tsunami was under 3m.

A small desalination plant is associated with the Kudankulam plant to produce 426 m^3/hr for it using four-stage multi-vacuum compression (MVC) technology. Another reverse osmosis (RO) plant is in operation to supply local township needs.

Kaiga 3 started up in February, was connected to the grid in April and went into commercial operation in May 2007. Unit 4 started up in November 2010 and was grid-connected in January 2011, but is about 30 months behind original schedule due to shortage of uranium. The Kaiga units are not under UN safeguards, so cannot use imported uranium. Rajasthan 5 started up in November 2009, using imported Russian fuel, and in December it was connected to the northern grid. RAPP 6 started up in January 2010 and was grid connected at the end of March. Both are now in commercial operation.

Under plans for the India-specific safeguards to be administered by the IAEA in relation to the civil-military separation plan, eight further reactors were to be safeguarded (beyond Tarapur 1&2, Rajasthan 1&2, and Kudankulam 1&2): Rajasthan 3&4 from 2010, Rajasthan 5&6 from 2008, Kakrapar 1&2 by 2012 and Narora 1&2 by 2014.

In mid-2008 Indian nuclear power plants were running at about half of capacity due to a chronic shortage of fuel. Average load factor for India's power reactors dipped below 60% over 2006-2010, reaching only 40% in 2008. Some easing after 2008 was due to the new Turamdih mill in Jharkhand state coming on line (the mine there was already operating). Political opposition has delayed new mines in Jharkhand, Meghalaya and Andhra Pradesh.

A 500 MWe prototype fast breeder reactor (PFBR) is under construction at Kalpakkam near Madras by BHAVINI (Bharatiya Nabhikiya Vidyut Nigam Ltd), a government enterprise set up under DAE to focus on FBRs. It was expected to start up about the end of 2010 and produce power in 2011, but this schedule is delayed significantly. Construction was reported 94% complete in February 2013. Four further oxide-fuel fast reactors are envisaged but slightly redesigned by the Indira Gandhi Centre to reduce capital cost. One pair will be at Kalpakkam, two more elsewhere.

In contrast to the situation in the 1990s, most reactors under construction more recently have been on schedule (apart from fuel shortages 2007-09), and the first two – Tarapur 3&4 – were slightly increased in capacity. These and future planned ones were 450 (now 490) MWe versions of the 202 MWe domestic products. Beyond them and the last three 202 MWe units, future units will be nominal 700 MWe.

The government envisages setting up about ten PHWRs of 700 MWe capacity to about 2023, fuelled by indigenous uranium, as stage 1 of its nuclear program. Stage 2 – four 500 MWe FBRs – will be concurrent. Construction costs of reactors as reported by AEC are about $1200 per kilowatt for Tarapur 3&4 (540 MWe), $1300/kW for Kaiga 3 & 4 (220 MWe) and expected $1700/kW for the 700 MWe PHWRs with 60-year life expectancy.

India's Nuclear Power Problem

In January 2010, before the nuclear disaster in Fukushima, Japan, and before the anti-nuclear protests in India spread nationwide, Anuradha Talwar was tallying up a demographic survey of the people of Haripur, a rural coastal village in West Bengal. Sitting on a tiled veranda, alternating between using her cell phone and directing the small army of young women sifting through spreadsheets, Talwar was determined to count every man, woman, and child who would lose their homes to accommodate a 10,000 megawatt nuclear reactor complex, the largest on the subcontinent. According to a senior government official, Haripur is an inhospitable environment where "most of the land [has] a high saline content and cannot be used for agriculture." Talwar knows better. The nuclear power complex would in fact evict some two hundred thousand farmers and fishermen. She dismisses the government's claim that Haripur is a barren wasteland by recalling the sumptuous meal of home-grown vegetables and fragrant fish curry that villagers prepared for her the previous evening.

A plump, soft-faced, middle-aged woman with thinning grey hair and sizeable *bindi,* she does not come across as someone who would lead the opposition against the West Bengal state government's attempted land grab. But Talwar, whose surname means "sword" in Bengali, has spent decades fighting for human rights and sustainable development in sectors as diverse as health care, gender equality, labour practices, disaster relief, malnutrition, and starvation. To her and to the villagers in Haripur, nuclear power is nothing special. They are not impressed by the prospects of developing a carbon-free energy system that would mitigate climate change. Nor are they drawn into the debate over the risks and uncertainties of generating nuclear energy. To them, what matters is that livelihoods are in jeopardy.

Similar scenes of resistance are rippling throughout India as the government of Prime Minister Manmohan Singh undertakes a massive expansion of the nation's nuclear energy program. In communities affected by India's growing nuclear power infrastructure, activists like Talwar are conducting surveys, handing out pamphlets, forming committees, contacting journalists, and staging protests. In some places, including Haripur, resistance to nuclear energy plans has even turned violent.

What is noteworthy about the bourgeoning local activism is how often it differs from the campaigns led by established anti-nuclear groups, who typically focus on the morality of nuclear weapons or the risk of a cataclysmic nuclear power plant accident. Instead, India's new grassroots activists are struggling against the government's nuclear energy plans for a wider variety of reasons, ranging from ingrained distrust of the government due to corruption and lack of accountability, to tangible local concerns such as losing land rights and economic livelihoods. The affected communities, largely comprised of farmers, fisherman, and miners, are essentially concerned with the broad and deep issues of democracy, citizenship, and government responsibility. At its core, the resistance is challenging the distribution of power and how it governs relationships between the state, citizens, and private interests.

A dramatic case in point is the rising furor over the Koodankulam nuclear plant in the state of Tamil Nadu, at the southern tip of India. Protests that intensified after the Fukushima accident forced officials to delay the commissioning of the plant, scheduled to go critical last December. In March, hundreds of protesters from farming and fishing communities, many of them women, converged on the nearby village of Idinthakarai in an effort to halt construction activities at Koodankulam. Led by local resident and long-time anti-nuclear activist S. P. Udaykumar, they organized demonstrations and began a relay fast. In response, authorities placed Idinthakarai under martial law and arrested some two hundred protesters. Reports say that activists were beaten and subjected to religious profiling and open mob violence, while Singh apportioned the blame for the protests against Koodankulam on foreign hands. The stirring of Indian unrest over a program ostensibly intended to boost India's broad economic fortunes and reduce the nation's contribution to global warming is a cautionary tale of what can go wrong when policies are formulated primarily around technological considerations at the expense of profound concerns related to community well-being, culture, and justice.

In undertaking a massive project destined to directly impact the lives of millions of citizens, the Indian lesson shows it is essential that governments bolster democratic institutions and foster a transparent airing of all concerns. These would include questions about whether and how land should be acquired for nuclear infrastructure development, what kinds of compensation and rehabilitation would be due to displaced communities, how the government should recognize tribal identity and sovereignty over resources, and what responsibilities the government has towards safeguarding the health of communities, such as uranium miners, who are embedded from the very start in the nuclear economy. The debate from the community to the national level should include the question whether nuclear energy is even the right choice for Indian energy security.

3

India: Making of Superpower

The rise of this growing nation will change the balance of power in Asia—and potentially the world. With nearly 1.1 billion inhabitants, India is the second largest country on earth in population, and seventh largest in geographical area, over 1.1 million square miles. This is almost 1,000 people for every square mile of area nationwide—much denser than even China.

Since achieving independence from British rule in 1947, it has seen its share of conflict, struggle and setbacks. Although India still faces many challenges, it is now poised to reach a higher position on the world scene than at any previous time.

The Indian economy has grown an average of around 6% annually over the past decade and 8% per year over the past three years—among the fastest rates in the world. It boasts an emerging middle class and increasing gross domestic product, exports, employment and foreign investment. This is complemented by a roaring stock market (index value up by a third in 2005 and by 200% since 2001), low external debt and large foreign exchange reserves.

Recent visits from leaders and officials from the United States, France, Germany and Russia have spotlighted India's rise. These wealthier nations see India as a trading partner with enormous potential.

Although it has not yet matched the financial performance of China—currently the fastest-growing economy in the world—according to some analysts, India shows even more long-term potential for rapid growth. Leaders from both nations have discussed the creation of a Chinese-Indian common market based on the European Union model. Although only an idea at present, if realized, it would be the largest economic system in the world, home for about 2.5 billion consumers—almost 40% of the human race (or 3 of every 8 people on earth)!

India's growth becomes more impressive in light of the fact that it is driven by a fraction of its population. Much of the nation remains a picture of rural poverty. Nearly all foreign investment in India goes to its six most urban states, with 22 other less developed states virtually ignored. This gap between city and country is keenly felt in places such as Gurgaon, a suburb of the Indian capital New Delhi: "In a land still plagued by deep poverty and backwardness, Gurgaon has become a renowned home of international call centers, business-processing operations, and information-technology firms. There are gleaming, glass-paned high-tech towers, condominium blocks, multiplexes, and shopping malls, where Indians dine at Ruby Tuesday, browse for Samsung electronics, or kick the tires at a Toyota, Ford, or Chevy dealer. If one overlooks the dusty pockets of poverty nearby, a few water buffaloes picking at garbage near shantytowns, the look is more Southern California office park than the India of yore" (*U.S. News and World Report*).

Despite the problems seen in India's underdeveloped countryside—for example, massive unmet infrastructure needs; more illiterate citizens than any other single nation—there are several areas in which the nation excels. These particular specialized talents have allowed a tiny percentage of the populace—perhaps less than 1%—to spearhead its move toward a higher standing in the world order.

INTELLECTUAL CAPITAL

India's economy is divided between agriculture (which accounts for a quarter of the gross national product), manufacturing (constituting another quarter) and the high-tech service sector, which now makes up fully half of the gross national product. Striving to become a "knowledge superpower," it hopes to skip the intermediate step of industrial development that has preceded other nations' march into the Information Age. Scientific and information technology companies from around the world are opening research and development labs in India—more than 100 in the past five years. One mainstay of the new economy is software development, with ever more global firms outsourcing to India the time-intensive work of programming. Businesses worldwide also rely on the country for customer service—phone calls from around the world are directed to call centers in Indian cities such as Bangalore. Other developing markets include pharmaceutical and biotechnology research. Currently, the majority of top American companies send some of their IT work to India, and there is little evidence of a slowdown in this trend.

The business world is also looking in India's direction. Graduates of the nation's business programs are in high demand among multinational corporations, with each graduating class commanding a higher average salary than the one before. Those who complete MBA degrees at schools such as the Indian Institute of Management can now expect starting salaries ranging from $75,000 (USD) at Indian firms to over $200,000 outside the country. This is comparable to graduates of top American business schools such as Harvard, Stanford and Dartmouth—testimony to the market value of Indian talent in this area of study.

Military Buildup

As its clout has grown, India has placed a high priority on improving its military capabilities as well.

New Delhi has not joined 187 other nations in signing the Nuclear Non-proliferation Treaty (NPT), and appeared on the world's radar screen as a nuclear-armed nation in May 1998, with the detonation of five warheads in the desert near the border of Pakistan. This disturbed many governments around the globe, naturally including that of Pakistan, which responded with nuclear tests of its own. This stand-off was the turning point that began India's pursuit of a full-fledged nuclear weapons program. According to *The Bulletin of the Atomic Scientists*, additional nuclear missile tests occurred in the summer of 2004; since then, the Indian Defense Ministry has earmarked $2 billion annually to build 300 to 400 weapons over the next 5 to 7 years.

India maintains a "no first strike" nuclear policy, and asserts that it only seeks enough nuclear weaponry to effectively deter aggressors. U.S. President George W. Bush, during a March 2006 visit with Indian Prime Minister Manmohan Singh, announced cooperation between the two countries on civilian nuclear programs, and had previously called India a "responsible" nuclear nation (*Der Spiegel*). These measures drew an American diplomatic line between India and other nations that have nixed participation in the NPT, such as North Korea and Iran.

Whatever its nuclear aspirations, the country has a long military shopping list. Last year, it announced plans to build the first aircraft carrier ever put to sea by a developing nation, and to lease two nuclear submarines from Russia. America has openly discussed the sale of naval vessels, combat aircraft, patrol aircraft and helicopters to India. One former U.S. ambassador to India opined, "Of course we should sell advanced weaponry to India. The million-man Indian army actually fights, unlike the post-modern militaries of many of our European allies" (*The Economist*).

A Turning Point in Relations With China?

Many have compared India's pattern of growth to its neighbor, China. The countries have much in common—physical borders, immense populations, similar challenges, ancient civilizations, and quickly-rising economies. India also measures itself against China, coveting its economic power and international standing, including its permanent seat on the United Nations Security Council.

Though a degree of tension does remain between the two nations, with lingering memories of the brief 1962 war in which China soundly defeated India, the relationship between these two Asian giants is warming up. Trade between them is now increasing at a vigorous pace, and diplomatic relations are at a post-1962 highpoint. Chinese Prime Minister Wen Jiabao, during a recent visit to New Delhi, hailed cooperation between the two nations as the driving force of a new "Asian Century." Indian Prime Minister Singh spoke of the potential for India and China to rearrange the world order by working together.

Many have pointed out that their economic strengths seem to be tailor-made for a partnership. India seeks to be a major player in the computer software world in the same way that China is in the area of hardware. Cooperation between Beijing and New Delhi could prove a dominant force in the information technology market.

Both nations have a voracious appetite for natural resources, and a recent energy deal neatly symbolized the new Sino-Indian dynamic: India acquired a 20% share in the development of the largest onshore oil field in Iran. The venture happens to be operated, and 50% owned, by Sinopec—China's state-run oil company.

However, India could seek to undercut China's manufacturing prices (as China did with many Southeast Asian countries in the 1990s). But it is more likely to pursue a different segment of the world market by producing higher-quality goods, as well as entirely different products.

Time will tell exactly how the relationship will mix competition and cooperation. These two nations both aspire to "first-world" status—and economic gains could be the incentive for a more tightly allied Asia.

Between East and West

With its newfound power, India faces a dilemma: Should it ultimately pursue closer ties with Western nations, or with other Asian countries?

After India gained independence, its first prime minister spoke of an Asian renaissance, envisioning a tightly bound continent changing the post-World War II landscape. Though premature at the time, the idea is now more feasible than any time since the Cold War era. Along with the improving relations with China, India is also friendly with Russia and Japan. And, as of 2004, the value of India's trade with other Asian nations surpassed that of exchange with the United States and Western Europe put together (*International Herald Tribune*).

But the United States—after courting India's arch-rival Pakistan as an ally in the war on terror after the September 11 attacks—is now distancing itself somewhat from the current Islamabad regime led by Pakistani President Pervez Musharraf, focusing on India instead. India's common ground with the U.S. includes liberal democratic government, capitalism and, among the more educated urban residents, the English language. However, America's courting of India is viewed by some as a way to limit and contain Chinese influence in Asia. Some Indians resent this perception of their nation as a pawn of the U.S. Though they appreciate the American lifestyle and culture, much of the Indian population still sees this lone superpower as a bully.

While it may be able to dance with both partners alternately for a while, India will eventually be forced to choose. Which way will this nation turn?

"Kings of the East"

We need not merely guess where world events will ultimately lead. While many of the details remain to be seen, the overall framework of the future has been recorded in advance in one book—the Holy Bible.

In nations such as India, the size of population alone pulls them toward superpower status. Bible prophecy describes global power blocs—superpowers, or groups of superpowers—that will be prominent at the end of the age, shortly before Jesus Christ returns.

These powers will be based in the north (Europe), the south (the Arab world), and the "kings of the East"—a group of Asian nations that will band together, eventually fielding a standing army of*two hundred million* (Rev. 16:12; 9:16; Dan. 11)!

The nations of the West, including the United States, are headed for hard times as a result of their national and personal sins against the God that inspired the Bible. He reveals that they will be forsaken by their allies, called "lovers" in Scripture:

"And when you are spoiled, what will you do? Though you clothe yourself with crimson, though you deck yourself with ornaments of gold, though you rend your face with painting, in vain shall you make yourself fair; your *lovers* will despise you, they will seek your life…All your *lovers* have forgotten you; they seek you not; for I have wounded you with the wound of an enemy, with the chastisement of a cruel one, for the multitude of your iniquity; because your sins were increased" (Jer. 4:30; 30:14). India is today one of these "lovers," but one that will soon prove to be something very different. So will other nations that Western countries now consider to be allies. Keep watching India's growth toward superpower status—just one part of the inevitable rise of Asia!

MAKING INDIA AN IT SUPERPOWER

We can do it!

India has come a long way from the days it was considered a land of snake charmers and oriental bric a brac! Today, the images that are getting conjured up in the minds of global citizens have more to do with hi-tech software development facilities, cutting-edge R&D centers and 24x7x365, constantly humming, offshore outsourcing environments that represent a giant, ever-expanding IT hub.

Even a chatty, New York cabbie will tell you that the software programmers that Silicon Valley is reputed for are from a techno-Shangri-la called India. Without a doubt, India has arrived on the global map and it's been all thanks to the country's two-decade old, relatively young but vibrant IT industry.

Clearly, the nexus between India and IT is getting stronger with each passing day. For a country that lagged behind in the industrial revolution, this rapid catching of the technology bus has been nothing short of a miracle. Riding high on the global IT wave, India has not only managed to keep pace with the rest of the developed world, it has even moved ahead in the hotly competitive technology race. India is now a well-recognized face on the world IT firmament. It is a country that is being increasingly identified with high-quality IT products, services and processes as well as a wealth of skilled manpower that ranks among the best in the world. India's vast pool of trained computer professionals is fuelling the growth of the fast-paced IT sector in the country.

By the looks of it, there's no stopping the Indian IT juggernaut!

India as IT Superpower?

It is no longer a question of whether India has arrived in the world-wide IT marketplace, but about whether the country can assume the leadership position in this segment. Whether it can emerge as the Superpower in the global IT arena, ahead of the more experienced, mature competitors such as the USA, UK, Australia and other hot-blooded young turks such as China, the Philippines, Malaysia, Ireland and the Latin American bunch.

The answer to the question might lie in the countless studies conducted by Indian and global IT industry associations, in the projections set forth by well known business intelligence majors and global consultancy firms and in the faith vested by the Indian Government in this burgeoning sector. That the Indian IT industry is set to achieve higher goals and cross more momentous milestones appears to be the viewpoint binding these disparate think tanks. Crystal ball gazing related to the IT industry is marked by positivism. Current day oracles are *gung ho* about the future fortunes and prospects of India's most sizzling industry and certain it is meant for bigger things.

India's IT software and services exports alone are estimated to cross an ambitious US$ 50 billion by 2008 *(the NASSCOM-McKinsey 2003 Report)*.

India's existing fact sheet on the IT sector also indicates a rosy picture for the industry. Here's what the Indian IT segment has going for it:

- Impeccable credentials in the global markets based on the successful customer engagements of Indian IT industry stalwarts. Today, one in three global companies outsources its IT software development or business processes to India
- Mature processes (based on global standards such as ISO, SEI CMM Level 5 and CMMi Level 5), that have given the Indian IT sector a high quality, state-of-the-art-orientation
- A liberal regulatory and policy framework that encourages investment by multinationals and creates a conducive climate for making India a preferred offshoring IT services and ITES-BPO destination
- A global-class and constantly improving telecommunications and physical infrastructure (transportation, real estate, etc.) that is catalyzing the growth of the IT industry, particularly the software export segment

- A ready supply of qualified, high quality, engineering and IT manpower, one of the most crucial ingredients for a successful IT sector
- A huge base of English-speaking graduates that forms a strong platform supporting the ITES-BPO industry
- A large number of IT professionals with relevant domain knowledge (expertise in financial, accounting, banking, insurance, healthcare, telecommunications, retail and other areas)
- A ready supply of professionals with relevant IT skills from both formal and informal sector institutions

India's IT manpower forms the crucial link

While the above mentioned factors are all contributing towards enhancing India's chances of achieving world-wide IT supremacy, it is the manpower factor that will finally determine the country's ascendancy to the Number One slot within this global segment.

It will finally be the contribution made by India's young IT talent that will tip the global scales in the country's favour and establish it as a "superpower" in the market. However, it will not be IT skills alone, but rather "relevant, industry-oriented IT skills" that will enable the Indian IT sector engine to gather steam. What this means is that the youth of the country have not only to turn to IT as a meaningful and preferred career destination, they also have to focus on building the correct skill sets through appropriate training. Countries like Taiwan, that managed to achieve leadership in the IT hardware design and production segment, offer us interesting insights on the role education can play in achieving global success. The Taiwanese model of higher education was virtually focused on "mass-creating" electronic engineers-manpower that was ably harnessed by the nation's export-centric semiconductor, personal computer and smart devices industries.

India too needs to take such a focused approach to manpower building for the IT sector. Both the formal and non-formal educational institutions have to work collaboratively to meet the broader IT manpower goals and create curriculum and IT training programs that are in tune with the requirements of the industry.

Tips for Young India

Young India, meanwhile, has to opt for IT training that comes from the premier IT education schools-training that is high quality, reliable, cutting edge and complete.

Such training will not only equip students to participate in the job-rich, IT and non-IT sectors, it will also allow existing IT professionals to reskill themselves with more up-to-date technology knowledge.

Leading training institutions such as NIIT, Asia's Number One IT/ITES education tiger, are working in close partnership with Indian software industry players to create and provide specific skills and relevant, hands-on IT abilities.

The Indian IT training pioneer has developed an awesome mix of IT training programs targeted at almost every kind of learner. From school children entering the IT world, to students wanting to build a career in IT, to professionals learning new skills-NIIT has something for everyone.

Of particular importance to India and Indian students, is NIIT's flagship IT career program, GNIIT.

Recently refined and refurbished, the program is bringing additional specializations within the IT domain, creating manpower that possesses very specific, high-level IT expertise.

GNIIT helps create industry-ready professionals through its one-of-a-kind, 12-month Professional Practice that places students in a live, enterprise environment. It's no surprise then that India's CIOs and IT HR heads prefer to recruit GNIITians *(Dataquest HR survey 2001-03)*.

With manpower continuing to remain the key input in India's global IT success formula, the entire country-students, the IT industry, the formal and non-formal computer training institutions-has to gear up and work towards attaining the targeted landmarks.

The lesson in this for Young India is to go out there and Just Do It! With Gen Next by its side, India can live its dream of becoming a global IT superpower. By all accounts, we can certainly do it!

Statistically Speaking

The statistics, put forth by business intelligence firms, merchant bankers and leading IT industry associations such as NASSCOM, McKinsey & Co., Goldman Sachs, among others, seem to point to a robust, high growth Indian IT industry in the future. Can India make it to IT Superpower status?

- India's knowledge-worker population grew to 650,000 software and services professionals in 2003-04 from 6800 in 1986
- India's IT workforce could grow to 2 million in 10 years (a Goldman Sachs 2004 study)
- According to a NASSCOM-KPMG study, there will be a manpower requirement of around 0.97 million in the IT export services segment. The ITES sector, will need 2.72 million professionals by 2012
- By 2012, the ITES/IT industries could provide direct employment to about 5.1 million people, of which around 3.7 million would be for IT services and IT-enabled services
- The IT sector currently contributes three percent to India's GDP but is slated to account for 8-10 percent of the GDP by 2008
- The software and services export clocked an annual growth of 30 percent in 2003 and constituted 32 percent of the total exports. This was despite the challenging global IT environment and world-wide economic downturn
- The ITES-BPO sector grew in excess of 50 percent during the 2002-04 period. The industry is expected to maintain this rate of growth
- Estimates of the potential number of US offshorable professional services jobs range from 3-4 million over the next decade. Even if this number were doubled to consider potential offshoring jobs from other parts of the world, that would only represent 1.5 percent of India's labour pool
- Beyond IT, offshoring opportunities exist in a number of IT assisted roles in industries like accounting, financial services, medical services and pharmaceuticals.

GLOBAL POWER BALANCE 2020

The global power balance has been in a churning state ever since the turn of the millennium. The disintegration of the Soviet Union enabled the United States global strategic predominance to be unrivalled and unquestioned. Concerned by United States unilateralism., Russia and China as the two nations most strategically affected set in motion two significant initiatives to offset the US predominance.

Russia under the dynamic leadership of President Putin set Russia on a course of strategic and military resurgence. This was facilitated by rising Russian oil revenues. China with significant economic resources at its disposal embarked on a strategic build-up of its strategic assets and military upgradation. The United States decade-old strategic global predominance was now to be under challenge by Russia and China. This strategic challenge by these two nations became further accentuated as a result of United States getting inextricably tied down militarily in Afghanistan and Iraq.

The current global economic turbulence has prompted many strategic analysts to re-examine the short-term global balance of power perspectives with 2020 taken as a more identifiable time frame. Some would like to believe that the current economic melt-down could affect the global power balance and the inter-se strategic equations between USA, Russia and China. They would like to suggest that the United States as the strongest economy in the world could weather the storms, but Russia and China, and especially Russia's resurgence and its strategic challenge to the United States could be diluted.

This Author would like to maintain that the economic meltdown today is globalised in its dimensions and would therefore affect USA, Russia and China without any exception. However, Russia and China's strategic programs directed at altering the global power balance would not be diluted. This besides other reasons, is valid, because Russia and China are not involved in any costly strategic distractions like the United States in Iraq and Afghanistan, requiring a significant outlay of financial resources.

Otherwise too, it is conceded by many economists that economies of the world surface more strongly after economic depressions. Strategically, the historical evidence cannot be ignored that the Second World War took place within a decade of the Great Depression in which the United States was the most vitally affected.

Therefore, in strategic analysis such economic depressions may act as "speed breakers" but definitely do not bring global strategic power rivalries to a "dead end".

With the above as an introductory background, this Paper attempts to analyse "Global Power Balance 2020: Perspectives" under the following heads:

- Global Power Balance 2020 Will be Bi-polar in Nature
- Multi-polarity is a Political and Strategic Myth
- United States Would Have Strategic Edge Over Russia in a Bi-polar World
- A New Cold War is Inevitable.

Global Power Balance 2020 Will be Bi-polar in Nature

Assertions of this Author in this direction stand examined in fair detail in earlier SAAG Papers and particularly those dealing with Russia's resurgence. This Author firmly believes that the global power balance in 2020 would be bi-polar in nature with the United States and Russia as the two poles.

Russia is being dismissively discussed in US and Western think-tanks and Russia's resurgence is de-emphasised and devaluated. This dismissive attitude is not born out of realistic strategic analysis but wishful thinking that Russia does not emerge as a strategic challenge to United States global predominance.

The moot question that needs to be considered is that who amongst Russia and China is more strategically potent to challenge United States global predominance?

Even on current analysis the following strategic realities suggest that Russia is the foremost candidate to challenge USA and not China (1) Russia's existing strategic nuclear weapons arsenal outnumbers the United States whereas China's nuclear arsenal at about 400 warheads is a remote comparison (2) Russia's existing power projection capabilities extend far beyond its immediate neighbourhood, in all dimensions – land, sea and air. China's power projection is limited to her periphery and limited to ground forces dimensions only (3) Russia is an "energy self-independent" state and this is an essential pre-requisite of national power. Japan and Germany lost the Second World War because they were not "energy self-reliant" (4) Russia has existing strategic partnerships with many countries across the globe. China has no "natural allies" to boost her strategic power (5) Russia's resurgence has been welcomed in many regions and more importantly in the Middle East. China is not viewed as a credible strategic challenger to the United States.

More importantly Russia has been a practitioner of global power politics in the bi-polar environment of the Cold War and successfully provided countervailing power to the United States for 45 years. Further, it needs to be noted that Russia was not defeated by the United States in the Cold War; it was Russia that defeated itself.

Russia's current strategic and political resurgence is precisely aimed in this direction once again, namely, to reclaim her former superpower status. It has won recognition in Europe, Middle East, Central Asia and South East Asia too. Reading between the lines one gets a sneaking feeling that the United States may prefer China as a manageable strategic rival rather than Russia. But the strategic realities indicate that the United States would in 2020 have to accept a bi-polar world with Russia as the second pole.

Multi-polarity is a Political and Strategic Myth

Multi-polarity as a desirable state in the global power balance was forcefully enunciated by China to begin with in the immediate period following the demise of the Soviet Union. To begin with, in the early 1990s, China advocated a multi-polar world incorporating China, India, Iran and Syria with Pakistan added. Later inducements were to include France and Germany. This enunciation never took off though being repeated periodically.

So the initial Chinese model of multi-polarity comprised Asian nations with no strong strategic linkages with USA as the unipolar power. China then as the only nuclear weapons state in this grouping may have been led to believe that it would emerge as the natural leader of its proposed multi-polar grouping.

Russia today also talks of multi-polarity but one suspects that it is more for political reasons in favor of China than any strategic conviction. Russia would strategically prefer a bi-polar world at the global level and without frowning on multi-polarity at the regional level.

China, Japan and India even with the full development of their strategic strengths cannot hope to equal the strategic potential of being super-powers in the classical sense of definition of the term.

They can sit on the global powers high table as associate global players, but not as "super powers". China, Japan and India therefore are incapable of emerging as multiple poles to bring about a multi-polar world. Only the United States and Russia qualify to be superpowers. Available indicators suggest that the United States and Russia would be the two super-powers in 2020 and no scope exists for any of the other global players intruding into that league.

4

Challenges of Foreign Policy and Super Power in India

INDEPENDENCE OF FOREIGN POLICY

India's capacity for autonomous action in foreign policy is of fundamental importance to nationalists. This has taken on different policy manifestations at different times, including as "non-alignment" during the Cold War and more recently as "strategic autonomy." As Foreign Minister S.M. Krishna noted in a September 2009 speech, "Our main objective is ensuring a conducive international environment for consolidating our strategic autonomy." Nationalists tend to see New Delhi as being under constant pressure to submit India's interests to those of other major powers.

This usually means from the United States, though at different times it has also meant from the West in general or China. Nationalists see foreign policy as an arena of conflict, with major powers constantly seeking to subvert India's pursuit of its national interest to force New Delhi to follow policies that are in the interests of other powers.

For example, some commentators charged that India's passivity towards Pakistan over the last decade, despite evidence of Pakistani complicity in terrorism directed at India, was made at the behest of the United States because of Pakistan's importance to U.S. interests—in other words, that Indian policy was being dictated by Washington. This criticism is often invoked by nationalists on issues as varied as India's position at the Cancun climate change summit in December 2010, where India was seen as bending to U.S. pressure to accept legally-binding emission cuts, or its February 2006 vote to refer Iran to the UN Security Council. This was also one of the key objections that nationalists had to the U.S.—India civil nuclear deal. As one analyst noted, "We are forgetting that we are being sucked into a situation that will hobble the independence of our foreign policy." Nevertheless, it is important to note that there were some differences within the nationalist camp on the nuclear deal, and some who could be characterized as nationalist did support the deal.

The fear of losing independence in foreign policy is the primary reason why nationalists oppose any alliance-alliances are seen as a way of subverting Indian interests to those of others. It was this deeply-held value that Prime Minister Manmohan Singh was referring to in September 2010 when he said that "India is too large a country to be boxed into any alliance." The idea that alliances are constraining rather than a way of security burden-sharing explains the Delhi elite's enduring suspicion of great powers, especially the United States. This does not mean that India has no interests in common with other powers, but such common interests are likely to be on particular issues rather than in general. Thus, nationalists prefer foreign policy cooperation on a case-by-case basis to long-term alliance relationships which could tie India down.

Opposition to Power Politics

Nationalist opposition to balance of power politics has its roots in the tradition of Jawaharlal Nehru, the country's first prime minister. Even though Nehru's ideological reasoning may have withered away, an analyst recently noted that "the Nehruvian instinct of staying away from balance of power considerations has not.... it is fair to say that balance of power is not the default common sense of Indian strategic thinking." Jasjit Singh, a leading Indian strategist, echoed that thought, saying, "Indian strategic culture does not accept conflict as inevitable." Writing about India's policy towards China, Singh continued that India's central goal in relation to other powers is "to address potential adversarial relations through political and diplomatic efforts to improve relations and rely on cooperative engagement as the primary instrument of strategy... [N]onalignment itself was pursued as a strategy to diffuse the strategic challenge posed by China." This opposition to power politics grows out of the strongly held belief that "India can and must play its role as conscience-keeper of the world." Thus, there is frequent invocation of alternative paradigms such as "comprehensive security" that are designed to be "cooperative, multilayered and multi-lateralized."

The nationalist opposition to power politics also makes for continuing controversy and considerable discomfort about episodes in which India has reached out to other countries to counter a threat. Nehru's desperate plea to President John F. Kennedy for U.S. military assistance to deal with the Chinese invasion in the fall of 1962 is particularly noteworthy because the opposition to power politics owes so much to Nehru himself.

The streak of moralism which runs through this opposition to power politics has another manifestation: a strong and abiding commitment to global nuclear disarmament. India's commitment to nuclear disarmament is usually treated with some skepticism outside the country, and indeed even by some within the country. But even if there is posturing in India's diplomatic positions, there can be little doubt about the sincerity of the sentiment regarding nuclear disarmament among sections of the Indian strategic elite.

India's Innate Importance

India's economic growth, information technology prowess, and rising power have reshaped global perceptions of India and India's perception of itself. A decade after India's nuclear tests, India's global relations have dramatically improved and New Delhi is increasingly wooed by major powers. Indian commentators have not been slow to notice that leaders from all of the permanent members of the UN Security Council visited India in 2010. For nationalists, this was a recognition of India's importance which called for a "noiseless celebration."

The possibility exists, however, that at least some of India's strategic elite are inflating India's capabilities and attractiveness. Yashwant Sinha, a senior Bharatiya Janata Party (BJP) leader and former Minister for External Affairs, expressed this overconfidence well when he argued, in the context of the recent visit by President Obama to India, that "the U.S. needs India more" than India needs the United States. For instance, the United States was forced to lift the sanctions it imposed on India after the 1998 Indian nuclear tests because "these sanctions were causing more damage to the U.S. than India." This belief that India was so important that other powers would not stand by idly if India was invaded-possibly even leading to a world war is presumably one of the reasons why Nehru thought that China would not attack India militarily in 1962. The sense of India's intrinsic importance is also reflected in India's push for a permanent seat on the UN Security Council. Though all shades of foreign policy opinion in India broadly support a permanent seat for India, nationalists tend to emphasize such demands more.

Equity and Democratic Global Governance

A key determinant of nationalist positions on specific foreign policy issues is their claim that India must stand for democratic global governance. Nationalists support the UN as the key global multilateral forum "which embodies the collective will of its member states and the rule of law." What this means in the abstract is not often clear, but it is usually invoked in reference to the actions of other global powers rather than to India's own behaviour.

For example, though nationalists strongly support multilateralism, this rarely extends to issues that might impact Indian interests and sovereignty such as Kashmir or arms control. Nationalists generally tend to equate democratization of world politics with multi-polarity.

Thus, nationalists propose working together with other powers in groups such as the IBSA Dialogue Forum towards a multi-polar world order. Equity in international interactions is another fundamental concern of nationalists, leading many times to legalist rather than political arguments on international issues. This should not be surprising since the Indian government has often been criticized for just such a predilection, and many of those who would hold nationalist views are former Indian diplomats.

This was the basis of much of the opposition to the U.S.—India nuclear deal among some nationalists, who joined with other critics from both the left and the right of the political spectrum in parsing every statement and document for signs of U.S. perfidy. For example, they pointed out that the United States had unilaterally altered or reinterpreted a previous nuclear cooperation agreement for the supply of nuclear reactors to the Tarapur nuclear plant in the 1970s.

This emphasis on equity can also be seen in the focus on the rights of states, especially developing ones, rather than obligations. Such legalism tends to make nationalists inflexible and dismissive of arguments based on political changes.

Rising Pragmatism

The end of the Cold War led to new challenges and new debates about India's foreign policy. Some Indian strategists, referred to here as the pragmatists, argued that India's traditional foreign policy was no longer relevant to the post-Cold War world, and pushed for the unabashed consideration of the Indian national interest rather than global justice or ethics.

The Primacy of National Interest

One of the key arguments made by the new pragmatists is that Indian foreign policy has for far too long been driven by ideological positions which have not promoted India's national interest. Therefore, they argue that national interest rather than global concerns or ideology should guide Indian policy. Pragmatists have, for example, wondered why India is so committed to the UN. T.P. Srinivasan, a former Indian diplomat, noted that "India's commitment to multilateralism and the U.N. is firm and absolute... And yet, India has very little to show in reciprocal advantages, which India has gained over the years from the U.N." Pragmatists tend to be skeptical of the UN in general, though they are not averse to the idea of India in the UN Security Council. They tend to be much more realistic about the prospects of any such entry in the future, however, and dismissive of the urgency with which such demands are made in the Indian debate, characterizing these as "immature yearnings."

Morality and Compromise

Pragmatists tend to be impatient with moral claims in foreign policy. As Shashi Tharoor, who would become India's junior foreign minister, put it once, traditionally India "seemed to take greater satisfaction in being right than being diplomatic." More recently—and controversially—he criticized Nehruvian foreign policy for being a "moralistic running commentary." But direct criticism is not the only tack that pragmatists have used to argue against the moralism in Indian foreign policy.

Others have argued that Indian foreign policy was actually not particularly moralistic, which also is an argument to suggest that there is little reason for Indian foreign policy today to try to live up to such traditions. Pragmatists tend to blame misplaced moralism for India's previous strategic missteps, such as not conducting a nuclear test in the 1960s so that India could join the nuclear Non-Proliferation Treaty (NPT) as a nuclear weapon state. In contrast, nationalists dismiss these new claims, suggesting that those who proclaim themselves as realists have "little awareness of what real politic means."

Pragmatists argue that India should be flexible in the pursuit of its national interests, especially on ideological issues. They believe that Indian policy is often geared towards consistency with past positions without recognizing India's changed circumstances, especially in the aftermath of the 1998 nuclear tests. This is particularly visible in India's nuclear policies. Pragmatists find the deeply held Indian opposition to the Comprehensive Test Ban Treaty (CTBT) and many other nuclear arms control policies outdated and suggest that India take a fresh look at such issues.

But as strategist C. Raja Mohan suggested, Indian foreign policy debates are so focused on semantics that "they have little time for the 'grammar' of global power politics." He argues that this focus on semantics was understandable when India was weak, when "rhetoric compensated for power," but unnecessary for an India that has become far more consequential in global affairs. Pragmatists think that New Delhi should carefully weigh foreign policy choices, assessing the overall benefit rather than costs alone.

Alliances

Pragmatists are much less doctrinaire about alliances than nationalists are. While nationalists make non-alignment the basis for Indian foreign policy, pragmatists are not as concerned about that foreign policy heritage. Although they are critics of the excessive focus on non-alignment, pragmatists do not necessarily suggest that India needs to align with other powers.

For example, while pragmatists tend to be strong supporters of closer U.S.—India relations, they do not see the relationship as an alliance. A hostile China may bring the United States and India together in the near term, but "it is far from certain on which side of the U.S.—China divide India's long-term interests lie." Nevertheless, pragmatists suggest much closer U.S.— India cooperation not only on political and military issues, but also on issues of the global commons. But pragmatists also suggest closer military ties with powers other than the United States, such as Russia, as a way of hedging against any potential threat from China. In essence, though they have not suggested that India should ally with other powers, this appears to be more because they do not yet see the necessity for such alliances rather than because of any ideological opposition.

International Treaties

Pragmatists do not share the suspicion which nationalists have of many international treaties or agreements. For pragmatists, while there might have been good reasons for India not to accede to particular international agreements in the past, India's changed global circumstances should also lead to changes in its approaches to international treaties. This is particularly true for various arms control agreements and initiatives. Pragmatists have not only supported signing the CTBT, but also initiatives such as the Proliferation Security Initiative (PSI). Similarly, pragmatists suggest that India should prepare the groundwork for the Fissile Material Control Treaty (FMCT) rather than simply opposing the treaty. Since the key objection to the treaty is not having sufficient fissile materials, India should decide how much fissile material it needs and how to acquire it prior to an FMCT coming into force.

Opposing Perspectives, Disputed Policies, and Implications

These opposing perspectives have led to far greater disagreements over India's foreign policy than at any time in the past. Below are four specific policy disputes, all of which have particular policy relevance for the United States.

U.S. Relations

India's policy towards the United States has become increasingly contested. Pragmatists want closer ties—they see the United States as being useful to India right now—while nationalists remain suspicious that the United States seeks to contain India.

For the nationalists, "there is a fundamental contradiction between U.S. and Indian long-term foreign policy objectives" because while "the U.S. wants the current so-called unipolar world order to continue, India believes that the world should be multipolar, with India itself as one of the poles." Others suggest that the key problem is the U.S. dependence on Pakistan. As a former Indian Foreign Secretary asked, "If the U.S. has a long-term strategic partnership with a Pakistan that remains unremittingly hostile to India, how does it reconcile that reality with its strategic partnership with India?" Pragmatists, on the other hand, are willing to push for closer relations with the United States, even if that increases the possibility that it could lead to greater difficulties with other powers such as China.

They suggest that it is in India's interest to build up ties with the United States, given the close relations that China has had with Pakistan for decades and the fact that India is an attractive partner for the United States, both because of U.S. worries about a rising China and the clout of India's burgeoning market.

The debate over the U.S.—India civil nuclear deal is an illustration of the growing clout of the pragmatists. The Indian decision to go ahead with the deal finally owed more to Prime Minister Singh's determination to push it through than to pragmatist success in the public debate over the issue. Nevertheless, the debate over the nuclear deal demonstrated for the first time that the pragmatists could mount a credible challenge to the traditionalist dominance over a key area of foreign policy. There is little indication that the dispute over the appropriate type of relations which India needs to have with the United States will be resolved in the near future.

Arms Control

India's arms control policy is a second area of conflict between these two perspectives. Nationalists continue to be suspicious of many arms control agreements, holding out for nuclear disarmament as the right way forward. To the extent that they are willing to consider arms control measures, they require that such treaties directly contribute to nuclear disarmament rather than simply be stand-alone measures. Nationalists tend to be particularly opposed to treaties such as the CTBT and the FMCT, which are seen as non-proliferation measures rather than steps towards nuclear disarmament.

On CTBT, for example, nationalists would suggest that India should not sign the treaty unless all others do and add conditions such as the treaty being nondiscriminatory with a clearly-established link to nuclear disarmament. In essence, these conditions would suggest that India will not sign the CTBT in the foreseeable future. But pragmatists want India to be more open to considering a different approach. For example, arguing that India took the lead on CTBT in the 1950s, pragmatists have argued that India should rejoin discussions about nuclear non-proliferation rather than dismiss them. Similarly, pragmatists suggest that India should be more open to working with the nuclear non-proliferation regime, even if the NPT itself is considered unacceptable.

Iran

India's position on Iran, specifically on Iran's dispute with the United States and the international community on the nuclear issue, has become another hotly contested foreign policy issue. The most serious conflict over Iran is between the pragmatists and leftist opinion-makers, who see the Iran nuclear issue through their traditional anti-American prism. The left has traditionally had little influence on Indian foreign policy, but was influential in the first Singh government because Communist parties were part of the ruling coalition and the government depended on their support to stay in power.

The nationalists have made common cause with leftists on this issue, dismissing U.S. claims that Iran is seeking nuclear weapons and supporting Iran's right to develop civilian nuclear technology. The nationalists are not necessarily united in their views on Iran, however. Some see Iran as "a neighbour with which India is linked by many centuries of economic, cultural and even civilizational ties." Other nationalists tend to worry about Iran's links to Pakistan, especially on the nuclear black market, and are suspicious of Iran's efforts to compare their illegal nuclear programme with India's.

It is not that nationalists are particularly supportive of closer ties with Iran, but their objection is to what they perceive as U.S. pressure on Indian foreign policy, of which Iran is only one manifestation. Writing about the purported U.S. pressure on the stillborn Iran—Pakistan—India gas pipeline project, one former senior official wrote that "the pipeline never was really a brilliant idea... But that apart, it was India's decision—good or bad, right or wrong." Thus, India's Iran policy has become an important test of whether Indian foreign policy is sufficiently independent from the United States, with critics of the government claiming that New Delhi kowtows to Washington. Pragmatists tend to defend India's taking a position against the Iranian nuclear programme, such as voting against Iran at the International Atomic Energy Agency (IAEA), by pointing out that Iran had not lived up to its obligations and India had little reason to support Iran. Rejecting charges that such a position represented giving in to U.S. pressure, one analyst characterized the Indian position as "Enlightened Independence." This is another dispute that shows little sign of ebbing.

INDIA'S SAARC SATELLITE PROPOSAL AND POLICY

Indian Prime Minister Narendra Modi undertook a two-day official visit to Nepal on August 2–3. Surprisingly, no Indian prime minister had visited Nepal—with whom India shares more than 1,700 kilometers of borders—for 17 years. Modi articulated his vision for Indo-Nepal relationship with four C's: cooperation, connectivity, culture, and constitution. As a part of his vision, he also spoke about developing a satellite to assist India's neighbors. Naturally, Modi is looking at satellite technology as a tool for cooperation and connectivity.

Narendra Modi became India's prime minister on May 27. On June 30, after witnessing the launch of PSLV-C23, carrying the French earth observation satellite SPOT-7, he addressed India's rocket scientists. While congratulating the Indian Space Research Organisation (ISRO) for the successful PSLV launch, he also outlined his vision for India's space program. He argued in favor of changing the perception that India's space program has an elitist agenda. He emphasized that space technologies are being used for socioeconomic development and, over the years, have proved their utility for common people.

During his speech, Prime Minister Modi also argued for the need to share India's space expertise with its neighbors. He proposed to develop a "SAARC satellite" for the region and also to expand the footprint of India's satellite navigation program to South Asia. This indicates that generally New Delhi is keen to use India's expertise in space as an instrument of foreign policy. It's worth examining and deliberating about the possible design of such a vision in the context of SAARC.

The South Asian Association for Regional Cooperation (SAARC) was established in 1985. This organization has a key focus on economic and developmental issues. SAARC has eight members: Afghanistan, Bangladesh, Bhutan, India, Maldives, Nepal, Pakistan, and Sri Lanka. Additionally, there are some nations with observer status, including the United States, Australia, Japan, and China. Myanmar (Burma) also has the status of an observer, but is keen to become a full member. This country shares more than 1,600 kilometers of borders with India. Owing to geographical and political realities for this discussion, Myanmar is thus considered as a part of SAARC. Over the years, SAARC has evolved various areas of cooperation, and science and technology is one such area of interest. They have developed a cooperation mechanism that includes areas like environment, energy, education, and media. In the areas of science and technology cooperation, SAARC established a Meteorological Research Centre (SMRC) in

1995. It undertakes collective research in meteorology in the SAARC region. It has a modern and advanced observing system with a reliable and timely communications network. Also, there is a network for regional cooperation on subjects like hydrology, oceanography, seismology, and atmospheric science. Obviously, such networks rely on satellite-derived data.

Amongst the SAARC member states, India is the only spacefaring nation with a number of satellites operating in various orbits. Pakistan is another state with reasonable interest in space field. However, in spite of its early start and its knowledge of "rocket science" (it has a well-developed missile program), Pakistan has not made much progress in space arena. Their space agency, known as Space and Upper Atmosphere Research Commission (SUPARCO), was established during 1961 as a committee and was granted the status of a Commission in 1981. Badr-1 (Badr-A) was Pakistan's first indigenously developed satellite and was launched from China on July 16, 1990. This satellite is no longer operational. Pakistan's second satellite, BADR-B, an Earth observation spacecraft, was launched on December 10, 2001. Subsequently, Paksat 1, its first geostationary satellite, was acquired in 2002. China launched Paksat-1R, a communication satellite for Pakistan, on August 12, 2011. In November 2013, a CubeSat called iCUBE-1 was launched in a polar orbit to take low-resolution images of the planet.

There are two other SAARC states with satellites in their inventory. One is Sri Lanka. Its first satellite is actually a commercial satellite and was launched by China in 2012. Otherwise, Sri Lanka is likely to launch its first geostationary communications satellite by 2015, in collaboration with a Chinese company. The other nation is Afghanistan, which started using its first satellite in May of this year. This satellite, called Afghansat 1, was acquired to boost the telecommunications sector. This is an orbiting Eutelsat satellite that was launched in December 2008 and with is designed to last until 2020. Afghan's Ministry of Communications and Information Technology is renting this satellite for US$4 million per year.

Apart from these two nations, Bangladesh has shown some interest in research related to space. The Bangladesh Space Research and Remote Sensing Organization (SPARRSO), established in 1980, is a state agency concerned with astronomical research and the application of space technology. They propose to launch their first satellite, called Bangabandhu-1, around 2015. There are some unconfirmed reports that Maldives could be assisted by China to evolve their space agenda in near future.

This is the existing "SAARC space footprint" that is providing assistance to a limited population. By contrast, India's proposed SAARC satellite would be serving the interests of entire SAARC population, almost 1.5 billion people. The SAARC region included many nations plagued by poverty and conflict. In this region, in a relative sense, India is an island of prosperity surrounded by states fighting to win over security and economic challenges. At the same time, within India there are also visible disparities between rich and poor. It's also worth noting that two nuclear weapon states are the part of this grouping and there are some inherent security contradictions amongst some of the states in the region.

The geography of the SAARC region is unique, with coastlines, forests, deserts, and mountains. It has one of the youngest mountain ranges in the world, the Himalayas. They influence the major rain providing system for the region, the monsoon. The major rivers in South Asia are the Ganges, the Indus, and the Brahmaputra. Major deserts include the Thar Desert, which covers large areas of both Pakistan and India, with an approximate area of 175,000 square kilometers. Mainly tropical weather systems influence the Indian peninsula and other island states. Extra-tropical weather systems influence the survival of people staying close to Himalayan region. The region is prone for earthquakes, and a few tsunamis have taken place in the recent past.

These geophysical and geopolitical realities of the region should be taken into account before suggesting any model for the SAARC satellite. India needs to evolve a joint mechanism involving representatives from all member states to decide on the expectations from the proposed SAARC satellite. Before designing such a satellite, it would be important to identify and zero in on the specific and urgent needs of the nations in the region. Broadly, the various socioeconomic challenges of SAARC nations could be at least partially addressed by communications satellites, weather satellites, and remote sensing satellites.

Considering the issues like necessities of member states, cost, time, and expertise required for development and launch of a satellite, the best option for India could be to develop an Earth observation satellite as the first SAARC satellite. Basically, such a satellite could be of much use for land and water resources management for the entire region. India would also be expected to assist member states to develop ground infrastructure and create expertise. Some analysts believe that, at times, SAARC gets held hostage to the divergence of the India-Pakistan relationship. In fact, satellite technology could come very handy to silence such critics. As confidence building measures, such technology could be used to undertake joint surveillance of the border regions and resolve issues related to infiltration, water sharing, and more.

India's Regional Satellite Navigational Network is likely to become operational by the end of 2015. As suggested by Prime Minister Modi, India could offer these facilities to the SAARC states as well. To assist civilian aircraft for navigation and non-precision approaches over India airspace, ISRO has developed a GPS-Aided Geo Augmented Navigation (GAGAN) system. India could also allow access to this system to aircraft operating within SAARC airspace.

Presently, what is important for India is not to limit itself with the idea of a SAARC satellite but instead to effectively use its existing capabilities in space to assist the various SAARC members. Most of these nations, being novices in the field of satellite technology, may not be in a position to ask India for specific assistance. India needs to become proactive and share with these nations imagery and other relevant data. In 2005, the Asia-Pacific Space Cooperation Organization (APSCO) was established, which is the only multilateral space mechanism presently available for the region. Among the SAARC members, only Bangladesh and Pakistan are members of APSCO and, from the SAARC point of view, such a body is not of much use. India could take a lead to establish a SAARC space cooperation mechanism, which could also bring more transparency into the system. Such agency could play a major role towards coordinating various data sharing and training related activities.

In SAARC, India is the dominant player; in the space arena, it is the only player. It is important for India to guard against developing any form of so-called "big brother attitude." While establishing a relationship with other nations, India should not play only the role of assister. India needs to develop a system where these nations could be made partners in various activities. To reduce rivalry (if any) and promote solidarity among members, India could engage these nations in important space projects to create a sense of belonging. Presently, India is working on a program to develop Astrosat, a dedicated astronomy satellite that is likely to be launched in 2015. India could involve SAARC members in this project and could call this satellite "SAARC Astrosat." Also, with the Sri Lankan government, India could undertake a feasibility study for developing a joint spaceport in that country.

SAARC region is bound together not only by geography but also (in some sense) by culture, ethnicity, traditions, religion, and languages. At the same time, this region has various strategic fault lines with strong differences on issues among some member nations. Any proactive collaboration in the outer space arena is unlikely to resolve all issues of differences. However, in an era of tremendous growth in information technologies, the Internet, mobile telephony, and social media, satellite technology could form the basis to establish a common SAARC identity.

Saarc: India needs to lead the way

The upcoming summit of South Asian Association for Regional Cooperation (Saarc) will be held against the backdrop of important global and regional developments. On one hand, it is increasingly clear that the advanced Western economies are unlikely to see off the economic downturn in the short-run. This will have a knock on economic effects on South Asian countries in the form of weakening the demand for their products.

On the other hand, the context in the subcontinent is changing in a manner that augurs well for closer regional economic linkages. Taken together, these trends could provide an opportunity to infuse a muchneeded sense of purpose to Saarc. India should take the lead in re-programming Saarc for the next decade and ahead.

South Asia is one of the least economically integrated regions of the world. Intra-regional trade is just about five per cent of total official trade. The contrast with other sub-regions of Asia — let alone other parts of the world — is sobering. For instance, intra-regional trade in East Asia accounts for over 50 per cent of total trade. The current situation in South Asia seems all the more stark when we set it against its past record as well as its future potential. Before 1947, this region boasted of more or less open borders, allowing for easy movement of goods and services.

Furthermore, the subcontinent also enjoyed close economic ties with other parts of Asia. The regional arc stretching from Kolkata to Singapore was a vibrant network of trade, finance and entrepreneurs that formed the economic heartland of the British empire in Asia. South Asia does not have to rest on its history. It continues to have tremendous potential to grow through trade. The region has the highest population density in the world. It has a large number of cities close to the borders. And there is considerable cultural, ethnic and linguistic overlap of populations across the borders.

What, then, has prevented closer regional and sub-regional economic integration? At one level, the answer can be found in the economic policies and outlook of the countries of South Asia since independence. The experience of colonialism led the newly independent countries — with the notable exception of Sri Lanka — to regard the idea of an open trading system with some suspicion and to pursue more autarkic economic policies and plans.

India and Pakistan also struggled to come to terms not only with the political consequences of Partition but also with its economic implications. The two countries were at odds on economic issues ranging from division of assets to exchange rates — differences that put paid to the idea of free trade between them. The problem was compounded by India's propensity to treat its borders as fences to keep others out rather than using them as gateways for the movement of goods, people and ideas. The under-development of India's own border areas, which were wont to be seen as buffer zones, undermined India's ability to promote regional trade.

These economic issues have been overlaid by political differences. Reconciling the two is not all that simple. Economic affairs tend to have a win-win logic. It is easy to see how cooperative exchange could work to the material benefit of all parties. But in politics moral considerations such as identity and honour can outweigh material interests. This is a problem that India faces with almost every one of its neighbours. What's more, if political differences have a national security angle to them, it becomes all the more difficult for the logic of economic integration to assume primacy. Economic affairs are about absolute advantages accruing from interchange, but security affairs are about relative advantages gained by one side or another.

Here too, India's immense lead in size and power as well as outstanding political disputes have worked to reduce the attraction of closer economic ties in the subcontinent.

The issues will not go away any time soon. But there are some indications that South Asian countries are willing to try according greater importance to economic linkages as opposed to political and security considerations. For one thing, India's economic growth in the last two decades has positioned it to credibly play the role of a regional dynamo. India's neighbours are slowly realising the tremendous opportunity that India presents for their growth prospects. India's free trade agreements with Sri Lanka and Bhutan, and the trade and transit agreement with Nepal have highlighted the potential benefits of regional economic integration.

It is not surprising that Bangladesh wants to greatly enhance trade and connectivity with India, or that Pakistan has at last agreed to confer "Most Favoured Nation" status on India. In the context of the continuing economic downturn in the West, India could become rather more important to its neighbours. For another, India too has understood the fact that allowing its neighbours to partake of its growth is essential both to draw the sting from political differences and to enable India to play a role on the global stage. Once the largest recipient of foreign aid, India now extends aid and developmental assistance to most of its neighbours. These bilateral programmes are important, but India needs to help institutionalise pan-regional economic cooperation and eventually integration. The South Asian Free Trade Agreement (Safta) needs to be worth more than the piece of paper on which it was written. It's time India took concrete measures to hasten the implementation and expand the provisions of Safta.

The New Identity for the SAARC

With one-fifth of the world's population, the countries of South Asia face formidable challenges resulting from poverty, underdevelopment, and conflict within and among themselves. Their low levels of production, unemployment, and population pressures are not helped by historic exploitation and other adverse legacies. In an historical, cultural, physical and linguistic sense, South Asia is an integrated region, but any commonality across nations has been made impossible by deep-rooted divisions and animosities across the whole region. The latter is hugely polarized, and it has to grapple with gross violations of human rights. Consequently, governments in the region lack the effective initiative and political commitment needed to meet their obligations to respect, protect, and fulfil human rights and fundamental freedoms. Internal conflicts, civil strife, poverty and so-called state anti-terror legislation and measures have resulted in violations of the civil liberties of the people.

The South Asian Association for Regional Cooperation (SAARC) was established in 1985 with the objective of promoting regional cooperation between seven South Asian countries: Bangladesh, Bhutan, India, Nepal, the Maldives, Pakistan and Sri Lanka. Despite the extremely slow pace at which SAARC moves and its very limited achievements, the association did receive an increase in its membership when Afghanistan became the 8th member in 2007. However, the Association has from its very beginning been up against hard politics, mutual fear, and a strong sense of rivalry between its two principle members: India and Pakistan. One reason for SAARC's unimpressive progress is a lack of agreement among the member states on what should be the guiding force towards regionalism. SAARC has consequently been unable in any way to achieve its basic objective of promoting regional cooperation and solidarity. It is a disgrace that after nearly 30 years it has nothing to show and nothing to celebrate.

Even now SAARC is still trying to steady itself. It may not have made any great mark, but at least it has not been disbanded and it continues to function, albeit in a haphazard manner. Sadly, the presence of this regional organization has done nothing to remove historical irritants between members or to lower the levels of suspicion and distrust among neighbors.

Disputes between member states have led to outright wars, low-intensity conflicts, cross-border terrorism, a debilitating arms race and some very hostile propaganda. SAARC has failed to prevent any of these and they in turn have held up SAARC's progress. Belonging to a regional forum for nearly 30 years has led to no shared values or norms and, despite some points of commonality in the past, the member states have been unable to map out a common future.

South Asia today is a black spot for the gross violation of human rights and civil liberties. The people of Bhutan have as yet seen no glimpse of democracy, and they are deprived of all kinds of freedoms under the rule of an assertive kingship.

Pakistan enjoys a pseudo democracy. Nepal has been faced with a serious political crisis from more than a decade: it has no proper government, no constitution, a dead civil society, and a puppet media.

India, a so-called growing economy and the largest democracy on earth, faces political crises and internal instability from Kashmir to Assam. Kashmir is regarded as 'a legal black hole' in terms of human rights violations perpetrated by the armed forces.

Most importantly, throughout the SAARC region, the poor are getting poorer and the rich richer: the gap between the two is widening further while the dynastic political elite and business people can enjoy whole states' welfare facilities and opportunities. Why is this happening?

Why there is so much that is unjust in this region? Is it not time for a radical rethink? Who is responsible? Is it not high time for the people of SAARC as a whole to seek common answers to common problems?

Despite a serious human rights crisis throughout much of the region, SAARC has not even given thought to adopting a specific, detailed and uniform human rights convention or charter despite the existence of these in all other major regions of the world. Is it not high time then for SAARC states to think seriously about it?

What is required is a widespread formal commitment to human rights across the whole region. This should take the form of bills of rights, the establishment of national human rights institutions, declarations by IGOs, and the establishment of regional human rights regimes. The latter would be relatively independent but coherent human rights sub-regimes operated within the larger framework of international human rights practice. Examples of major regional mechanisms are the European human rights monitoring mechanism, the Inter-American system, and the African system. All these regional mechanisms have created, under their human rights charter, bodies such as a commission and a court of human rights. These have broad mandates to monitor human rights compliance by states parties, to receive reports from states, to receive complaints from individuals and states, to investigate and to order interim measures to prevent any escalation of human rights violations. They also provide appropriate reparations for victims by the violators, and they publish their findings and make recommendations to pressurize the state parties concerned.

Many questions need to be asked today: has SAARC achieved anything in nearly three decades of existence? Why, compared with other regions, are they so backward in terms of everything? In almost every other region there is some kind of regional human rights mechanism: since a fifth of the world's population resides in the SAARC region, why have the SAARC nations never thought having one? Can a region so politically, socially, and economically volatile afford to go on ignoring this issue? Most importantly, can South Asia gear itself for real regional cooperation? Can national and regime interests become sufficiently harmonized in order to promote cooperative trust and mutual confidence among the power elites of the region? The very diversity of South Asia demands the gradual implementation of conceptual steps that build towards a distinct regional identity. One such conceptualization could well be the establishment of a SAARC regional human rights mechanism.

Towards Setting up a South Asian Human Rights Mechanism

Many questions need to be asked: Why is a separate charter for the promotion of human rights so important for the SAARC region? What would it add to existing practices? SAARC countries have signed already several conventions on narcotics, trafficking in women and children for prostitution, promotion of child welfare, and there have been several agreements on food security and various social issues.

However, there has been no regional agreement that specifically focuses on human rights and fundamental freedoms. A regional instrument would be regarded as an appropriate complement to the universal human rights instruments of the United Nations. Such regional human rights mechanisms are already established in the Americas, Europe, Africa and most recently the Arab States: the last major geographic area, therefore, without its own mechanism is the SAARC region. The Council of the League of Arab States adopted its own Arab Charter on Human Rights in 2004, and it has been in force since 2008. The Charter grants a number of human rights and fundamental freedoms to the people, and it provides for the election of a seven-person Committee of Experts on Human Rights to consider states' reports and to monitor states' compliance with the Charter.

Most SAARC countries have common problems concerning torture, trafficking, internal displacement due to conflict, refugees, rights over resources, urban shelter and demolition, domestic violation against women, the practice of the death penalty, and extra-judicial detention and forced disappearances. A few countries of SAARC have national human rights institutions. All SAARC countries have, or in the case of Nepal should soon have, a written constitution under which human rights are recognized as fundamental. Despite these provisions and initiatives, however, there is a deteriorating human rights situation in the region brought about by the anti-terrorism measures adopted in some South Asian countries, by internal political crises and civil strife and by the hostility of governments towards human rights despite their claims to be democratic. The SAARC region has suffered for centuries from the absence of a rule of law and constitutionalism and from a culture of impunity that affects almost all the countries. Is there not then an urgent need to formulate a regional human rights mechanism?

The majority of SAARC member states have still to ratify the optional protocols to the International Convention on Civil and Political Rights (ICCPR) and the Convention on the Elimination of All Forms of Discrimination against Women (CEDAW). Moreover, Bhutan has still to ratify the ICCPR, the International Convention on Economic, Social and Cultural Rights (ICESCR), and the Convention against Torture.

Even where treaties have been ratified, though, implementation has been restricted by the reservations of some countries that follow a narrow interpretation of treaties relating to civil and political rights, and by a limited political commitment to implement economic, social, and cultural rights. An effective regional human rights mechanism would ensure the protection and promotion of human rights in the region especially common issues including the rights of migrant workers, human trafficking, minority rights, the right to development, and, most importantly, it would challenge the existing culture of impunity and lawlessness in the region. Such a mechanism could also provide a less costly, more accessible and effective redress alternative to existing international processes and procedures.

Not all SAARC nations are democratic and those that claim to be on the way to being so easily slide into authoritarianism, as in the case of Bangladesh, Pakistan, and Nepal. The prospect, therefore, of ideological homogeneity across the region would seem to be anything other than bright. With over sixty per cent of its population still forced to survive below the poverty line, how could this region even claim to be democratic? Moreover, how could it claim to have a fully-fledged democracy until human rights are protected and enshrined in the international covenants?

The SAARC region faces serious challenges in consolidating democracy and strengthening and promoting human rights and the fundamental freedoms of its people. SAARC should now seriously consider establishing a regional human rights mechanism similar to those of the Inter-American or European Systems. The mechanism would certainly help states to promote and protect rights and freedoms effectively within their jurisdiction. It would ensure that international human rights laws were respected and promoted effectively throughout the SAARC nations. Moreover, such a mechanism could help people in the region to develop a common understanding of universal human rights issues, norms, values and perspectives.

By way of example, the Organization of American States governs human rights protection in the Americas. Both states and individuals can file cases and complaints. Under the American Convention on Human Rights, two bodies protect, promote and monitor human rights: a) The Inter-American Commission whose the primary function is to make a complaint to the Inter-American system whenever an American state is proved to have violated individual human rights; and b) The Inter-American Human Rights Court, which has jurisdiction over contentious cases mostly forwarded by the Commission. In the Inter-American system, both the Commission and the Court have made a major contribution to recognizing human rights, developing human rights jurisprudence and protecting human rights in the Americas. Elsewhere, the Council of Europe drafted a European Convention on Human Rights after Second World War in response to a call issued by Europeans from all walks of life. The Convention was designed to incorporate a traditional civil liberties approach to securing effective political democracy. The Convention created the European Court of Human Rights in Strasbourg, and any person, who feels that a state party has violated his or her rights under the Convention, can take a case to the Court. Judgments confirming violations are binding on all. To be credible and able to meet both the promotion and protection requirements effectively and practically, a future regional human rights mechanism for SAARC, based on a human rights charter, should have a minimum set of characteristics. These would include an ability to receive and decide upon individual and interstate complaints of human rights violations by the state party. It should have the potential to develop additional mechanisms such as special procedures and subsidiary bodies on thematic issues, working groups, etc. There would be a SAARC Human Rights Commission, with broad powers to investigate, make site visits, receive reports and complaints by states and individuals, and a SAARC Human Rights Court empowered to make binding decisions on human rights issues and grant reparations for victims of human rights violations by states. The human rights mechanism, as with other regional practices, would be able to cooperate with international human rights mechanisms. This would permit reinforcement of the existing human rights framework and the overcoming of procedural and institutional weaknesses in domestic jurisdictions as well as in the international system. It would also help to overcome any lack of expertise or experience in human rights jurisprudence and to ensure effective implementation and enforcement of human rights norms and standards.

National human rights mechanisms are more important and effective in addressing local issues: the regional mechanism would play a complementary role, especially with regard to cross-border matters. The regional mechanism would also be a useful platform for South Asian countries to utilize opportunities under the United Nations's Universal Periodic Review system, which monitors the human rights performance of all UN members. A future SAARC charter on human rights, similar that of the Inter-American system, would be a great breakthrough for the SAARC region.

A Human Rights Culture in the Region

Enough is enough—SAARC must no longer be a hostage of rival powers in the region. The South Asian states have been too reluctant to take forward the regional project in a manner that it deserves. The provisions of the SAARC Charter have been ignored. Regional cooperation remains at a very rudimentary stage, and there is little evidence of any desire to act regionally by building trust and avoiding force. Prominent Nepalese Professor Lok Raj Baral has argued: 'So whatever commonalities and shared values exist in the region, they hardly matter for making SAARC more meaningful for the peoples of the region. Unless the South Asian regimes are reconstructed (and this is perhaps a challenging task for South Asian power elites who come from a variety of backgrounds) for transforming the nature of the region, SAARC cannot make headway.' In the absence of the right political atmosphere no economic, political or social integration is feasible. Establishing a proper regional human rights mechanism could provide an alternative way of establishing a favorable political environment and of reconstructing the region politically, socially and economically.

Of course, there would be enormous challenges in establishing a regional human rights mechanism in South Asia because of the legal and geo-political hurdles. The politics of the South Asia continue to be affected heavily by the continuing tensions in Indo-Pakistan relations. There are contentious issues, too, in South Asia—such as water, migrant workers, trafficking, minority and indigenous communities, refugees, and border disputes—which need to be settled through bilateral and multi-lateral mechanisms. If the SAARC countries fail to address these factors, its very future is bleak. Most importantly, political commitment, sincerity, and establishing a culture of human rights and the rule of law across borders are essential. Now is the time to create a SAARC Charter on Human Rights in treaty form, a consensus document. This must be the primary focus of all SAARC nations. It is essential. It needs to be the departure point for all SAARC agendas; it needs to be the alpha and omega for SAARC's future plans, programs and cooperation. The basic norms and values of human rights guaranteed by the international human rights covenants and national constitutions has to be the guiding force for any economic, social, developmental, and political cooperation among the South Asian countries. Human rights must also be the guiding force for South Asian politics and for its democratic processes. These values must be above partisan politics and above the narrow interests of one or two nations. It has to be the means to common goals and agendas. Establishing the proposed human rights institution to monitor, promote, and consolidate human rights will bring the

SAARC nations together to achieve common aims and ambitions towards peace and prosperity. The new future human rights body must be the common forum and a milestone to bring the South Asian society together as a single body of humanity regardless of religious, political, cultural or ideological differences. The essence of human rights has the power to mend all differences!

INDIA'S FOREIGN POLICY CHALLENGES IN 2014

China

Since the new millennium, relations between India and China have been characterised by 'hot economics and cold politics' or 'cooptetion'—economic cooperation and political competition. In recent years, tensions between the two countries have increased due to the border dispute. According to Dr Harsh Pant at King's College London, "the lingering border dispute between India and China continues to be the single-most important impediment, though increasingly the larger context of this relationship is undergoing a transformation. As the balance of power in Asia changes and India strives to manage the rise of China with its own blend of internal and external balancing, this will assume a bigger profile in Sino-Indian bilateral ties." It is highly unlikely that relations between the two rising giants will improve in 2014, and will continue to be characterised by 'cooptetion' and military confrontation in the medium term.

Pakistan

The enduring Indo-Pakistan rivalry is well known. The Kashmir conflict and cross-border terrorism have historically led to tensions between the two countries. The beheading of an Indian soldier along the Line of Control (LoC) in January this year and incessant ceasefire violations since have vitiated relations between the two countries. LSE Professor Sumantra Bose avers that "cross-border incidents as well as terrorist incidents are symptoms of the deeply conflictual nature of the India-Pakistan relationship. The Kashmir dispute is real and important, but has simply provided a focal point for a multifaceted and deeply rooted antagonism." The emphasis on security obscures other aspects of the relationship, including a growing appetite on both sides of the border for increased bilateral trade. In the context of increasingly adverse domestic political environments in both countries – the jingoistic right-wing in India and Pakistan's irredentist military – hindering the diplomatic process, there is an even greater need to re-think India- Pakistan relations in 2014.

Afghanistan

India and Afghanistan have historically enjoyed friendly relations. According to Dr Shanthie D'Souza at the National University of Singapore, the most significant aspect of the India-Afghanistan relationship is that the "long history of cultural and civilisation linkages have been further strengthened by a decade of development assistance, capacity building initiatives and economic opportunities." India and Afghanistan have mutual economic and strategic interests—as Professor Bharat Karnad at the Centre for Policy Research, New Delhi, puts it: "India needs natural resources, access to Central Asia through Chabahar Port (in Iran), and the mineral-rich Hajigak region as a base for intelligence operations and, if needed, to squeeze Pakistan. Kabul needs Indian capital, technical assistance, development aid, and military assistance."

However, terrorism and resulting regional instability pose a serious challenge to the relationship. The "challenge remains in terms of establishing regional trade, transit and connectivity by making Afghanistan a land bridge connecting South with Central Asia from which both Afghanistan and Pakistan would derive tremendous economic benefits," adds Dr D'Souza.

United States

On the eve of Prime Minister Manmohan Singh's meeting with President Obama in Washington on 27 September, 2013, the media painted a gloomy picture of India-US relations. There were assertions that the relationship between the two largest democracies in the world was 'oversold' and experiencing a 'drift'. Indeed, there is no paucity of disagreements between the two countries: Pakistan, Afghanistan, UN reforms, permanent membership for India of the UN Security Council, and economic challenges such as India's unwillingness to open its markets. Professor Brahma Chellaney at the Centre for Policy Research underlines that the "India-US strategic partnership is somewhat lopsided and unbalanced because of India's structural and strategic limitations." In the new year, Dr Pant believes that "New Delhi and Washington will face the challenge of maintaining stable ties as the United States prepares to leave Afghanistan with help from the Pakistan military. But on larger strategic issues, there is a convergence between the two states that is as striking as it is potent. The relations are likely to only improve over the long term."

Iran

India has long pursued a careful balancing act between its relationships with Iran and the United States. In recent years, India and Iran have been trying to manage their economic, energy and political cooperation in the shadow of US and European Union sanctions. A potential US-Iran rapprochement will likely ease existing diplomatic and economic pressure on India in this context.

Iran under President Hassan Rohani is expected to enhance cooperation with India in the areas of energy, connectivity, trade, and on the issue of Afghanistan. Both countries also seek to enhance connectivity through the International North South Transport Corridor (INSTC) and the Chabahar Port. However challenges remain in the bilateral relationship. "The biggest challenge for India-Iran relations is that India does not have a clearly articulated foreign policy strategy towards Central Asia or the Gulf," explains Professor Lawrence Sáez at SOAS. "At a bilateral level, India does not engage directly with Iran, partially as a result of US pressure and mostly as a result of India's own inertia and strategic incompetence. At an international institutional level, India has shown little enthusiasm for including Iran as an active participant in SAARC."

Sri Lanka

India and Sri-Lanka have had cordial relations in the new millennium. LSE's Dr Rajesh Venugopal explains that "security cooperation, trade and investment, China and the Tamil situation are important factors in India-Sri Lanka relationship." Human right violations against Tamils and rehabilitation of Tamils in the national mainstream in Sri Lanka after the end of the civil war have strained diplomatic relations between the two countries. Ceteris paribus, Dr Venugopal believes that "relations are unlikely to improve in the next year simply because India will enter into election mode, and every party will be under pressure to attack Sri Lanka in order to win the Tamil Nadu vote." However, defence ties between the two countries would continue as usual through joint training, sharing of warfare expertise and military exchanges.

Vietnam

Bilateral ties between India and Vietnam have improved significantly in recent years. Due to its antagonistic relations with China, Vietnam is a key component of India's 'Look East' policy. Although the two countries have enhanced their political and security cooperation, there is still a need to strengthen commercial and economic ties. Both countries need to think creatively about expanding investment opportunities, especially in the energy, steel and pharmaceutical sectors. This can be done by establishing stronger institutional mechanisms that review and develop the economic relationship on a regular basis. The burgeoning relationship between the India and Vietnam raises concerns in China and may have repercussions on Sino-Indian relations in 2014 and onwards.

Bangladesh

Since Sheikh Hasina and her Awami League came to power five years ago, there has been tremendous goodwill for India in Bangladesh. There is a wide consensus that Sheikh Hasina has largely delivered on Indian security concerns by cracking down on terrorism directed against India from Bangladeshi soil. However, contentious issues remain in the bilateral relationship: the division of common river waters, the land corridor that India wants through Bangladesh to connect West Bengal to the north-eastern states, the continuing influx of undocumented migrants from Bangladesh through the porous border and the continuing presence of anti-India forces in Bangladesh despite the recent crackdown. "India's giant size and Bangladesh's smallness mean that it is difficult to negotiate equally to reach fair outcomes between the two countries," says LSE's Professor David Lewis. "The long border means Bangladeshis feel encircled and enclosed by India, leading to distrust and border tensions."

Nepal

In recent years, the increasing dominance of Maoism in Nepal's domestic politics, along with the strengthening economic and political influence of China, has led the Nepalese government to gradually distance itself from India. Nepal has also become a haven for terrorists and separatists operating in India: the recent arrests of two high profile terrorists – Abdul Karim Tunda and Mohammed Ahmed Sidibappa – have brought the India-Nepal border into sharp focus. India has been seeking Nepal's cooperation in managing the border through several bilateral mechanisms. However due to domestic political turmoil, lack of political will and a resource crunch, Nepal has been unable to effectively cooperate with India. But that could change if Nepal sees increasing political stability in 2014.

Burma

Political developments in Burma over the last two years have opened a new chapter in India-Burma relations. Burma, like Vietnam, is an important pillar in India's 'Look East' policy. Burma's internal political dynamics will determine the course of bilateral relations: Burma's transition from authoritarianism to democracy, communal and ethnic violence and implementation of bold reform initiatives presents immense challenges as well as opportunities for India. Challenges include the long-running border problems (compounded by the diplomatic row over pillar number 76 in the north-eastern Indian state of Manipur), Indian support for pro-democratic forces, China's influence and active role in state building in Burma and the uninterrupted flow of weapons from Burma for the rebels in north-east India among others. On the commercial front, India would like to gain access to Burma's oil and gas reserves but faces competition from other countries especially China. But given the limitations of Indian public sector investment in Burma due to bureaucratic hurdles, private-sector investment would have to increase in the new year in order to consolidate ties.

INDIA'S FOREIGN POLICY OPPORTUNITIES AND CHALLENGES IN MID-2014

India's foreign policy opportunities and challenges in mid-2014 under the leadership of India's new Prime Minister Narendra Modi will expectedly acquire bold and audacious contours dispelling the earlier ten years of appeasement and timidity. India's foreign policies in the 2004-2014 periods failed to exploit the strategic leverages that were being bestowed on India, internationally and regionally, in recognition of India's emerging major power potential in the process of crystallising till mid-2004.

Perceptionaly, what is evident in mid-2014 is the debris of collateral damages of obsessive Pakistan-centric and China-centric Indian foreign policy with no gains visible for indulging in appeasement of these two prominent India's military adversaries. Perceptionaly again, India during the preceding ten years seemed to have outsourced and mortgaged its foreign policy directions to Washington which was more sensitive to Pakistan's and China's sensitivities than Indian national security interests.

Prime Minister Modi's opening move even before oath-taking as PM was South Asia-centric and not Pakistan-centric as was being made out by the Indian media.

PM Modi made a significant and imaginative political outreach to the SAARC Nations when he invited their leaders for his oath-taking ceremony. That all of them came was a measure of the Indian Prime Minister's personal leadership waiting to unfold and his underlying objective of attaching first priority to India's SAARC neighbours.

They all came despite the very negative propaganda and demonization of Mr Modi indulged in by India's then ruling Congress Party from 2002-2014. PM Modi's opening foreign policy act was therefore well conceived by him as in light of the above negative campaign it gave an opportunity to SAARC leaders to personally size-up PM Modi and vice versa.

In a further act of reinforcing his India's neighbourhood-priorities policy it has been announced today that PM Modi's first foreign visit would be to Bhutan, a nation strategically important for India because looming large over it is China. Nepal having been lost to China by the flawed policies of the previous Government, India cannot afford to let Bhutan slip under China's influence likewise because of Indian insensitivities. Now moving to the larger canvas of India's opening moves under the new leadership of PM Modi, one would like to advocate that India's foreign policy initiatives to be classified in two major categories.

Category I nations would be those nations which present promising "Opportunities" to India in terms of evolution of more robust and substantial partnerships and in which their past record does not carry any baggage of discord or tensions with India. Such nations would also be those nations which in the contemporary global security environment enjoy strategic convergences with India and can hopefully be strategic assets in India's ascendant power trajectory.

Category II Nations would be those nations which are not likely to shape or emerge as "Opportunities" for India but would always be "Challenges" for India's foreign policy decision makers. Such countries have a record of discord, strategic distrust of India and many irritants exist in their relationships with India. They cannot be wished away but nor can India afford to allocate disproportionate time and effort to win them over.

In Category I Nations for Indian foreign policy attention I would like to include Japan, Vietnam, Indonesia, Israel and France and possibly Germany. In Category II Nations I would primarily classify and include USA, Russia, China, and Pakistan. These nations do not present opportunities for India to ascend the power-trajectory and more often than not would impede that process.

So as PM Modi starts planning his diplomatic calendar of foreign visits, it is the Category I Nations that should figure first. Japan should be PM Modi's' first foreign visit as both countries enjoy significant strategic convergences on Asian and Indo Pacific security and stability. A strong Strategic Partnership exists between the two nations and these need to be reinforced significantly, by

Japan being PM Modi's first port of call. Needless to state that in Asia there are only three major powers, namely, China, Japan and India. China is not willing to cede or share strategic space in Asia neither to Japan nor India. Further China is in a conflictual relationship with both Japan and India.

Vietnam has long and historic ties with India and also a Strategic Partnership with India. Geostrategically located, it is also a significant geopolitical player in South East Asia and ASEAN region. Combining his visit to Japan with a visit to Vietnam on the return leg would be a significant step for India and Asian security.

France also has been a good friend of India and has been a reliable and trusted supplier of arms and armaments to India, besides a substantial Strategic Partnership. The Indian Ministry of Defence has for far too long sat on and impeded the126 MRCA Rafael Fighter aircraft. This has seriously affected India's cutting edge defensive and offensive aerial combat capabilities. PM Modi with his dynamic style should prod the Indian Defence Ministry to finalise the deal within three months as it stood finalised a number of years back but for some nit-picking by the previous Government.

The United States has been placed in Category II because its intentions' and approaches to India have always been ambiguous and at times contentious. Its National Security Strategy in the past has included references to prevention of rise of hegemonic nations in Asia including India. Except for the short span of 2-3 years in the md-2000s the record is not of substantive support to Indians national security interests despite a much-touted Strategic Partnership. United States has still not forsaken playing balance-of- power games in the Indian Sub-Continent by balancing Pakistan against India. Too many trade irritants also exist. India would be well advised to go-slow in rushing head-long into a resuscitation of the Strategic Partnership and let it be reinforced by the pressure of the unfolding international power-dynamics.

Russia too has been placed in Category II because Russia in terms of Asian security still persists in giving weightage to China strategically over India. Gone are the days when Russia stood as a bulwark in India's favour as a countervailing power. India can afford to wait till geopolitically the Russia-China strategic nexus wears thin.

Lastly one comes to India's military adversaries namely China and Pakistan. No Nobel Peace Prizes await any Indian Prime Minister for a breakthrough in their adversarial relationships and postures against India. Without wasting disproportionate time on both of them, India should follow the policy of "Congagement" with Pakistan and China. 'Strategic Distrust' would continue to predominate for a long time to come until their domestic political dynamics bring about radical transformations in their political cultures.

PM Modi can be expected to bring about a radical transformation in India's military capabilities and higher defence structure endowing an inclusive role to India's military hierarchy in national security affairs. This would make India's defence capabilities that much stronger and enable India to withstand any military coercion or destabilisation by China or Pakistan besides making Indian foreign policy that much more robust.

Concluding, one can only refer to the pointers that are coming where China is making the first moves to establish contacts and dialogues with the new Modi Government in India and Pakistan would follow suit. Pakistan is not India's long term threat. It is China that is India's long term and potent threat and this strategic reality should not be wished away in our foreign policy making.

In terms of systemic changes in India's foreign policy structures, PM Modi should dispense with the system of Special Envoys system (a slot for retired IFS diplomats), Track II initiatives and so many other Tracks which foul up the foreign policy making structures. Let institutionalised foreign policy be the rule and if dramatic results are to be achieved it should be the prerogative and be coming from the dynamism of PM Modi himself. With so much on the plate to be handled in terms f India's foreign policy by Prime Minister Modi as he sets out to map India's foreign policies, it is incumbent that India's foreign policy objectives be prioritised and be categorised into "Opportunities" and "Challenges" in relation to India's national security interests. In the field of foreign policy formulation "Opportunities" are always fleeting and need to be grasped instantly. "Challenges" will always abound and must wait till geopolitical dynamics offer leverages to convert challenges into opportunities.

INDIAN FOREIGN POLICY UNDER NARENDRA MODI

The likely defeat of the Congress Party in India's 16th general election has prompted considerable debate about the impact a change of guard in Delhi will have on foreign policy. What would India's foreign policy look like in the event of the Hindu nationalist Bharatiya Janata Party (BJP) government coming to power, either on its own or with the support of allies?

Many in India and abroad believe that India's foreign policy is poised for a "sea change" under a BJP government, especially one headed by the strident Narendra Modi.

According to Sreeram Chaulia, professor and dean at the Jindal School of International Affairs in Sonipat, India, foreign policy under Modi-led government will see greater emphasis on commercial diplomacy, "more assertive actions in response to [Pakistan backed] cross-border terrorism," greater attention to long-term policy planning with a view to formulating grand strategy for scenarios in 2020 and beyond, "a bigger role for the military in shaping India's national security and formulating doctrines," and a greater say for the states in the government's formulation and execution of foreign policy.

Not much is known of Modi's foreign policy thinking. Even the BJP's election manifesto, which is said to carry his "definite imprint," sheds little light; just a over a page of the 52-page document is devoted to foreign policy.

A controversial and polarizing figure, Modi has often poured scorn on the Congress-led United Progressive Alliance (UPA) government's "soft" response to terrorist attacks emanating from Pakistan and to Chinese incursions into Indian territory. This has contributed to a widely held perception that he will be tough in his response to Pakistan-backed terrorism and would not baulk at the use of force. Modi is also expected to take a tougher stand in dealing with India's territorial disputes with Pakistan and China.What "tough" might mean in practice is unclear at this point, and how far Modi will go is hotly debated. Some have even argued that he may reserve the right to use tactical nuclear weapons against Pakistan in response to a major terrorist attack. Most, of course, don't go that far.

According to Chaulia, in dealing with terrorism emanating from Pakistan, Modi could go for "clinical counter-strikes" and covert operations, including targeted assassinations of key figures in the Pakistan-based, anti-India terrorist network. But he "will try to avoid war with Pakistan at all costs because of the obvious danger of nuclear exchange," he says. While agreeing that Modi will appear tough with Pakistan, T P Sreenivasan, a former diplomat who spent 37 years with the Indian Foreign Service, argues that "this toughness will not go beyond a point" as he will realize soon that with "war not an option anymore, a tough approach will go only so far."

In fact, foreign policy under Modi, Sreenivasn says, "will not change in any significant way." It would be "continuity rather than change, because former diplomats would be advising Modi, foreign policy not being his forte." Changes if any will be in nuance and not fundamental in nature.

Indeed, a striking feature of India's foreign policy is its continuity. Certainly there have been shifts, but as Manjari Chatterjee Miller points out in a recent article in *Foreign Affairs*, "the broad shape of Indian foreign policy has remained the same for nearly five decades." Even when shifts do occur, they are not "sudden," "have rarely, if ever, been political," and "have had little to do with the prime minister's political ideology."

It is in emphasis and style rather than substance that the Modi government's foreign policy will differ from that of the UPA. Modi will be less patient with Pakistan and can be expected to base his relations with all of India's neighbors (and not just Pakistan and China) on reciprocity.

But like another BJP prime minister, Atal Bihari Vajpayee (1998-2004), Modi would try to reach a final settlement with Pakistan on Kashmir, Chaulia says.

In fact, Modi is reported to have already reached out to Pakistan by sending his emissaries to confer with its leadership. Vajpayee was assertive in his conduct of foreign policy. Within three months of coming to power, his government conducted a string of nuclear tests, declared India to be a nuclear weapon state, and abandoned the decades-old policy of nuclear ambiguity. His government's relations with Pakistan were often tense; the two countries fought a near-war at Kargil in 1999 and tensions soared repeatedly over major terrorist attacks in India. Following a terrorist attack on India's parliament in 2001, the Vajpayee government ordered a massive, year-long mobilization of the security forces along the India-Pakistan border to push Pakistan to dismantle the anti-India terrorist network on its soil.

This toughness notwithstanding, Vajpayee also set in motion a peace process with Pakistan, engaged in dialogue with it at the highest level, reached a ceasefire agreement that remains in force and initiated a direct bus service between the two countries.

So will Modi mix toughness with talks in dealing with Pakistan as did Vajpayee? Modi's critics point out that unlike Vajpayee he is not liberal in his outlook and has not demonstrated the vision that would be required to pursue a lasting peace.

What could force Modi to moderate his positions, however, is the priority he is expected to give economic development at home. That will require regional stability if it is to succeed and could force Modi to tone down his confrontationist approach and reach out to India's neighbors. Sreenivasan says that Modi's emphasis on economic matters will require him to adopt a "soft policy towards the rich countries." In this, the U.S. will be of "primary interest" to the Modi government, he says. Indeed, shared economic interests will see Modi and the U.S. put aside past differences – since 2005, the U.S. has denied Modi a visa over his complicity in the Gujarat riots of 2002 – and do business with each other.

However, it is with Asian powers such as Japan, China and Singapore that Modi's economic diplomacy will be the most energetic. Having established strong economic ties with these countries as chief minister of Gujarat, he is likely to build on this foundation. In this Japan will hold special appeal to Modi. Not only is it a rich non-Western country in Asia, and thus more acceptable to the BJP's thinking, but Japanese Prime Minister Shinzo Abe's own nationalistic and militaristic policies will strike a chord with Modi.

Modi's efforts to attract foreign investment to Gujarat are revealing of his likely economic diplomacy as prime minister. As chief minister he built a strong relationship with China, visited it at least four times and successfully attracted Chinese investment into Gujarat. Neither his nationalist outlook nor national security concerns stood in the way of his wooing of Beijing. As prime minister, he can be expected to court China for investment, setting aside the "expansionist attitude" with which he has labelled Beijing.

Modi is expected to allow state governments a greater say in the formulation and execution of foreign policy. He has said that states that have special links with other countries, whether due to shared borders, historical links, or cultural commonalities should be consulted in framing policies and crafting strategies with that country. He has spoken of India's 30 states as partners in his government's execution of foreign policy and of wanting to entrust them with "the task of forging beneficial foreign relations with at least 30 corresponding partner countries."

However, it is doubtful that Modi would treat non-BJP state governments, especially those of the Congress, as partners in his foreign policy execution. He may cede to demands from non-BJP regional parties in power in the states that are his allies in government. For instance, should the All-India Anna Dravida Munetra Kazhagam, the party in power in Tamil Nadu, join his government, Modi could be expected to allow its views to prevail in the crafting of India's policy to Sri Lanka. But much will depend on how dependent he is on the AIADMK.

Overall, Modi is likely to be comfortable with federalizing foreign policy only with regard to the states courting foreign investment. On other matters it will be his government that calls the shots. Of course, all this assumes that Modi will be able to form a government, on its own or with allies. Should that assumption prove false, then India may well end up with a coalition of regional and national parties. Such a coalition is very likely to be unstable, with little in common among its constituents. Preoccupied with survival and pulling in different directions, expect Indian foreign policy to be somewhat chaotic, lacking the robustness or purpose that could be expected of a strong BJP government.

NARENDRA MODI NUANCES FOREIGN POLICY APPROACH AHEAD OF BRICS SUMMIT

Prime Minister Narendra Modi today nuanced his government's foreign policy approach seeking an aggressive Indian engagement on global issues to address regional crises and security threats for restoring global peace and stability while advancing economic stability. Modi, who arrived here amidst light drizzle for an overnight halt en route to Brazil for participation in the sixth summit of the five-nation grouping BRICS, said in his departure statement in Delhi that he also hoped that negotiations at the summit would lead to establishment of the BRICS Development Bank.

Modi was received at the airport by Indian Ambassador to Germany Vijay Gokhale and senior officials from the German Foreign Ministry. Berlin was preferred to Frankfurt for a transit halt on Germany's request for a possible bilateral meeting with Chancellor Angela Merkel but their team's entry into the FIFA World Cup has rendered it a mere stopover for sleeping off jet lag.

Merkel is in Brazil to watch the World Cup final. Usually, Indian Prime Ministers transit through Frankfurt for further journeys across the Atlantic.

Modi's departure statement appeared to be giving a new thrust to India's foreign policy approach when he spoke of New Delhi's engagement on global issues. "I look at the BRICS summit as an opportunity to discuss with BRICS Partners how we can contribute to international efforts to address regional crises, address security threats and restore a climate of peace and stability in the world.

"I also look forward to our discussions to further advance intra-BRICS economic cooperation and our collective efforts to advance global economic stability and prosperity. In particular, I look forward to the successful conclusion of major BRICS initiatives like the New Development Bank and the Contingent Reserve Arrangement, which have seen significant progress since their launch in New Delhi in 2012," Modi said.

"These initiatives will support growth and stability in BRICS and also benefit other developing countries," he said. The BRICS Development Bank with an initial corpus of USD 100 billion was decided in principle at the Durban summit last year. India and China are said to be vying for getting the headquarters of the bank in New Delhi or Shanghai. Preparing for his first multilateral engagement with world leaders, Modi said they were meeting at a time of political turmoil, conflict and humanitarian crisis in several parts of the world and persisting weakness and risks in the global economy.

ASIAN FOREIGN POLICY OF NARENDRA MODI GOVERNMENT

The most significant initiative made by the Narendra Modi government is the focus on neighbouring countries and major Asian powers coupled with emphasizing on the two decades old Look East Policy. Asia being the major focus area of his foreign policy, Modi and his foreign minister chose several Asian countries for their initial bilateral visits. He has made state visits to Bhutan and Nepal and Japan within the first 100 days of his government and also hosted Asia leaders like Chinese President Xi Jinping and Australian Prime Minister Tony Abbott apart form inviting SAARC leaders in his inauguration ceremony. External Affairs Minister Swaraj has also made official visits to Dhaka, Bangladesh,Kathmandu, Nepal, Naypidaw, Myanmar, Singapore, Hanoi, Vietnam, Manama, Bahrain, Kabul, Afghanistan, and Dushanbe, Tajikistan.

Asian Century

Time and again Modi emphasized his believe on 21st century being the Asian century and also asked whether it would be the Indian Century. China, Japan and India being the first, second and third largest Asian economy respectively are among the most likely candidate to lead the strategically important Asia in the later part of this century. But China's increasingly assertive postures in the region recent years have raised concerns in the respective quarters. It seems Modi's foreign policy is focused on improving bilateral relations to higher levels with strategically located Asian countries like Japan, Vietnam, Australia without forging any formal security alliance in the Indo-Pacific region to avoid direct confrontation with China. India, due to its good relation with both Russia and United States, is often considered to be the swing state in the race for strategic dominance in Asia between the democratic alliance of Japan and US and China-Russia club on the other hand.

Relations within the Indian subcontinent

Even before becoming the Prime Minister Narendra Modi hinted that his foreign policy will actively focus on improving ties with India's immediate neighbours which is being termed as neighbourhood first policy in the media and he started well by inviting all heads of state/heads of government of South Asian countries in his inauguration and on the second day on office he held bilateral talks with all of them individually which was dubbed as a mini SAARC summit by the media. Later during a launch event at ISRO he has asked Indian scientists to take the endeavour to develop a dedicated SAARC satellite to share the fruits of the technology like tele-medicine, e-learning etc. with the people across South Asia to complement the currently operating Indian Technical and Economic Cooperation Programme program in the region.

Bhutan

Narendra Modi made his first foreign visit to Bhutan following an invitation by King Jigme Khesar Namgyel Wangchuck and Tobgay. The visit was called by the media as a "charm offensive" that would also seek to check Bhutan-China relations that had recently been formalised. He also sought to build business ties, including a hydro-electric deal, and inaugurated the India-funded Supreme Court of Bhutan building. While talking about the visit, Modi said that Bhutan was a "natural choice" for his first foreign destination because of the "unique and special relationship" the two countries shared. He added that he was looking forward to nurture and further strengthen India's special relations with Bhutan.

His entourage included Foreign Minister Sushma Swaraj, National Security Adviser Ajit Doval and Foreign Secretary Sujatha Singh. He was further set to discuss the insurgency in Northeast India, and China.

Nepal

Modi arrived for a two-day visit to Nepal on 3 August. The last visit of an Indian prime minister to Nepal was 17 years ago in 1997 by I. K. Gujral. The talks with Nepal were focused on reviewing the 1950's Treaty of Peace and Friendship, India-funded 'hydroelectricity projects' in Nepal and other infrastructure projects in Nepal, although the much anticipated Indo-Nepal power trade agreement (PTA) could not get signed due to technical problem in the draft agreement. Following Jana Andolan, that marked the beginning of constitutional democracy in 1990, Modi became the first foreign leader to address the Parliament of Nepal. The Western media read it as a shift in foreign affairs for India, as well as a Nepal policy shift. He did *puja* at the fifth century Hindu Pashupatinath temple (where he donated Rs. 25 crores and the head priest, Mool Bhatta Ganesh Bhatta, said: "I told him that we see him as a mascot for Hinduism, and appreciate his efforts in saving Hindu culture"). Further he pledged not to interfere in Nepal's internal affairs (following controversy of appointment of Indian priests at a Nepali temple), Modi announced a credit assistance programme of US$1 billion to Nepal and said "Nepal can free India of its darkness with its electricity. But [*sic*] we don't want free electricity, we want to buy it. Just by selling electricity to India, Nepal can find a place in the developed countries of the world." He also told Nepali MPs he wanted to turn India's "hostile borders benign and ultimately gateways for free trade and commerce...borders must be bridges not barriers." The *Kathmandu Post*reacted in writing: "Modi mantra warms Nepal's hearts." The *New York Times* also suggested the lack of a meeting with former King Gyanendra signified that India would not support a return to monarchy despite the lack of a new constitution of Nepal. The commonality of a majority Hindu heritage was also played up.

Prior to Modi's visit, Swaraj made a three day visit to Nepal from 27 July 2014 and co-chaired the Indo-Nepal Joint Commission meeting and also prepared the ground for Modi's scheduled visit. The last visit by a foreign minister of India to Nepal was made 23 years before this.

Bangladesh

There was scepticism during election campaign about Bangladeshi illegal immigrants in India which raised concern in Bangladesh but it was Prime Minister Sheikh Hasina who made a remark: "I am delighted to see a great friend of Bangladesh leading an extremely friendly country, India, in the coming days." following Modi's victory in the general election. And the new Indian govt too were quick to realize the immense geo-strategic importance of Bangladesh in India's security paradigm and therefore Foreign Minister Sushma Swarajchose Dhaka for her first stand-alone foreign visit on 26–27 June 2014, where she met her counterpart Abul Hassan Mahmood and also called on Sheikh Hasina. Discussions were held regarding the land boundary agreement (LBA), the proposed Teesta water sharing pact, cooperation in eliminating extremist groups from North-East taking refuge in Bangladesh and illegal immigration. And taking a lesson from the previous UPA govt experience Swaraj had discussed contentious issues of Bengal with Chief Minister Mamata Banerjee before leaving for Dhaka, indicating a federal style of foreign policy.

Afghanistan

The first challenge before the new govt had come from Herat, Afghanistan where the Indian consulate was attacked by the ISI backed terrorist organisation days before Modi's inauguration. Visiting the war-torn country on 10 September Swaraj called "India Afghanistan's first strategic partner". and has committed to play a greater role in capacity building by strengthening the Afghan National Army but sighed away from possibility of sending troops or direct export of military hardware from India instead according to an arrangement made earlier India would pay for purchase of arms and ammunitions from Russia.

Potential re-emergence of the Taliban and al-Qaeda in the subcontinent following NATO withdrawal from the country by end of 2014 and the deadlock over the US-Afghan bilateral security agreement (BSA) have raised concerns among Indian security establishments. India is also in the process of reviving an old agreement for modernising the Chabahar Port in Iran. This is to provide an alternative sea access to Afghanistan which will help further the Indian investment in the country and bilateral trade which is so far restricted by Pakistan's hostile transit policy through Karachi Port.

Sri Lanka

Despite India being Sri Lanka's only neighbour the India-Sri Lanka relations faced stagnation in recent decades due to several reasons including the large scale civilian casualties in civil war in the Tamil dominated north of the island country and a growing Chinese influence in Sri Lanka. In fact there were hardly any high level visits between the two therefore inviting President Mahinda Rajapaksato the inauguration in Delhi, overcoming domestic pressures from Tamil Nadu based political parties, helped set the ball rolling. At the same time the Sri Lankan President announced the release of Indian fishermen jailed in Sri Lanka in a goodwill gesture. But when the two leaders met in Delhi Modi had reportedly asked for Rajapaksa's commitment for fast implementation of thirteenth amendment to the constitution giving more self-rule to the Sri Lankan Tamil people in Jafna.

However the Indian govt is in favor of a good relationship as part of a greater 'neighbourhood first' policy and now Modi is scheduled to visit Colombo in January 2015 and will be the first Indian prime minister to address the Sri Lankan Parliament in 35 years.

Pakistan

Modi has long been considered as a hardliner nationalist against enemy forces across the border sponsoring terrorist attacks in India while he was Chief Minister of Gujarat, a state bordering Pakistan, but post-election things have changed substantially when he decided to invite Nawaz Sharif in the swearing-in ceremony.

Foreign Secretary level talk scheduled on 25 August in Islamabad was called off last minute by India following a meeting with secessionist leaders from Jammu & Kashmir at the Pakistani high commission in Delhi. Later External Affairs Minister Swaraj averted the question of whether Prime Minister will meet Nawaz Sharif in New York on the sidelines of UNGA by saying that "there is no full stop in diplomacy".

Relations with East and Southeast Asia

From the very beginning the Modi led govt made it ample clear that India would focus more and more on improving relation with ASEAN and other East Asian countries as per India's Look East Policy which was formulated during Narasimha Rao's govt in 1992 for better economic engagement with its eastern neighbours but successive govt later successfully turned it into a tool for forging strategic partnership and security cooperation with countries in that region in general and Vietnam and Japan in particular. In her recent visit to Hanoi, Vietnam Sushma Swaraj has stressed on the need for an Act East Policy that she said should replace India's over two decade-old Look East Policyemphasizing a more proactive role for India in this region.

Japan

Japan occupies a very important place in Modi's Asian strategy, as India is looking toward Japan, at a time when it is becoming 'normal state' amending decades old pacifist constitution, to forge a security alliance to balance an increasingly assertive China in the Indo-Pacific region. Maritime cooperation is most likely and bilateral naval exercises are on the cards. Significantly in 2014 Japan participated in the Malabar, a primarily bilateral naval exercise between India and US, held in Sea of Japan. Negotiations progressed recently for selling of US 2 amphibious aircraft to Indian Navy and the long pending civil nuclear agreements which would eventually help strengthen the strategic partnership.

Modi visited Japan on a five day official trip from 30 August to 3 September which was labelled as his fist bilateral state visit outside thesubcontinent also by the media. His 2014 visit further strengthened the ties between the two countries and resulted in several key agreements, including the elevating the already established strategic partnership to the "Special Strategic Global

Partnership". Business ties are stronger than ever with a commitment of US$33.5 billion Japanese investment in India in the next five year. India is in the process of importing Shinkansen technology form Japan as part of Modi's Diamond Quadrilateral project for introducing high-speed rail in India.

His visit to Kyoto supervised the signing of a cooperation agreement between Varanasi and Kyoto both regarded as heritage city and cultural centre in their respective country.

China

Prior to election Modi had expressed reservation over alleged Chinese 'expansionism' into India's frontiers as India and China locked into bitter territorial disputes over last fifty years. During his Japan trip, Modi has said eighteenth century mind-set of vistaar-vad or expansionism won't work and vikaash-vad or peaceful development is needed for sustainable peace and tranquillity in the world which was read by a portion of media as a subtle jibe on China. But he is also in favour of enhanced economic partnership with China.

Economic activity defines relation with China as it is India's biggest trading partner in goods. Soon after taking office commerce MinisterNirmala Sitharaman has already made two visits to China. The two countries have forged a mechanism called 'strategic and economic dialogue' (SED) to discuss the trade and other economic issues. Modi has publicly expressed his willingness to enhance trade and economic cooperation with China. Describing the newly found activism in bilateral relation Modi said India China relation moving "INCH (India-China) towards MILES(Millennium of Enhanced Synergy) ".

India sent National Security Adviser Ajit Doval as a special envoy of Prime Minister Modi to Beijing to negotiate the agenda and the schedule of the presidential visit to India which is appreciated by the top Chinese leadership who are known to be fond of diplomatic decorum. President Xi Jinping, only third Chinese President to visit India, arrived in Ahmedabad, Modi's hometown, on 17 September which coincides with Modi's birthday. China is expected to commit investment over US$100 billion in India's infrastructure projects including in high speed trains and dedicated Chinese industrial parks to balance the huge trade deficit exists in China's favour. The two leaders had earlier met in Brazil this year on the sidelines of BRICS summit.

Vietnam

Vietnam, strategically located in the South China Sea, plays an pivotal role in India's Southeast Asian policy and it is often referred as the important pillars of its 'Look East Policy' by the Indian diplomats.. Defence and security cooperation in recent years define the strategic partnership along with fast growing bilateral trade which stands at US$8 billion in FY 2013.

Visiting Indian President Pranab Mukherjee called Vietnam, "a trusted friend and an important pillar of India's Look East Policy" which emphasized the depth of their strategic partnership. The leaders reiterated their desire and determination to work together to maintain peace, stability, growth and prosperity in Asia.

And the two side vouched for 'freedom of navigation' in the South China Sea, which China claims as its exclusive economic zone, and called the parties concerned to exercise restraint, avoid threat or use of force and resolve disputes through peaceful means in accordance with universally recognised principles of international law, including the United Nations Convention on the Law of the Sea-1982..

India-Vietnamese defence cooperation has multiplied in recent years with emphasize on maritime security which includes training of Vietnamese naval personnel with Indian naval ships making frequent port-call in Vietnam in past few years. Recently it extended a US$100 m Line of Credit for purchase of Fast attack craft for Vietnamese navy from India. Vietnam is also interested in acquiring Brahmos supersonic missiles, a Indo-Russian joint venture project, Vietnam has friendly relation with both Russia and India a precondition for exporting the missile system and talks regarding the deal is believed to be in the advanced level.

Agreements signed in oil exploration cooperation between India and Vietnam as it earlier offered India to explore strategically located oil blocks in South China Sea, which is disputed by Chinese claims. On the following day Chinese Foreign Ministry through an official media statement expressed its objection to India's activity in what it refers its exclusive economic zone. External Affairs Minister earlier during her Hanoi trip said the state-owned ONGC Videsh will exploit the opportunity provided in Vietnam, a development China sees as an aggression into its backyard. Economic ties are fast growing with US$8 billion bilateral trade and the two sides emphasized the need of increasing people to people contact which is set to get a boost with upcoming launch of direct flight between Delhi and Ho Chi Minh City and using Bollywood to promote Vietnam to Indian audience.

Singapore

Singapore is amongst the top source countries of foreign direct investment (FDI) coming to India. Economic cooperation dominates the India Singapore relations given Singapore's strategic importance in India's 'Look East' policy. External Affairs Minister Swaraj visited Singapore on 16 August where she held talks with her counterpart Shanmugam and Prime Minister Lee Hsien Loong regarding Singapore's investment in India and their potential role in Modi's pet smart city project.

Earlier Modi played host to Singaporean Minister for Foreign and Law K. Shanmugam where he recalled his policies as Gujarat chief minister to expand cooperation between the two countries in, amongst others, public housing for the middle and lower classes based on Singapore's expertise.

Former Singaporean Prime Minister Goh Chok Tong visited India on 10 September and held several high level meetings with Prime Minister and other Ministers, later in conversation with a selected members from the media he referred former Indian Prime Minister Vajpeyee as Scholar but Modi is "Man of Action", while reassuring once again his countries full cooperation smart city project.

Australia

Australian Prime Minister Tony Abbott was the first head of government to make a state visit to India in Modi government which shows the importance both side attaches to their relations.

The most significant event of his tour was the signing of a civil nuclear energy cooperation agreement for supplying uranium (Australia is believed to have one third of world's total uranium reserve) to India.

The nuclear deal is a further step toward India achieving international acceptability for its nuclear programme despite not ratifying the nuclear non-proliferation treaty, and follows similar agreements with the United States and France.

The two side also agreed to enhance Maritime security cooperation in the Indo-pacific region and future joint naval exercise in the Indian ocean. During the joint statement following the summit Australian PM Abbott referred India as a model citizen in terms of following International guidelines justifying the nuclear deal beyond the scope of NPT and called *India the emerging democratic superpower"*.

Taiwan

As Modi has identified economic cooperation as a major thrust area in his foreign policy and coined slogans like Make in India to invite foreign direct investment (FDI) in manufacturing sector, Taiwan was one of the first to respond to his call. India Electronics and Semiconductor Association (IESA) and Taipei Computer Association signed memorandum of understanding for local manufacturing of semiconductors and electronics, even there are plans to set up 'Taiwanese hardware park' in about 200-300 acres of land.

Although India was among the first few countries to recognize PRC therefore jeopardizing relation with the island but later developed an official relation with ROCwhich it maintains through "India-Taiwan Association" a De facto embassy in Taipei.

Relations with West Asia (Middle East)

Indian External Affairs Ministry refers the region as West Asia and not as Middle East which is a more popular attribution, particularly in the western countries.

The region plays a vital role in India's economy as it supplies nearly two third of India's total oil import, bilateral trade is also flourishing in recent years particularly with UAE and other gulf states. Over the years millions of Indian mostly working class have migrated to the gulf looking for jobs and they account for a sizeable share in the total remittances received from abroad.

Bahrain

Swaraj choose Manama, Bahrain for her first visit to the gulf. The visit marked the first high level exchange from Modi govt to any Arab states following apprehension of less priority given to the Indo-Arab relation under Modi administration.

The island country with a significant population of Indian origin people has extensive trade and business ties with India. There addressing at a business meet the minister reiterated "Our government is firmly committed to bring back growth, have clear policies which will facilitate business environment, transparency and speed, well thought out decisions".

Israel

Israel is one of India's most important strategic partner and major source of its military hardware. Relation is expected to flourish with Modi govt as the ruling BJP is known for its pro-Israeli stands and in favour of strengthening ties with Israel. Sushma Swaraj, who was chairperson of the 'India-Israel parliamentary friendship group', visited Israel earlier and publicly expressed her admiration for former Israeli Prime Minister Golda Meir.

2014 Israel-Hamas Conflict

At the height of the tension between Israel and Hamas in July India in offered a rhetorical condemnation holding both sides responsible for erupting violence and asked Israel to stop "disproportionate use of force" in Gaza which was read by many as departure from tradition of more vocal supports for the Palestinian cause.

External Affairs Minister Swaraj insisted that "there is absolutely no change in India's policy towards Palestine, which is that we fully support the Palestinian cause while maintaining good relations with Israel. " clarifying India's current position on the issue. That might sound like fence-sitting, but it's a policy shared by all Indian governments of the past 20 years following the establishment of formal diplomatic relation in 1992.

Sushma Swaraj, a seasoned parliamentarian, had herself blocked the opposition demand in Rajya Sabha for passing a resolution condemning Israel for 2014 Israel-Gaza conflict by saying that "India has friendly relation with both Israel and Palestine and therefore any such move may impact its friendship negatively".

Although later in a symbolic gesture India joined others BRICS nations in voting at the United Nations Human Rights Council for a probe into the alleged human rights violation in Gaza. Which generated mixed response among media and analysts in India.

5

India: the Emerging Asian Super Power

Singapore's defence minister Ng Eng Hen stated last month that his country wanted India to play a bigger role in the South China Sea. The leaders of Vietnam and the Philippines have also made similar statements in recent years. This "invitation" extended to India by the leaders of Southeast Asia to participate in that region's security affairs is tantamount to India's emergence as a great power in Southeast Asia, and by extension, in Asia itself.

Southeast Asia connects the Indian and the Pacific Oceans, and includes some of the most important maritime chokepoints, is likely to be the site of order-making in Asia in the context of the rise of China.

Thomas Donilon, who was the American National Security Advisor when the US said its "pivot/rebalancing" has explained that the pivot is not just about "rebalancing towards Asia" but also includes rebalancing "within Asia" as America has begun to focus "in a renewed way on Southeast Asia and Asean." Furthermore, the Asian-institutional architecture is Asean-centric and Asean-led.

Therefore, India's emerging profile in Southeast Asia is significant and marks its arrival as a great power.

Solid grounds

There are two main reasons that explain the benign perception of India's rise in Southeast Asia. First, there are no territorial disputes between India and its immediate neighbours in Southeast Asia. India has a land border with only one Southeast Asian state, Myanmar, which was fixed by their British colonial rulers in 1937.

India has maritime borders with three Southeast Asian states: Myanmar, Thailand, and Indonesia. India's maritime boundaries with Thailand and Indonesia were fixed through a trilateral agreement in 1978, while India's maritime boundary with Myanmar was finalized in 1987.

Second, India is not pursuing any unilateral or hegemonic policies towards Southeast Asia. In 2012, former Prime Minister, Manmohan Singh, explicitly noted that New Delhi believes that "Asean centrality is essential in the evolving regional architecture," endorsing Asean's leading role in regional diplomacy.

Similarly, at the military/maritime level, India not only prefers to be invited into the region , but former defence minister, Pranab Mukherjee, noted in 2006 that India was willing to assist the regional states in "any capacity" for security in the Strait of Malacca subject "to the desire of the littoral states."

In other words, despite India's more advanced military capabilities, New Delhi is not claiming the mantle of leadership there but prefers to work in accordance with the local norms and mores.

Therefore, it is not surprising that Lee Kuan Yew, Singapore's recently deceased statesman, welcomed India's presence in Southeast Asia in 2007 by noting that there was "no fear" that India had "aggressive intentions."

India has now transcended its home region of South Asia due to its growing power in Southeast Asia, thus becoming a key component of the Asian security architecture along with the region's other great powers: the United States, Japan, and China. Notably, all three Asian great powers also seem to be willing to work with India in Southeast Asia.

Strategic edge

US President Obama has urged India to "act East" on a number of occasions. Furthermore, the US and India released a joint vision statement earlier this year in which they specifically called for "safeguarding maritime security and ensuring freedom of navigation and over flight throughout the region, especially in the South China Sea." On his part, Japanese Prime Minister Shinzo Abe sees the India-Japan relationship as a "confluence" of the Indian and Pacific Oceans.

Notably, Southeast Asia is geographically — and geopolitically — located at this confluence. The Japan-India statement on their strategic and global partnership that was released last year especially noted the launch of their "bilateral dialogue on Asean affairs." Finally, China also seems to be willing to work with India, even if begrudgingly, in the region's economic and institutional affairs.

Through their 2008 shared vision document, China and India agreed to "explore ... a new architecture for closer regional cooperation in Asia, and to make joint efforts for regional integration of Asia." This statement, which explicitly identified the Asean-led East Asia Summit as an avenue where China and India can work together is significant simply because China was hitherto unwilling to recognize India as a major power in Asia beyond South Asia.

In other words, the regional states of Southeast Asia, as well as the great powers active in Southeast Asia, now seem willing to grant India the status of a great power in that region.

This has two noteworthy implications. First, these acts 'legitimise' India's status as a great power in Asia as well as its role in the security affairs of a region outside of India's home region in South Asia. As such, India is not seen as an interloper. Second, this empirically demonstrates that the rise of a new great power need not disrupt the extant order as is normally assumed. In fact, the rise of a new great power — in this case, India — can be seen as contributing to the maintenance of the regional order.

Security angles

India has three main security-related interests in Southeast Asia. First, as noted by Mukherjee in 2005, India's "Look East" strategy is based on the principle of "the maintenance of an equitable strategic balance."

India does not want Southeast Asia to be dominated by any single great power. Consequently, India is upgrading its naval and air assets in the Andaman and Nicobar Islands. Located at the mouth of the Strait of Malacca, India's maritime and air capabilities in the Andamans help India meet its second security interest in the region: the security of the Strait itself. Finally, India's growing maritime and air capabilities — cantered on diverse platforms such as the P-8I aircraft, the C-130Js, the C-17 Globemasters, Sukhoi-30 MKIs, aircraft carrier(s), nuclear submarine(s), and landing dock(s) — allow India to project military power into the South China Sea from the Andamans.

After all, India's third security interest in Southeast Asia is to ensure the freedom of navigation in the South China Sea. In fact, India's regional partnerships — including docking rights at Vietnam's Nha Trang port — may further augment India's capabilities.

At the same time, India has been providing a range of security-related public goods in Southeast Asia such as the provision of humanitarian and disaster relief assistance as well as military capacity-building in regional states.

Despite these modest but significant efforts, Southeast Asian states want India to "do more" pro-actively. The crucial question now is whether India's political leaders will grasp the geopolitical opportunity to ensconce India in the emerging Asian order or if a lack of vision and the exigencies of domestic politics will effectively force New Delhi to squander the chance to shape Asia.

At the very least, India needs to expedite its economic engagement with Southeast Asia while enhancing physical connectivity – land and maritime – in order to demonstrate its seriousness.

EMERGING ASIAN AND GLOBAL POWERS

Critical Political Economy and the Study of Foreign Policy

Critical political economy (CPE) is a dynamic perspective on the interplay between geo-political and geo-economic priorities in foreign policy. This approach recognizes a certain degree of nation state diversity, but equally insists that the focus of mainstream neo-realist and neo-liberal theories on national distinctiveness is ultimately misleading in that these established theories lose sight of essential similarities in national models of regulation that are substantially shaped by the external structural imperatives of capitalist accumulation. Moreover, the diversity of forms taken by various states conceals a generalized shift away from the Keynesian or other interventionist or regulative models with alleged national/ domestic rather than international/competitive orientations.

CPE goes beyond the perspective of the orthodoxies of neo-realism, neo-liberalism and some structural theories like world-system theory in which "historical change is assumed to follow a predetermined path regardless of historical context and human agency; with the result that theoretical argument dominates and displaces the complexity of history". In this sense, CPE sees social change as a dynamic and historical process and as a continuing creation of new forms and asks how existing social or world orders came into being; how norms, values, institutions, or social practices have emerged, and are perpetually contested and subjected to change. In this way, CPE rests on historical dialectics trying to discern not only the past but with a continual process of historical change and with exploring the potential for alternative forms of state and world order.

The dissolution of the Soviet Union in 1989 spelled the end of the Cold War and thereby the dominance of politics in command turned into economics in command. An important post-1989 effect was the shift from the primacy of military power to a greater role for economic power in shaping global geopolitics. Economic structural change has become the epitomization of globalization and it challenges "deeply embedded socio-cultural and political structures in critical ways that cannot be ignored, provoking dynamic responses of promotion, accommodation, and resistance". The classical interplay and dynamics between exercise of 'political authority', security issues and 'the distribution of wealth and production' cannot be analyzed as exclusive domains but at the present stage of history it is manifested that geo-economics has a dominant position in international relations.

No continent benefited more than Asia, as has been manifested in its dramatic economic rise, the speed and scale of which has no parallel in world history. It may be that the United States is engaged in a number of wars in Asia and the Middle East but it also seems to be losing in the areas of finance, trade and competition and in its attempt to impose Western 'good governance' and human rights.

The concept of geo-economics thus came into prominence after the end of the Cold War and it suggests interconnectivity but also unevenness of the economic and commercial opportunities, broader political and international relations, and a blurring of the boundaries of the state to pursue its strategic interests, including through military capabilities. This concept is rooted in the growing importance of economic factors in international relations and in a wish to dig deeper than neo-realism in order to provide an understanding of the nature and sources of power.

The CPE approach does not essentialize the state as a pre-constituted entity or a 'black box' of "national interests" interacting within anarchical international relations. Rather, CPE seeks to understand 'forms of states' as 'state/society complex' and asks how the prevailing order has come about and how it is changing. It is the interplay of particular configurations of contending social forces and alliances, including attempts at integration of a variety of class interests that defines "national interests" and characterizes inherent contradictions in the historical structure. We have to explore the boundaries of the state in its current conjunctures, its historical dynamic and the process of social change. In this way, we seek an understanding of the underlying and prevailing tensions between geo-politics and geo-economics in foreign policy. It is important to ask "who defines national interest" and who has the power to change it?

It is quite obvious then that India's and China's strategy of increasing presence in the global economy is actually the strategy of the dominant social groups, alliances, and class interests within these countries. Geo-economics emphasizes the importance of integrating China's and India's economic diplomacy in its multi-faceted relations with different countries and regions in the context of a rapidly changing world order. The essential question then is of the viability of the ability of the capitalist class to gather social consensus for achieving its ambition of greater global reach and whether this will happen despite the interests of the peasantry and the poor masses in rural and urban areas.

The question is also whether it is possible to establish a social consensus in India and China regarding the expansion and drive towards a more aggressive foreign policy to become world players and whether that entails a fundamental shift away from pre-existing norms and values.

It is power itself which is becoming more diffuse, diffracted through an increasingly complex, prismatic structure of socio-economic forces and levels of governance. The result is a hollowing out of the state even if it maintains the monopoly over the means of violence over a given territory and this gives space to a plethora of actors and institutions – not least financial capital - capable of influencing foreign policy and social change in Asia and the world.

Transnational issues including climate change, terrorism, cyber-warfare, pandemics, rush to secure energy and resource supplies, and difficulties in sustaining multilateral focus in trade and on economic issues through the completion of the Doha Round. All open up the foreign policy field and would, ideally speaking, denote a myriad of actors and influences from formal organizations such as transnational corporations to advocacy networks and think tanks 'epistemic communities' (networks of individuals and/or organizations based on authoritative claims to consensual knowledge). In the end, this blurring of the levels of 'sovereignty' and 'non-intervention' sanctioned by socio-political conflicts – internal and external to the state – concerns the classic problem in international political economy: 'Who gets what, when, where, and how'.

The monumental changes in the global economy helped promote not only an economic boom in Asia, but also led to an eastward movement of global power and influence, signaled by Asia's ascent to the world system and the possible emergence of a new multi-polar order. Global power shifts are now being triggered not by military triumphs or geopolitical realignments but by one factor unique to our contemporary world — rapid economic growth.

The CPE approach to foreign policy has a normative commitment—seeking to analyse phenomena through empirical evidence with an explicit theoretical purpose—and focused on the actual interplay of domestic and international agents and structures. Foreign policy decisions are made by agency but always within a set of structural constraints. Critical accounts of foreign policy pursue a holistic view of politics and avoid the pitfall of seeing politics as only involving governments and state actors. It is furthermore necessary to understand the constitutive and purposive nature of knowledge and questioning whether they serve particular interests as Cox (1981) remarks: "Theory is always *for* someone and *for* some purpose." Finally, CPE leaves room for alternative ideas and visions and includes a developmental and socio-economic perspective in foreign policy. Policymakers are constrained by societal contexts, but equally they do make decisions and are able to establish elaborate critique and policies against the current.

This type of approach constitutes a more holistic and open 'state/society complex' conceptualization including other relational interests, private, corporate, military, and civil society which can potentially impact foreign policy outcomes.

For instance, energy resources beyond borders may be accessed by trade, respectively by conquest, domination and changing property rights and in this way markets are not institutionally separated in international relations from states and the distribution of military capability.

This is neatly illustrated partly in India but in particular in China where there is strategic political decision taken by Beijing "to integrate China into the global political economy. During this process, they have allowed Chinese sovereignty, in the economic sphere at least, to become 'perforated', and thus increasing the number of actors in the policy spheres". This can also be seen in the pragmatic approach India has taken towards Myanmar and other non-democratic countries where commercial and geo-economic interests take precedence over ideology and idealism about human rights and democracy.

When it comes to the question about foreign policy in India and China these considerations lead to a number of inter-linked issues of strategic importance.

For instance, what are the links between energy security (oil, gas and water), trade and FDI flows in relation to more traditional issues of military security, encirclement and containment? What explains the fact that both countries share mutual interests in a number of global policy areas while the same areas retain a degree of rivalry and competition at the regional level? What is India's reaction to China having the hands on leadership role when it comes to economic investment and respect for sovereignty?

6

Globalization of Indian Economic Power

Indian Economic Policy determines the various initiatives that has been taken by the government, since liberalisation in 1991, for the benefit of different sectors of the Indian economy. India Economic Policy was influenced by a Fabian-socialistic approach with emphasis on protectionism, import substitution, industrialisation, state intervention in labour and financial markets, and central planning.

The government had strict restrictive economic policies over the private sector participation, foreign trade and foreign direct investment.

The first breakthrough came with Jawaharlal Nehru and statistician Prasanta Chandra Mahalanobis, who emphasised on more flexible economic policies involving both public and private sectors based on direct and indirect state intervention. However, India Economic Policy changed after 1980 with the removal of restrictions on capacity expansion for incumbents, price controls and reduction in corporate taxes.

The revolutionary change came with the economic liberalisation of 1991, undertaken by the then prime minister of India, P. V. Narasimha Rao and the finance minister Manmohan Singh. Considering the balance-of-payments crisis, they formulated a new set of economic policy in India, ending many public monopolies and allowing automatic approval of foreign direct investment in many sectors of the Indian economy.

The Indian Economic Policy at present comprise of:

- Civil Aviation Policy
- Foreign Direct Investment Policy
- Drug Policy
- Industrial Policy
- Broad Band Policy 2004
- National Electricity Policy
- New Telecom Policy 1999
- Foreign Trade Policy
- Exim Policy
- National Mineral policy
- Monetary and Credit Policy
- Non-Resident Indians (NRIS) Policy
- Current Export-Import Policy
- Current Monetary And Credit Policy
- Indian Direct Investment In Joint Ventures And Wholly Owned Subsidiaries Abroad
- Policies And Procedures For External Commercial Borrowings
- Overseas Venture Capital Investment In India
- Baggage Rules for Indian residents or foreigners residing in India.

At present, the India Economic Policy have made India as one of the most prosperous economy of the developing world. Indian economy is one of the most preferred destination for the foreign direct investments specially in the real-estate sector, in which from March 2005 onwards, FDI is allowed 100 per cent, as per the India Economic Policy.

Post-Independence

Indian economic policy after independence was influenced by the colonial experience (which was seen by Indian leaders as exploitative in nature) and by those leaders' exposure to Fabian socialism. Policy tended towards protectionism, with a strong emphasis on import substitution, industrialisation, state intervention in labour and financial markets, a large public sector, business regulation, and central planning. Jawaharlal Nehru, the first prime minister, along with the statistician Prasanta Chandra Mahalanobis, carried on by Indira Gandhi formulated and oversaw economic policy.

They expected favourable outcomes from this strategy, because it involved both public and private sectors and was based on direct and indirect state intervention, rather than the more extreme Soviet-style central command system.

The policy of concentrating simultaneously on capital-and technology-intensive heavy industry and subsidising manual, low-skill cottage industries was criticised by economist Milton Friedman, who thought it would waste capital and labour, and retard the development of small manufacturers. India's low average growth rate from 1947-80 was derisively referred to as the Hindu rate of growth, because of the unfavourable comparison with growth rates in other Asian countries, especially the "East Asian Tigers". The economic reforms that caused a surge in economic growth after 1980 can be attributed to two stages of reform.

The pro-business measures of 1980, initiated by Rajiv Gandhi, eased restrictions on capacity expansion for incumbents, removed price controls and reduced corporate taxes. The economic liberalisation of 1991, initiated by then Indian prime minister P. V. Narasimha Rao and his finance minister Manmohan Singh in response to a balance-of-payments crisis, did away with the Licence Raj (investment, industrial and import licensing) and ended many public monopolies, allowing automatic approval of foreign direct investment in many sectors.

Since then, the overall direction of liberalisation has remained the same, irrespective of the ruling party, although no party has yet tried to take on powerful lobbies such as the trade unions and farmers, or contentious issues such as reforming labour laws and reducing agricultural subsidies. Since 1990 India has emerged as one of the wealthiest economies in the developing world; during this period, the economy has grown constantly, but with a few major setbacks. This has been accompanied by increases in life expectancy, literacy rates and food security. While the credit rating of India was hit by its nuclear tests in 1998, it has been raised to investment level in 2007 by S&P and Moody's.

Future Predictions

In 1999, Goldman Sachs predicted that India's GDP in current prices will overtake France and Italy by 2020, Germany, UK and Russia by 2025 and Japan by 2035. By 2035 it is expected to reach as 3rd largest economy of the world behind US and China. Goldman Sachs has made these predictions based on India's expected growth rate of 5.3 to 6.1% in various periods, whereas India is registering more than 9% growth rate. However, the same report also shows there were large variation in its predicted gauging growth between 1960-2000, 7.5% predicted India's annual growth rate compared to the real average value of only 4.5% during that period.

Future Predictions

A Goldman Sachs report recently cited by BBC News stated that 'India could overtake Britain and have the world's fifth largest economy within a decade as the country's growth accelerates' Jim O'Neal, head of the Global Economics Team at Goldman Sachs, said on the BBC, "In thirty years, India's workforce could be as big as that of the United States and China combined".

However, the Goldman Sachs report ignores the effect of rapid decline in purchasing power parity ratios of economies as they approach maturity, resulting in purchasing power parities that eventually tend toward 1.0 (as compared to nearly 5.0 for India and China in 2007, *i.e.* the value of 1 US$ in India and China after conversion into local currency at current exchange rates was 5 times of that in the US due to their cheaper currencies).

This decline happens because of two reasons-(1) inflation, and (2) appreciation of the local currency. The two factors can happen simultaneously leading to exchange-rate level GDP growth rates that are phenomenal-hitting 20% a year or more. This results in a doubling of GDP in constant dollars every 3.5 years or so (an example of this phenomena happening on the Indian economy for 2006-07 is described below).

This has historically happened to Japanese, S. Korean, Taiwanese and other newly developed economies that rapidly industrialised and caught up with the western world in a few decades. There is no reason why such trend will not occur to the

Indian and the Chinese economies (some of this phenomena can be seen in the recent pressure on Chinese and India currencies to appreciate). For example, last year's GDP growth in India was 9.4 percent, currency appreciation was ~10%, and inflation was around 5%, resulting in a GDP increase as measured in "exchange dollars", of (=(1+(0.1+0.05))*1.094) approx. 26%. Even after adjusting for the 3% loss of value of the real US$ (due to inflation in US), these numbers in constant US$ still come to an over 22% per year of GDP growth. This is the reason why India's GDP went from less than 800 billion US$ in 2006 to over a trillion US$ in 2007.

These growth numbers fly in the face of computations by Goldman Sachs and others that use real GDP growth of a country in their projections (which corresponds to the PPP based growth), thus ignoring the effect of PPP ratio decline, but at the same time, use current exchange-rate GDP as the base economy size for their projections.

Any extrapolation of GDP growth based on past "local" growth that does not take into account the decline in PPP ratios as an economy develops would thus hugely underestimate the GDP growth at exchange rates that will actually occur, and the error will accumulate as the prediction is stretched further into the future. A more reasonable projection of future per-capita could simply be based on two compatible quantities-the current economy size as measured in PPP, and the real growth-rate.

Based on PPP growth, the Chinese GDP is set to cross the US economy to become the largest in the World between 2009 and 2010, in merely 2 to 3 years from now. Similarly India's GDP has already crossed Japan's to become the third largest.

Making projections into the future, India is set to cross US economy at PPP around 2024 (at 10 percent annual growth for India, 3 percent for US.

There is substantial evidence looking at Chinese, Taiwanese, S. Korean and Japanese history that India's economy has just crossed a growth bottleneck, and that the actual growth rates for India might be even higher and would sustain for decades, making this crossing even earlier and even more dramatic"). When India becomes larger than the US economy, India's per capita income would still be ~1/4 of US income at that time; for the reasons mentioned above, it is likely that it would still be growing at it's current pace when it crosses US to become the second largest economy in the World, 16-17 years from now.

SOCIO-ECONOMIC CHARACTERISTICS

Poverty

Wealth distribution in India, a developing country, is fairly uneven, with the top 10% of income groups earning 33% of the income. While poverty in India has reduced significantly, 17.59% (over 230 million) of Indians still live below the national poverty line. Since the early 1950s, successive governments have implemented various schemes, under planning, to alleviate poverty, that have met with partial success. All these programmes have relied upon the strategies of the Food for work programme and National Rural Employment Programme of the 1980s, which attempted to use the unemployed to generate productive assets and build rural infrastructure.

In August 2005, the Indian parliament passed the Rural Employment Guarantee Bill, the largest programme of this type in terms of cost and coverage, which promises 100 days of minimum wage employment to every rural household in 200 of India's 600 districts. The question of whether economic reforms have reduced poverty or not has fuelled debates without generating any clear cut answers and has also put political pressure on further economic reforms, especially those involving the downsising of labour and cutting agricultural subsidies.

Corruption

Corruption has been one of the pervasive problems affecting India. It takes the form of bribes, evasion of tax and exchange controls, embezzlement, etc. The economic reforms of 1991 reduced the red tape, bureaucracy and the Licence Raj that had strangled private enterprise and was blamed for the corruption and inefficiencies. Yet, a 2005 study by Transparency International (TI) India found that more than half of those surveyed had firsthand experience of paying bribe or peddling influence to get a job done in a public office. The chief economic consequences of corruption are the loss to the exchequer, an unhealthy climate for investment and a decrease in the cost of government-subsidised services. The TI India study estimates the monetary value of petty corruption in 11 basic services provided by the government, like education, healthcare, judiciary, police, etc., to be around Rs.21,068 crores. India still ranks in the bottom quartile of developing nations in terms of the ease of doing business, and compared to China, the average time taken to secure the clearances for a startup or to invoke bankruptcy is much greater.

The Right to Information Act (2005) and equivalent acts in the states, that require government officials to furnish information requested by citizens or face punitive action, computerisation of services and various central and state government acts that established vigilance commissions have considerably reduced corruption or at least have opened up avenues to redress grievances.

The latest report by Transparency International puts India at 70th place and states that significant improvements was made by India in reducing corruption.

Occupations and Unemployment

Agricultural and allied sectors accounted for about 57% of the total workforce in 1999-2000, down from 60% in 1993-94. While agriculture has faced stagnation in growth, services have seen a steady growth. Of the total workforce, 8% is in the organised sector, two-thirds of which are in the public sector. The NSSO survey estimated that in 1999-2000, 106 million, nearly 10% of the population were unemployed and the overall unemployment rate was 7.32%, with rural areas doing marginally better (7.21%) than urban areas (7.65%).

Unemployment in India is characterised by chronic underemployment or disguised unemployment. Government schemes that target eradication of both poverty and unemployment, (Which in recent decades has sent millions of poor and unskilled people into urban areas in search of livelihoods.) attempt to solve the problem, by providing financial assistance for setting up businesses, skill honing, setting up public sector enterprises, reservations in governments, etc.

The decreased role of the public sector after liberalisation has further underlined the need for focusing on better education and has also put political pressure on further reforms.

Regional Imbalance

One of the critical problems facing India's economy is the sharp and growing regional variations among India's different states and territories in terms of per capita income, poverty, availability of infrastructure and socio-economic development.

The five-year plans have attempted to reduce regional disparities by encouraging industrial development in the interior regions, but industries still tend to concentrate around urban areas and port cities.

After liberalisation, the more advanced states are better placed to benefit from them, with infrastructure like well developed ports, urbanisation and an educated and skilled workforce which attract manufacturing and service sectors. The union and state governments of backward regions are trying to reduce the disparities by offering tax holidays, cheap land, etc., and focusing more on sectors like tourism, which although being geographically and historically determined, can become a source of growth and is faster to develop than other sectors.

SECTORS OF INDIAN ECONOMY AND AGRICULTURE

More than 58% of country's population depends on agriculture, a sector producing only 22% of GDP. The agriculture and allied sector witnessed a growth of 9.1% in 2003-04, which fell steeply to 1.1% in the current fiscal year. Favourable monsoon facilitated an impressive growth rate of 9.6% in 2003-04 on the back of negative growth in the preceding year. However, deficient rainfall from the southwest monsoon is estimated to have caused a significant decline in kharif crops production in the current year.

While looking at some of the agricultural products, one finds that India is the largest producer of Tea, jute and jute like fibre.

India is not only the largest producer but also largest consumer of tea in the world. India accounts for around 14% of the world trade in tea. Indian tea is exported in various forms such as bulk tea, packet tea, tea bags, instant tea etc., to more than 80 countries of the world.

Among livestock cattle and buffalo are found maximum in India. Indian total milk production is highest in the world. India has also the privilege of having the 1st rank in total irrigated land in area terms in the world. Among cereals production, India is placed third, having second largest production in wheat and rice and the largest production in pulses.

However, the full potential of Indian agriculture as a profitable activity hasn't been realized yet. Agriculture upliftment will not only benefit farmers and a large section of the rural poor, but also will give fillip to overall growth of the economy through the backward and forward linkages of agriculture with the rest of the economy. Priority must be given to livestock's & fisheries, horticulture, organic farming, commercial crops and agro-processing, as these are the potential areas of high growth. Further, rationalization of minimum support price regime and introduction of other risk-mitigation measures, improvements in rural infrastructure are essential for sustaining high agricultural growth. It is conceived that reforms in legislation, strengthening R&D and improvements in post harvest management technologies will give a further boost to Indian agriculture.

While acceleration in agriculture growth to 4-4.5% is imperative, even with such growth rate; share of agriculture in total GDP is likely to reduce further. Therefore, there is a need to absorb excess agricultural labour in other sectors, notably industry. Rapid growth of agro-processing industry close to the agricultural production centres can bring about this shift without moving people from rural to urban areas. Also, public investment in agriculture needs to be augmented, especially in rural infrastructure, irrigation, and agricultural research & development. Better access to institutional credit for more farmers, is also high on priority list. The New trade policy gives focus to agriculture and all the hurdles in Indian agriculture will be crossed gradually.

Industrial Production

Index of industrial production which measures the overall industrial growth rate was 10.1% in October 2004 as compared to 6.2% in October 2003. The double digit in IIP was aided by a robust growth of 11.3% in the manufacturing sector followed by mining and quarrying and electricity generation. But industrial production saw a decline in Dec 2004 when IIP dipped to 8 %. Thus one of the critical challenges facing Indian economic policy consists in devising strategies for sustained industrial growth. Final phase-out of the MFA and India's conformity with the international intellectual property system from Jan 1st Jan 2005, have been two significant developments in the world of commerce & industry.

Textile industry is the largest industry in terms of employment economy from the current US $37 billion to $ 85 billion by 2010 creation of 12 million new jobs in the textile sector and modernization & consolidation for creating a globally competitive textile industry. With the phasing out of quota regime under MFA, from Jan 1st 2005, developing countries including India with both textile & clothing capacity may be able to prosper.

Automobile sector has demonstrated the inherent strengths of Indian labour and capital. The pharma industry and the IT industry are two sunrise sectors for India. Among the sectors that have experienced the greatest transformation in India, the pharmaceutical is perhaps the most significant.

India's WTO involvement during the last decade has encouraged our pharma companies to adopt a strategy of R & D based innovative growth. Indian pharma exports were 14000 crore Rupees & accounts for more than a third of the industry's turnover. Apart from manufacture of drugs, the pharma industry offers huge for out sourcing of clinical research. A vast pool of scientific and technical personnel & recognized expertise in medical treatment & health care are India's strength, India can take advantages of its strength once patent protection is given to the result of the researches. By participating in the international system of intellectual property protection, India unlocks for herself vast opportunities in both exports as well as her potential to become a global hub in the area of R & D based clinical research out sourcing, particularly in the area of biotechnology. The three main sub sectors of industry viz Mining & quarrying, manufacturing, and electricity, gas & water supply recorded growths of 5%, 8.8% and 7.1% respectively. Apart from infrastructure, particularly adequate and reliable power supply at reasonable cost and transportation facilities, there is need for stepped up investment in manufacturing. Industry needs to grow rapidly not only to boost the overall growth rate in the economy but also to generate gainful employment for the existing unemployed, as well as the new entrants. In a diverse range of industrial activities, several Indian firms have succeeded in getting integrated into global production chains and realized rapid growth of exports. This experience suggests that with appropriate scale, investment and technology, rapid industrial growth is indeed possible.

Services Sector

Service sector has maintained a steady growth pattern since 96-97, except into a fall in 2000-01. Trade hotels, transport & communications have witnessed the highest growth of level 10.9% in 2004, followed by financial services (With a overall growth rate of (6.4) % and community, social & personal services (5.9)% of all the three sectors, services have been the highest contributor to total GDP growth rate.

While in most parts of the developed world, the services sector's share of employment rose faster than its share of output in India there has been a relatively slow growth of jobs in the service sector. This is primarily because of the rise in labour productivity in services in sectors such as information technology that is dependent on skilled labour. Growth in tourism and tourism-related services such as hotels, holds a large potential for employment generation.

IT enabled services, such as Business Process Out sourcing have been growing rapidly in the recent past and will continue to rise. India's large number of English speaking skilled manpower has made India a major exporter of software services and software workers.

However, the emergence of somewhat inexplicable protectionist tendencies in some developed countries is a disturbing trend. At the same time it is important that India sees BPO in a larger perspective, than the Internet, as India's share is just $ 3.5 billion in December 2004 compared to the global market of US $ 178 billion. Also India out sourcing companies need to work more closely with their customers. In the complex BPOs, customers would like to have hybrid processes to control value. Indian companies need the right mix of domain expertise and process expertise, further, mere knowledge of English is not sufficient; management skills are also needed. Education for the offshoring industry needs to be given impetus too.

The beginning of New Year saw Tsunami, a worst ever disaster, which killed thousands of people in India, Sri Lanka, Indonesia & Thailand. Many of them were international tourists. The disaster was expected to have a negative impact on India's tourism in terms of large-scale cancellations of tourists to India but nothing of that sort was seen. In fact, tourist arrivals in India rose 23.5 percent in Dec. 2004 and tourist arrivals crossed 3 million mark for the first time in 2004.

THE INDIAN APPROACH IN CURRENT SCENARIO

Today India stands erect to face this financial crunch with many advantages and strengths. One of the major strength is its nuclear technology which will aid India to battle out its biggest problem-power. Cautioning against the use of word "recession" for Indian economy, Finance Minister P Chidambaram says India's growth would moderate in this difficult year, but would still be second-fastest in the world at the rate of 7-8 per cent. According to him a recession is defined as two successive quarters of contraction of GDP. He wishes to emphasize that India is nowhere near a recession. We may expect a moderation in growth rate in the current year to a level between 7 and 8 per cent. India would still be the second-fastest growing large economy in the world Chidambaram says.

Giving a positive projection on the country's economic scenario, P.M Manmohan Singh said India could regain its annual growth rate of 8% to 9% as the world's economy could recover partially the present crisis by September this year. According to the Planning

Commission Deputy Chairman, Montek Singh Ahluwalia, The global financial turmoil will not have any significant impact on the country's financial system as India is not exposed to the new and innovative financial instruments that triggered the meltdown. We have not been as exposed to these new and innovative instruments, which have been the source of financial distress internationally... So the direct impact on the Indian financial system is not going to be significant at all.

There will be indirect effect As regards to India, the country is fortunate to have large foreign exchange reserves and hence it would be able to tide over any short-term disruption in capital inflows.

The strengths of the Indian economy are substantial and capital inflows would eventually resume the normal course. As far as economic growth is concerned, the downturn in the world economy is going to have an impact on India and unlike the last year, the country would not get 9 per cent growth rate during the current fiscal. Still, the growth rate could fall below 8 per cent at 7.7 per cent, as predicted by the Prime Minister's Economic Advisory Council.

Positive Impacts on Indian Economy

Perhaps this is the first time during such crisis period when world's big economies like US is struggling to overcome this situation India was able to invest money for launching of chandrayaan-1. This is the time when world's most powerful economies are suffering more than Indian economy. It affected developed country economies more than developing country's economy. In USA Lehman Brothers has filed for bankruptcy, Merill Lynch has emerged with Bank of America, Washington Mutual Operations are being apprehended by FDIC and Wachovia is being auctioned by Citigroup.In comparison to such terrific conditions India is in a better place. It is worth underlining that we have a number of companies still reporting successes at this time. Some of the businesses bucking the trend at this stage have diversified into a number of areas and others have exposure to export markets. Whilst overseas markets are increasingly tough, but the businesses have been able to benefit from the weakness of the money value which has allowed exporters additional competitiveness with their international trade.

Expose of Weaknesses in the Economy

The major role of financial crunch is that it exposes the political, structural and financial weaknesses of an economy. It explores efficiency in the financial market, transparency and accountability of new or reformed organizations, opportunity for creating new jobs and technologies, sufficient fund for investment in R&D innovation and education.

During the financial crisis period, the extent of sufferance of an economy shows its weaknesses. Because if the rest of the world gets disturbed and capital flows and liquidity shrinks, there is bound to be spillovers not just on India but all over the world.. Regulators are trying to assess the situation and taking steps to insulate their economies from the unnecessary shock. The fact that we have not been affected reflects the merit of proceeding slowly. We have actually been reforming very slowly and gradual pace of reforms has some advantage and we should continue with that pace. India should endeavor to make the regulatory system more sophisticated to ensure that the country does not run into regulator gaps that precipitated the present global financial crisis. Our country pursued economic reforms in a calibrated manner and escaped the fallout of global financial crisis. So these expose of weaknesses will definitely help India's fast growing economy in the long run.

Cost Stabilization in Real Estate Market

Confederation of Real Estate Developers Association of India (CREDAI) and National Real Estate Development Council (NREDC), both builders association with around 3500members each across the country, have appealed the members to slash prices of their proporties. Builders feel that cutting down prices will spur buyers and restore confidence. This development will enable middle-class families to think of having their own homes as owning a house had become a distant dream because of unrealistic rise in real estate properties. By developing middle-class families it is for sure that Indian economy will be affected positively in long run. Because in comparison to any other country Indian middle-class families are significantly improving in monetary measures.

Rationalization of Salary Structure in IT Industry

This financial crisis will have a positive impact on the IT industry. This sector has seen an unprecedented rise in salaries and increments. But with this financial crisis this cannot go further. No economy can afford 25% to 30% salary hike per industry per annum. So now IT industry slowdown will ensure better quality of work and also prevent attrition. Today the IT professional will think twice before changing their jobs. Along with it funds spent on recruitment, training and development and retention of man power will come down considerably. Earlier the scene was quite different. With that lucrative growth rate of salary structure, IT professionals were changing jobs frequently. It had a bad impact on the job culture of the industry in particular. Frequent change of jobs also affected the overall productivity of the industry. But now the scene is totally reverse in nature. As a result of this financial crisis professionals are not only in favour of changing the job but also ready to work more with the same salary with the objective to keep his job secure. Definitely it would help in the improvement of this sector as well as the productivity of the IT industry.

Performance Appraisal is Gaining Ground

Today's businesses are under a great deal of pressure to perform. With increasing customer expectations, global competition, costs of goods and services and above all because of financial crisis, many companies struggle to meet profit forecasts. As a result, companies are beginning to discover the powerful link that exists between employee performance and financial success. Many companies are relying more heavily on human capital to address consumer demands while lowering operating costs, and improving financial position. Deploying employee performance appraisal programs that lead to measurable improvements in employee performance can provide the human capital leverage companies need to overcome many of today's business obstacles.

Earlier as the job opportunity was more for the people; the role of performance appraisal was less. To understanding how efficient your employees perform was critical to your business. Every year, thousands of businesses were losing millions of dollars in revenue due to inefficient employees.

Now as this financial crisis arises everyone is trying to save one's job. Watching the changed job environment use of Performance Appraisal is gaining its ground day by day. As a result, everyone is ready to give his 100% to his job. Fear of losing the job improves the performance of the employees as a whole.

Austerity is the Targeted Path

Today Warren Buffet advice of austerity is practically followed by many countries. Cost cutting seems to be the sole solution to this contemporary problem.

Starting from Govt. sectors to big private corporate sectors, cost cutting is there everywhere. Earlier when big MNCs were spending recklessly for promoting their business where staff luxury was of major portion, today they are taking a second thought before spending a single penny.

Splurge will no more be the watchword and greed will no more be good in corporate parlance. Financial crunch will force the companies to eliminate all forms of wastage and follow an austerity regime. India's greatest ability and strength is its tolerance and ability to adapt to difficult situations. It is now trying to tackle the issue of panic resulted out of depression and then pump massive amount of liquidity and confidence into the system. India's population plays the most crucial role here

Best Place for Out sourcing

"It is time to open up banking and insurance sectors for further foreign direct investments as multinational insurers and bankers are willing to invest more in India. There is a talk that FDI limit in insurance might be hiked to 49%. And this time is the best time to do it", Prabhu Guptara, Executive Director, Think-Tank of United Bank of Switzerland (UBS). According to Obama Govt. US's priority would be given to curtail costs, which would include cutting wage expenditure and there by outsource work to countries like India.

In view of high credibility, Indian banks should also expand retail and other businesses abroad. There is also a need for more innovative products and global competitiveness.

India continues to be the best place or top destination for out sourcing. Two factors are responsible for it. First when it comes to salary costs India is extremely competitive, second Indian out sourcing firms have now matured into true global companies that can offer best services at competitive prices. India is coming under the list of top out sourcing destinations with China, Brazil, Mexico, Malaysia and Chile. India has the second lowest Its-BPO salary base of $7,500-$8500 followed by China. Another advantage of India in this section is that India is having one of the largest producers of English-speaking graduates including management and engineering graduates. Such a huge number of graduates will definitely result in offering higher value-added services to the customers. Which is very weak in china as the number of youth is less here.. Today having the maximum no of youth our country is ready to adapt to this situation. Efficient young personnel are India's greatest asset here.

Opportunities for International Trade

When looking in particular at International Trade, there are huge opportunities for when the world economy begins to grow again and demand returns to foreign markets. The competitive position of Rupees only adds weight to the potential that can be realised. Today countries all over the world are interested for trading with India. It will have a great impact on our foreign fund reserve and forex market.

While it is uncertain how prolonged and deep the recession will be, it can be said with certainty that demand, and subsequently growth, will return. It is therefore imperative that, when this happens, policymakers have a recovery plan in place. This plan should act to foster growth in the short-term and lay the foundations for economic stability in the long-term. There is currently a high level of activity amongst the business support community with a key focus on ensuring businesses survive the downturn. A challenging and critical focus on the basics, or fundamentals of businesses, is likely to give local companies the best chance of survival over the next year.

The growth of the public sector and the narrow reliance on financial services for growth needs to change, with manufacturers and exporters having particular attention paid to them. After watching so many positive points we Indians can ourselves that we are quite in a safer place in comparison to many developed countries economy. To conclude lets hope for a stronger India by rectifying all its economic weaknesses after this so called financial crunch. -

GLOBALIZATION OF INDIAN ECONOMIC REFORMS

Presenting the central Government's budget for the year, 2001-02, the Union Finance Minister on 28/02/2001 said, "it is now 10 years since economic reforms began in 1991. During this period the economy has grown at an average rate of **6.4%** per year since 1992-93 compared to the 5.8% recorded in the 1980s. Poverty has fallen from 36 percent in 1993-94 to 26 percent or less now. Summarising the impact of the decade old reforms, the Minister, asserted" while economic reforms have placed the country on a much more secure and sustainable growth path, we still have sonic, serious concerns and can not afford to be complacent.

Investment is the driving force of economic growth. When investment with in the country is not adequate to accelerate economic growth. foreign direct investment (FDI) has a crucial role to play. The cumulative F.D.I in flows since 1991 increased to $ 26.89 billion Rs.1,03,636 crores, while approvals were at $ 72.98 billion-Rs. 2,67,798 crores till August 2001. India has received foreign direct investment of US $ 2 to 3 billion last year while China got $ 40 billion in FDI7. This is one of the salutary effects of liberalisation and globalization. Apart from Delhi, major recipients of FDI had been the states of Maharashtra, Gujarat, Karnataka, Andhra Pradesh and Tamil Nadu. However the flow of FDI at US$ 2.26 billion into India in 1998 was far lower than into countries like Singapore (U.S.$ 7.22 billion) China ($ 45.5 billion) and Mexico ($ 7.24 billion). While foreign investment, as a percentage of GDP was almost zero in 1990-91 and 0.1% in 1991-92, its average during 1992-2000 was 1.2 %. At the confederation Of Indian Industry partnership summit 2002 held in Bangalore European Commissioner said-with total Indian Software exports of $ 6.300 billion in 2000-2001 of which European Union accounts for 23 percent-a mere 0.42 % of the total European IT Market. India has still long way to go and areas of mobile communications C.R.M. back office management S.C.M. Solutions and e-learning segments. require Indian expertise. The growth of the Indian Economy in the post reform era in several sectors in quantitative forms is shown in the table given below; Savings and investment rates have remained more or less stable around 22/23 percent. Further these rates are lower than the comparable rates in Singapore at 51.4% and 34.5% and in China at 42.5% and 38.8% respectively. Moreover the negative rate of savings in the Govt. sector because of revenue deficits is a matter of concern.

Assessment

The foregoing account indicates the success and failure (short fall) of the Indian Economy in achieving measurable progress in quantitative terms relating to macro economic variables. The question whether the progress is satisfactory or not, whether the prospects are rosy or gloomy for the Indian economy depend not only on quantitative factors, but also the qualitative factors/the imponderables that influence the work ethos of Indians themselves. For long, Indians have been largely described as those that work very hard every where excepting in India (with exceptions). Punctuality, abiding interest in the work assigned, dedication and sincerity have an important role to play in increasing productivity, particularly in the services sector.

Similarly the linkage between increase in productivity and increase in wages should never be under estimated. Possible pursuit of incomes policy about which we were talking in 1970s along with the recommendations of Bhoothalingam Committee needs to be examined afresh. The query of the Eleventh Finance Commission (EFC) whether periodic appointment of pay revision commissions is warranted in view of the financial difficulties experienced by the union and state governments after the submission of the fifth pay commission, needs careful examination before such. Commissions are appointed in future. It should also be examined whether the "tyranny of the ten percent" in the Indian Economy namely the work force in the organised sector that resists all changes unfavourable to it has been a stumbling block in the pace of economic reform and growth.

Another factor that reduces the utility and productivity of large investments in India is the extent of leakages and the so called all pervading corruption for which India got 46th rank among 54 countries in 1996 surveyed by the Transparency International and GOTTINGEN UNIVERSITY. It is this that made Rajeev Gandhi, the former Prime Minister, to draw attention to the abysmally low percentage of benefits that reach the targeted groups-beneficiaries, out of every rupee spent by the government.

A number of persons of every description think that they are entitled to a share in the Governmental expenditure deprive the deserving of the benefits meant for then and rob the utility of public expenditure meant for development or reconstruction or social welfare. As a result the returns cannot be expected to be equal to the full value of the expenditures incurred by the Government while the objective of public expenditure is to make the governmental rupee go the farthest in terms of utility in practice in several cases it turned out to be futile and infructious expenditure.

Further limited government capacity and individual ingenuity in manipulating public programmes for private gain discredited the post war view that governments could directly replace the private sector to correct market distortions. It has to be recognised that the governments in India are neither omnipotent nor vigorous (hard) in the pursuit of declared state policies. Having recognised the limits of markets and the limitations of the government, the strategy for accelerating economic development has to be worked out. In his address to the FICCI on 05/12/2001 the Union Finance Minister himself admitted that the government was not always the best and most efficient spender of national resources.

It should also be noted that growth alone is not enough. It is not the be all and end all of all economic activity. Poverty anywhere in the world is a danger to prosperity every where. Over the past 40 years-(say between 1960 and 2000) the gap between the rich and the poor al lover the world has doubled-with incomes of the richest 20 countries now averaging 31 times, that in the poorest. In India the percentage share of income or consumption of the lowest 10 percent was 3.5% in 1997 where as the share of the highest was 33.5%. The Gini index was 37.8 in 1997.

Good Governance matters very much for economic growth and poverty reduction. Good governance also means the absence of corruption, which can subvert the goals of policy and undermine the legitimacy of the public institutions that support market. Good governance in fact is broadly the ability of the state to provide those institutions that support growth and poverty reduction. SMART Govt. advocated in Andhra Pradesh may be taken as a concrete expression of good governance. Above all, public enthusiasm is the lubricating oil of planning and petrol for economic development. So how far the public at large is enthusiasm for participation in development activities initiated by the government is a moot question. Among the 162 counties listed in the Human Development Report 2001, India ranks 115 with Norway topping the list and Sierra Leone occupying the last rank.

India therefore has to develop its own strategy for planning and development. In the race for economic development every country has to keep running even to stand where it is, that is, even to protect its relative rank among the comity of nations. To improve the rank, naturally, hard work, right policies effective governance, sincere implementation of programmes, transparency and accountability are essential. India has to distinguish itself increasingly as a leader in the services sector particularly in the IT Software, just as China has made a mark in the manufacturing sector and the Hardware segment of IT.

The Associated Chambers of Commerce and Industry (ASSOCHAM.) in a recent chapter says that what the country needs to day is good institutions to nurture its human capital. It has also warned that a sustained, accelerated economic growth will not be possible with out a significant improvement in the integrity and effectiveness of the governmental financial and other institutions on which the economy depends. it also emphasizes that governance is the key to India's future economic growth and lays emphasis on the need for strengthening the expenditure framework. It is to be noted that even in 1999-2000 and 2000-01 about one percent of GDP (1.32% & 1.04%) has been the estimated share of subsidies and more than 4.6°/o of the GDP was the estimated expenditure on interest payments in the central governments total expenditure of around 15.5% of GDP while total revenue expenditure was nearly 13% of the GDP. Plan expenditure, capital expenditure developmental expenditure. Expenditure on social and economic, infrastructure need to be increased significantly to achieve durable and sustainable growth. It should be noted that in the post reform era, though the consumer has not become the "king" his importance has increased. He has a wide variety of goods, particularly consumer durables to choose among competing products at fairly competitive prices. In several cases the service attached to the products has also improved. The exhibitions and "melas" that are organised for most part of the year in several parts of the country is proof positive of the effort to woo the consumers, who were earlier confronted with a sellers market. But then the importance of sovereignty of the consumer depends on the quantum of the purchasing power he commands. While those who are fortunate to have a job to sustain themselves are in a fairly comfortable position, for those who expected to get a secure and stable government job of any description, life seems to have become a nightmare. On a rough estimate for every 100 persons that are employed in the organised sector, more than 142 persons are waiting to be employed without any guarantee that even when posts fail vacant (on account of retirement or other reasons) they would be filled because of the policy of the right sizing the government. Unemployment is the one word that no one in the Govt. dared to utter in recent months.

Prolonged unemployment leads to unemployability and frustration and misery lead to hatred of the lucky ones, if not militancy. In a fast changing technological society where acquired skills become irrelevant and obsolete very soon, the challenge is to keep oneself ready to change and learn newer skills. Knowledge is power.

For producers, the days of complacency and sellers markets seem to be disappearing. To produce properly and wisely, quality goods at competitive prices or to perish seem to be the choice open to them. The days of protectionism are almost over. Buyers are no longer passive and are more knowledgeable than at any time. Markets have become global. Trading environment, power and expectations of buyers have changed. So the producers and traders should be willing to take up the challenges or else will be pushed to the wall. As Dr. Y.V. Reddy wrote tomorrow's problems cannot be solved with yesterday's strategies and can not be even understood with day before yesterday's knowledge. Hence the need for "Vivekavardhini" & "Vivekavyapti". Similarly we must remember that "Sparadhaya Vardhate Vidya"-Cut throat competition and not all round altruism is the characteristic of business. If education is the basis for empowerment and prosperity it is necessary to discriminate between good and bad and take the right decisions at the right time ("Sadasadviveka Chatliuratha" is Education) with the help of strong institutions. Honesty is the best policy is not only an ethical proposition, but a business proposition.

That the economy is poised for growth and is on the road to prosperity are not in doubt. How high the rate of growth will be, depends on all of us governance, people and proper exploitation of resources. Even for 2001-02 the GDP growth rate is expected to be around 5% in spite of the known constraints. Given political stability and peace it should not be difficult to achieve growth rate of 7 to 9 percent in the next decade. But, Govt. should ensure (the old adage) that death and taxation are the only certainties in the world in the sphere of resource mobilisation through proper tax collection. Effective tax collection and expenditure management are the prerequisites for growth, among others.

In the context of the future of the Indian Economy we may recall what poet Shelley said namely that "we look before and after and pine for what is not". The imperative now is not to pine but try fine tune the economy think and implement vigorously an effective plan for the development of the country-Statesmen should think and act that they are trustees for the future not merely for the present or for themselves.

INDIA AND GLOBAL ECONOMY

Challenge for Human Capital Management?

In recent years there has been significant change in the way labour is pooled across the globe. The influences of technology and growth have effectively caused industry leaders to have to change their focus from the brute force of labour (factor of production of traditional Economics) to the actual quality of the workers available globally (Global Outsourcing). This has produced a shift in tactics for those who manage Human Resources. It is now pertinent to devise strategies to develop the working population by educating them and developing their technological skills so that they can contribute to the organization requirements adequately. High mobility of workers globally (The knowledge or technical workers), wage differentials across countries, borderless business models and cultural fusion problems are some issues involved in HCM.

Transforming Employee into Productive Asset

It is important today that organizations understand the value of increasing a laborer's output capability by investing in, and adding worth to, his or her abilities, rather than finding a mass of labourers who are willing to work yet who are unqualified to excel in today's highly technological business environment. Simply put, the idea is that, contrary to the old HR theory that emphasized people as the most fundamental asset to a company, *Human Capital Management*, or *HCM* is focused on the right kind of people to get the job done.

Our first and foremost objective is the transformation of a worker into a resource that is competitive. The entire Human Resources industry is scrambling to keep up with this trend, and the most successful are those who proactively seek to mold new labour into an asset that is potentially profitable to a company.

Those who achieve high levels of success in managing human capital are those who can harness the power of excellent leadership. But how does an HR firm or manager actually go about successfully leading workers to a place where they are able to confidently proffer their services to companies eager to employ? Likewise, what does it take to guide a company to a position in which it can be ready to hire the right talent at the right time?

Finding Leaders

The failure of good leadership in the management of human capital is one of the primary causes of bad employment processes, sagging profit margins and, potentially, the overall failure of a company. In today's competitive and dynamic labour market, it is vitally important for HCM to focus extensively on the strengthening and development of excellent leadership skills. All too often programs designed to develop and improve employee capabilities are destined to fail for one simple reason – they lack the backing of a strong leadership team. That is why it is crucial to set up a proactive leadership team, developing a roster of professionals with advanced leadership skills. A number of Indian companies too have been complaining about not getting adequate team work, innovative capability and Leadership qualities even in Best B schools graduates. Kind of soft skills needed to keep organization ticking to demand of dynamics of markets.

If a company's management is unsure how to begin, it will be wise to pay close attention to the skills that really do pay off. One of the most valued leadership skills in the HR industry is trust building. If Human Capital Management cannot deliver on promises it has made, both its corporate base as well as its labour pool will quickly slip away. One US Company, for instance, recruited a large number of programmers from a developing country. Dreaming to work for a U.S. company they gladly committed to the training courses provided, assuming there would be work for them after they were finished. Unfortunately, by the end of the training courses the company could only support half of positions sought by these potential workers, brutally dismaying those left behind. While the number eventually employed was still enormous by industry standards, the company lost out by the amount of negative press received.

Many companies fail by inadequately training their employees, leaving them once they are sent to work and generating a higher than expected employee turnover rate while reducing fiscal profitability. This is caused by employees being left with a sense of distrustfulness towards their employer, something that is extremely important to prevent (Issues of building Employee loyalty and emotional bond with the supervisor(s).

Development Strategy

While there are several issues involved, one of the advantageous aspects of having a dynamic and changing labour pool is the availability of large number of younger, tech-savvy recruits who are, more likely than not, more susceptible to be influenced by charismatic leaders who fit with their ambition and role model. Thus leading upfront and creating a kind of dramatic work environment where experiments and newer ways are allowed would sure bring opportunity to build leadership (I have used this repeatedly during my tenures in Industry, galvanizing work environment with excitement and achieving things.

College grads between the ages of 21 and 28 in most major tech industries respond incredibly well to *Human Capital Management* programs headed up by engaging and personable leaders. It has been found that leadership success comes most often from those who have a certain level of the "big brother" or "big sister" approach to the younger recruits, guiding them in a nurturing manner that inspires a sense of loyalty and trust. It should also be mentioned that a similarly charismatic approach should be taken with members of the other age groups, although adjusted somewhat so as not to demean them. Yet while other age groups do also respond well to good leadership, the salient quality of the younger demographic is its ability to adapt to the constantly evolving technology of their respective fields. When hiring for senior positions in HCM teams, it is important to focus primarily on the level of leadership skills demonstrated.

With globalization shrinking the world map on a daily basis, technology stepping ahead at a rate that is difficult to keep up with and a work force that is often hard to recognize, Human Resources Management (*HRM*) is in a state of great upheaval and constant change. It is important to remember, however, that this dilemma is nothing new. In manufacturing sector globalization, as we know it today has been in the works for decades, and people have long seen the need to adapt to the increasingly fluid labour pool, using the racing growth of technological development to connect employers to the work force, rather than isolate them. Still, the speed at which things are changing leaves many at a loss, providing Human Resource Management with a great opportunity to step in and lead the way – all it takes is a positive attitude and the ability to sail through uncharted waters.

Outsourcing from Overseas Markets

One of the biggest temptations for North American businesses has been to send jobs overseas. The trend is picking up, no one willing to miss the boat (All most 50% cost reduction in many industries}. With recent university graduates in developing nations earning wages anywhere from a fifth (Comparing 75000$ to 15000 $ a year in India, typically for IT technicians) to a tenth of an American worker, all kinds of work can be sent out at incredibly cheap rates. Such jobs include outsourcing call centres, credit card processing, legal transcription, genetic codes analysis, invoicing, scanning of medical records-anything that has a set of simple instructions that an employee can repeatedly follow throughout the work shift. This is the direct product of the gift of technology, thanks to Internet, wireless and high speed satellite based communication channels which has made it possible to decentralize the processing of information, and has provided access to an entire world of workers (virtual classrooms, live chats and video conferencing and high speed FTP data transmission).

Outsourcing Human Resources

Indeed, there is no shortage of such workers, as India and China-the population boomers-lead the way for American and now European outsourcing. In addition, cheap labour pool is available in the former Soviet Union, South and Central America (Mexico, Brazil), and the Philippines. With such an abundance of worker resources opening up to the market, those involved in the management of Human Resources are struggling to stay ahead. If it succeeds in connecting workers with employers in a way that is beneficial to both parties, HRM could be one of the foremost beneficiaries of globalization. For many employers, the cheap labour pool provided by globalization has finally offered to make their wildest dreams come true (IBM, GE, HSBC and so many others). Profit margins have the potential to soar as wages are cut dramatically, worker benefits are stripped and stringent U.S. labour laws do not have to be adhered to (as compared to non existent laws in India). But many are finding out that overseas jobs aren't turning out to be as profitable as expected. It is not all success stories, however. There are too many failures, which no one talks about. In an increasingly unpredictable market, if a company does not effectively map out a strategy of how to account for the common problems that overseas jobs bring with them, they are bound to shipwreck. Unfortunately, however, many companies are completely unaware of what they are to expect from pooling labour abroad.

If a company invests heavily in onsite human resource management and training and allows time for the establishment of a cohesive and secure setup, the chances of failure are greatly reduced. Perhaps the heady fantasy of labour obtained practically for free has to be remitted by overzealous executives so that a solid foundation can be put down and tangible savings can be experienced. What outsourcing does to domestic labour is a very complex problem for Human Resource Management. Workforce planning has always been an in-depth process of statistically determining the age and skill factors of a given labour potentiality. With globalization in the mix, the data field becomes much larger. The HRM statistician needs to balance the skills and wage requirements of a U.S. college graduate against those of a worker from abroad, and when choosing one over the other, the trade offs are significant. For instance, while many companies choose to have telephone operators with limited English skills in India and Pakistan receive questions from American customers, the rate of customer satisfaction drops (off late customers have been reacting violently). With high rates of turnover for these foreign operators (35-40% attrition rate in India in some sectors of outsourcing), the level of satisfaction for American customers does not auger improvement. Still, however, many companies choose to continue with foreign labour, experiencing a certain level of profitability regardless of various blemishes.

Implications for Work Force

One of the major realities facing labour in USA is the rapid decrease in the salary and benefits expectations a U.S. worker can have while going into the job market. With a vastly increased labour pool to compete against, the U.S. worker must be prepared to develop and hone skills that otherwise might not be necessary. However, this is increasingly the case, as workers must seek to differentiate themselves from the workforce abroad. Indeed, technology, information and English skills can be the battle cry of labourers redeployed into the domestic U.S. market. In addition, many workers must face contract options that place them in a more unstable position in terms of employment guarantees from companies, leading them to rely less on one employer and more actively seek other contract positions as well. This lack of worker commitment is a major factor in Human Resource Management today.

The Indian Companies are also soon going to face similar issues. More number of foreign employees will be found here. Indian companies would do well to rope in large talent pool of NRIs technocrats who are ready to work in global wok environment with advanced training and skills.

GLOBALIZATION IN INDIA

India had the distinction of being the world's largest economy in the beginning of the Christian era, as it accounted for about 32.9% share of world GDP and about 32.5% of the world population. The goods produced in India had long been exported to far off destinations across the world. International trade in India reached 24% of GDP by 2006, up from 6% in 1985.

Trade

International trade as a proportion of GDP reached 24% by 2006, up from 6% in 1985 and still relatively moderate. India currently accounts for 1.2% of World trade as of 2006 according to the World Trade Organization (WTO). Until the liberalisation of 1991, India was largely and intentionally isolated from the world markets, to protect its fledgling economy and to achieve self-reliance. Foreign trade was subject to import tariffs, export taxes and quantitative restrictions, while foreign direct investment was restricted by upper-limit equity participation, restrictions on technology transfer, export obligations and government approvals; these approvals were needed for nearly 60% of new FDI in the industrial sector. The restrictions ensured that FDI averaged only around $200M annually between 1985 and 1991; a large percentage of the capital flows consisted of foreign aid, commercial borrowing and deposits of non-resident Indians.

India's exports were stagnant for the first 15 years after independence, due to the predominance of tea, jute and cotton manufactures, demand for which was generally inelastic. Imports in the same period consisted predominantly of machinery, equipment and raw materials, due to nascent industrialisation. Since liberalisation, the value of India's international trade has become more broad-based and has risen to Rs. 63,080,109 crores in 2003–04 from Rs.1,250 crores in 1950–51. India's major trading partners are China, the US, the UAE, the UK, Japan and the EU. The exports during April 2007 were $12.31 billion up by 16% and import were $17.68 billion with an increase of 18.06% over the previous year. India is a founding-member of General Agreement on Tariffs and Trade (GATT) since 1947 and its successor, the World Trade Organization. While participating actively in its general council meetings, India has been crucial in voicing the concerns of the developing world. For instance, India has continued its opposition to the inclusion of such matters as labour and environment issues and other *non-tariff barriers* into the WTO policies.

Despite reducing import restrictions several times in the 2000s, India was evaluated by the World Trade Organization in 2008 as more restrictive than similar developing economies, such as Brazil, China, and Russia. The WTO also identified electricity shortages and inadequate transportation infrastructure as significant constraints on trade. Its restrictiveness has been cited as a factor which has isolated it from the global financial crisis of 2008–2009 more than other countries, even though it has reduced ongoing economic growth.

Payments

Since independence, India's balance of payments on its current account has been negative. Since liberalisation in the 1990s (precipitated by a balance of payment crisis), India's exports have been consistently rising, covering 80.3% of its imports in 2002–03, up from 66.2% in 1990–91. Although India is still a net importer, since 1996–97, its overall balance of payments (i.e., including the capital account balance), has been positive, largely on account of increased foreign direct investment and deposits from non-resident Indians; until this time, the overall balance was only occasionally positive on account of external assistance and commercial borrowings. As a result, India's foreign currency reserves stood at $285 billion in 2008, which could be used in infrastructural development of the country if used effectively. India's reliance on external assistance and commercial borrowings has decreased since 1991–92, and since 2002–03, it has gradually been repaying these debts. Declining interest rates and reduced borrowings decreased India's debt service ratio to 4.5% in 2007. In India, External Commercial Borrowings (ECBs) are being permitted by the Government for providing an additional source of funds to Indian corporates. The Ministry of Finance monitors and regulates these borrowings (ECBs) through ECB policy guidelines.

Investment

Foreign direct investment in India has reached 2% of GDP, compared with 0.1% in 1990, and Indian investment in other countries rose sharply in 2006.

As the fourth-largest economy in the world in PPP terms, India is a preferred destination for foreign direct investments (FDI); India has strengths in information technology and other significant areas such as auto components, chemicals, apparels, pharmaceuticals, and jewelry. Despite a surge in foreign investments, rigid FDI policies resulted in a significant hindrance. However, due to some positive economic reforms aimed at deregulating the economy and stimulating foreign investment, India has positioned itself as one of the front-runners of the rapidly growing Asia Pacific Region. India has a large pool of skilled managerial and technical expertise. The size of the middle-class population stands at 50 million and represents a growing consumer market.

India's recently liberalized FDI policy (2005) allows up to a 100% FDI stake in ventures. Industrial policy reforms have substantially reduced industrial licensing requirements, removed restrictions on expansion and facilitated easy access to foreign technology and foreign direct investment FDI. The upward moving growth curve of the real-estate sector owes some credit to a booming economy and liberalized FDI regime. In March 2005, the government amended the rules to allow 100 per cent FDI in the construction business. This automatic route has been permitted in townships, housing, built-up infrastructure and construction development projects including housing, commercial premises, hotels, resorts, hospitals, educational institutions, recreational facilities, and city-and regional-level infrastructure.

A number of changes were approved on the FDI policy to remove the caps in most sectors. Fields which require relaxation in FDI restrictions include civil aviation, construction development, industrial parks, petroleum and natural gas, commodity exchanges, credit-information services and mining.

But this still leaves an unfinished agenda of permitting greater foreign investment in politically sensitive areas such as insurance and retailing. FDI inflows into India reached a record US$19.5bn in fiscal year 2006/07 (April-March), according to the government's Secretariat for Industrial Assistance. This was more than double the total of US$7.8bn in the previous fiscal year. The FDI inflow for 2007-08 has been reported as $24bn and for 2008-09, it is expected to be above $35 billion. A critical factor in determining India's continued economic growth and realizing the potential to be an economic superpower is going to depend on how the government can create incentives for FDI flow across a large number of sectors in India.

7

India's Superpower Delusions

There is a thin line between the audacity of hope and grasp of reality. India's middle-class, with its fond dream of India as a Superpower, is like a trapeze artist walking that very thin line. Despair too much, and your case is hopeless. Daydream too much, and you topple into a delusionary void.

Over the past decade or so, it's the latter which has been the bigger danger. India the Infotech Iron-pumper. India the Nuclear Non-aggressor. India the Space Scorcher. India the Cricket Conqueror. India the Massive Market. India the Enormous Economy. India the Growth Giant… you get the drift. With a flying cape and coloured briefs, it's an India ready to make the world spin the other way round on its axis. At the top level, the dream was articulated by an optimist-in-residence at the Rashtrapati Bhavan itself, former President APJ Abdul Kalam. With his technocratic training straight from the rah-rah realm of rocket science, he went forth and set a deadline: 2020. And then got little children all across the land waving little tricolours to pledge their support.

The Millennium Goal to beat all millennium goals! The future that was promised! The glory that was destined! Each success has brought another bout of delirium, India's lunar mission being a fine example. There's ice on the moon, Jai Hind!

So many have grown so fixated on the target, that should we miss our date with Superpowerhood, we might need group psychotherapy for decades to come. But delusions of grandeur, some think, are best cured by grander delusions of grandeur. So, with some digital jugglery—Infotech Imperialism has its privileges—the deadline has been reset to 2012. As if the poor hungry child in drought-ridden Bundelkhand just has to wait for the clock to tick past the midnight of 31 December 2011, and he'll be reborn in the land of milk and honey.

The Will To Power

That a sizzling economy can fuel hysteria has been a new learning. In a way, this is understandable. For a generation of Indians who remember the humiliation of PL-480 food aid from America, a five-year wait list for a scooter, a phone as a symbol of authority, and a working phone as a sign of cosmic rarity, the emergence into this bright new world of choice and plentitude is cause enough for exhilaration. And with $280 billion in the treasure chest and a nuclear bomb in the basement, nobody dare take it away.

The 'Hindu rate of growth' of 3 per cent has been replaced by a robust 8 per cent. There is 'feel good' in the air, and it is making us heady. "There is a feeling that the next generation will be better than the previous one," says Pratap Bhanu Mehta, president of Centre for Policy Research, a think-tank, "In itself, the fantasy is not a bad thing, but to believe that you have arrived can be dangerous. India has a very vast underclass and this just cannot be wished away."

One aspect of the fantasy is the belief that India has finally secured a seat at the high table of global power. After all, the G-8 has become the G-20, coordinating stimulus packages to save the world. As for wielding a veto over world affairs, don't forget India has achieved parity with the Big Five, having found a cosy place in the Nuclear Club at long last, even if the official membership card is still in the mail.

With heft such as this, it is puzzling to have Bangladesh defy India in letting terror camps run amok. Or ragtag pirates thumbing their nose at Indian flag carriers on the high seas. Or even Indians opting for foreign citizenship at the slightest chance. As any international traveller will tell you, all passports are not created with equal prestige. Perhaps it is no surprise that non-resident

Indians have played a big role in formulating the fantasy. Oblivious to starvation deaths in Madhya Pradesh but delighted to find Laxmi Mittal as Britain's richest man, unaware of the scarcity of potable water in Uttar Pradesh but at their loudest holding wine glasses the size of watermelons, they have become India's cheerleaders. India's moment, they exult, has come. If only.

"Nation building is a hard grind," says Lord Bhikhu Parekh, political scientist, "Rhetoric, on the other hand, is easy. The Superpower Fantasy thus is an escape from reality. In the Nehruvian era, elections were won on the premise that 'we cannot offer you a great today but hard work will assure that your tomorrow is better'. This has been replaced by the rhetoric of 'India Shining'."

This is not the first time that India's elite has been in a euphoric mood. In 1947, Nehru's 'Tryst with Destiny' had everyone agog. It was supposed to turn this ancient civilisation into a beacon of enlightenment for the world. The 1962 humiliation by China was a cold shower, and a bitterly sobering one at that. In 1971, it resurfaced. India famously won its first war in a thousand years and split Pakistan. Internally, Indira Gandhi's 'Garibi Hatao' was the great new adrenalin shot. It ended in a nightmare called the Emergency. Today's delusion has its origin in the BJP's atomic muscle flexing at Pokhran. From 'desert vibrating', the country was taken in five years to 'India Shining'—a slogan that lost an election but gave the middle-class an ego kick. Resplendence, it would seem, is like transcendence. Fold your legs, chant the mantra, and you're there.

Get Real On The Vision Thing

So, can India realistically hope to be a superpower by 2020 or even 2050? This is not a prefix one can buy with $280 billion in hard currency or wrest with a bomb. If power is the ability to exert one's will, a superpower is understood as having the ability to exert itself globally, or at least beyond one's territorial borders. In world history, expansive empires have done this, from the Persian, Greek, Roman and Mongol expanses to the latter-day Chinese, Russian and British empires. From the mid-20th century onwards, America has been the Big Superpower.

Only, the information revolution of the modern era has been making it harder and harder to exert power without the consent of those affected, most pertinently that of people within one's own borders. In other words, there is no question of achieving or sustaining real power—super or not—if the basic aspirations of your own citizens go unfulfilled.

After decades of adhering to Mao's four-word 'keep a low profile' dictum, China has just begun to assert itself globally. America is America, of course, still in charge. So, where does that leave India?

For one, with an urgent need to align vision with realism. To be sure, given the grim scenario in South Asia, India has the makings of a regional power. Missiles and money count, but one neighbour neutralises the warheads and the other has more moolah. This limits India's influence in its immediate littoral, the big reason why the 'super' prefix eludes the country. Can India overcome Pakistan, at the very least, as a critical constraint?

In 2009, India was the world's second largest arms importer. But it's still an importer. Frontline tanks, fighter jets and warships, they're all foreign made. This means dependency. China, in contrast, is now among the world's five top arms exporters. India's own defence development efforts since 1947, barring the odd missile, so far have been a scandalous waste. This tardiness retards the country's power projection capability in hard military terms.

Then, there is the question of economic emergence. At last count, this country of 1.14 billon people had the world's largest number of malnourished children. India also has more people who can't write their name, more malaria deaths and more jobless youth than any other country. To most statisticians at human development organisations, the very aspiration of superpowerdom is a crude joke.

Gung-ho Indians, meanwhile, are counting on the 'demographic dividend'. By this conventional wisdom, India will still be youthfully energetic while the developed world ages into its drone years. This view ignores the fact that a majority of India's young are illiterate and underfed, and unfit to do anything except the most ill-paid of jobs. The dividend could well turn out to be a disaster. The third superpower paradigm involves the State and its institutions. While Indian democracy is often hailed highly for its 'soft power' appeal worldwide, it masks a bad case of dysfunctional politics, a reality that strikes the elite only in occasional spasms. Instead of delivery of results, electoral politics is all about retention of power and dispensing of patronage. Unlike the revitalised US democracy, India's capacity for self-renewal seems much too weak for the country's good.

Worse, the resolve to attain the grand goal India has set for itself is in sparse evidence. Internally, the Superpower Project is hollow. Take a look around. The fissures of petty politics block attempts to win elections on national issues. Nor can these become priorities of governance. Superpowers, on the other hand, have always upheld issues that are vital to them in a broad sense.

So why does this fancy persist? Says Shiv Vishwanathan, a sociologist, "There is a fantastic urge within the middle-class for upward mobility. For status. This is fuelled equally by the expatriate Indian cousins when they visit or hold 'India' days. It is a dangerous fantasy because it is taken as manifest destiny. Bear in mind that a lot can still go wrong in the India story. If the middle-class insulates itself in the superpower ivory tower, it will invite reactions."

There are sniggers in the dark, scowls in the aisles. Read The White Tiger. Or watch Slumdog Millionaire. Though aimed at Western audiences, they are reminders of the mockery that comes the way of India's middle-class consensus on Superpowerhood. And indeed, there is much that should make the country squirm. There is nothing 'super' in having to declare a quarter of the country's districts tormented by Naxal violence. There are people out in the jungles who are taking up guns to overthrow the State, an entity they see as increasingly hostage to the mollycoddled middle-class and its fancies.

Matter Of Self Belief

So, can no good come of hallucination? It could depend on how the energies are channelled. In Meiji Japan, or Imperial Britain, the State took national ambition to new heights. "Some good does come out of the fantasy," says Gurcharan Das, "It gives a sense of self-belief. But it is critical to direct this positive energy, for otherwise it can lead to a dangerous disconnect of the elite from the concerns of a transforming country." India must wake up.

INDIA'S RISE AS A GREAT POWER

In considering India's rise as a great power, this chapter focuses specifically on India's relations with its strategically significant neighbours, Pakistan and China. Though India's increasing projection of influence may change the regional dynamics, the fundamental balance of power among India and its neighbours will not change dramatically in the near future. Pakistan is already overwhelmed by the military strength of India, thus its strategic outlook will remain unchanged, while China and India have increasingly intertwined relations and evenly-matched conventional and nuclear forces, ensuring relative regional stability.

Analysis

The Problem of Pakistan

India's geographically closest and most frequently problematic relationship is with its neighbour and prodigal twin, Pakistan. India's rise as a great power will have its most immediate impact on the extremely dangerous stalemate which exists between the two states. Many security concerns converge in Pakistan, as: the state has been a key supporter of the Taliban in Afghanistan, factions of which the Pakistani Army is now fighting in a de facto civil war; elements within the state support Islamic terrorist organisations that periodically attack India, provoking regional crises; and, the Pakistani Army has a growing nuclear arsenal, which could be vulnerable to misuse by malicious elements within the state. India and Pakistan engaged in wars in 1965 and 1971, with crises about continuing Pakistani support for insurgents in the disputed Indian state of Jammu and Kashmir erupting periodically, and threatening war in 1990. Following Indian and Pakistani nuclear tests in May 1998, Pakistani incursions across the Line of Control in the Kargil region of Kashmir led to another limited war, and the veiled nuclear threat by Pakistani Foreign

Secretary Shamshad Ahmed that, 'We will not hesitate to use any weapon in our arsenal to defend our territorial integrity.' Major terrorist attacks in Jammu and Kashmir on 1 October 2001 and in the Indian capital Delhi on 13 December 2001 again threatened war, though merely resulted in major military manoeuvres by India, code-named *Operation Parakram*. The lack of military retaliation by India despite grave provocation seems to suggest that India is successfully deterred by Pakistan's nuclear capability, and this in turn only fuels the eagerness of some elements within Pakistan to provoke India. Pakistan has adopted an "asymmetric nuclear escalation posture", which has deterred Indian conventional military power and thus enabled Pakistan's 'aggressive strategy of bleeding India by a "thousand cuts" with little fear of significant retaliation.'

India is four times larger and seven times more populated than Pakistan. As Pakistan averages only 300 miles in width, it is susceptible to a central assault that would split the country in two. A number of important Pakistani cities also lie close to the international border in the Indus River basin. As Pakistan is thus extremely vulnerable to conventional attack by India's larger military, it defines such an attack as an existential threat to the Pakistani state. Pakistani Lt. Gen. Khalid Kidwai thus outlined that Pakistan would use its nuclear weapons if: India attacks Pakistan and conquers a large part of its territory; India destroys a large part of Pakistan's land or air forces; India blockades Pakistan in an effort to strangle it economically; or, India pushes Pakistan into a state of political destabilisation. This asymmetric escalation posture is designed for a rapid first use of nuclear weapons against conventional attacks, thus leaving India without the ability to punish terrorist attacks through conventional retaliation. As elements within Pakistan continue to provoke India, this creates an extremely dangerous imbalance reliant on India's restraint to maintain peace.

India and Pakistan escalating to the use of nuclear weapons within the first 12 days. New analyses of this eventuality reveal that a conflict between India and Pakistan, in which 100 nuclear bombs were dropped on cities and industrial areas within the two countries, would kill more than 20 million people from the blasts, fires and radioactivity. In addition, the explosions could produce enough smoke to cripple global agriculture. Smoke generated by burning cities could create a climatic response that immediately reduces sunlight, cools the planet, and reduces precipitation worldwide. This "nuclear winter" would reduce or eliminate agricultural production over vast areas, simultaneously decreasing crop yields nearly everywhere. Approximately one billion people worldwide today live on marginal food supplies and would be directly threatened with starvation. While some analysts maintain that nuclear weapons would be used in only a measured way, the chaos, fear and interruption of communications that would follow nuclear war's commencement leads some to doubt that attacks would be limited in any rational manner. Additionally, Pakistan could face a decision to use its entire nuclear arsenal quickly or lose it to Indian forces which seize its military bases. Thus, unrestrained nuclear war in South Asia potentially has cataclysmic regional and global consequences.

Following the terrorist attack by Kashmiri militants in December 2001 and the subsequent military standoff with Pakistan in *Operation Parakram*, the Indian Army announced a new limited war doctrine in April 2004 called the Cold Start doctrine, which aims to allow conventional retaliation without posing an existential threat to Pakistan. Under Cold Start, the Indian army would avoid delivering a catastrophic blow to Pakistan, and instead make shallow territorial gains, 50-80 kilometres deep, that could be used in post-conflict negotiations. This doctrine aims to deny Pakistan the justification of "regime survival" for employing nuclear weapons in response to a conventional Indian attack. However, Walter C. Ladwig III foresees that, 'An operational Cold Start capability could lead Pakistan to lower its nuclear red line, put its nuclear weapons on a higher state of readiness, develop tactical nuclear weapons, or undertake some equally destabilising course of action.' The danger of escalation is further compounded by the relatively immature "command and control" and early warning systems of both the Indian and Pakistani nuclear arsenals. There also remains the danger of nuclear accident as, if one nation accidentally detonates a nuclear warhead on one of its own military bases, it probably will not have adequate surveillance intelligence to know that it has not been attacked by its enemy, and thus may falsely "retaliate" against the other country.

Meanwhile, in the context of the continuing conflict in Afghanistan, Pakistan believes that the United States would intervene to prevent war, as it relies on Pakistani troops along the Afghan border and supplies for American forces are transported through Pakistan. Thus, Pakistan believes the only potential military action available to India is air-strikes against Islamist training camps, which itself is not a serious problem, and may actually help Islamabad by killing destabilising jihadists while generating massive support among Pakistanis for their government. The dual problems of nuclear escalation and American reliance on Pakistan for counter-insurgency meant that following terrorist attacks in Mumbai by Pakistani group Lashkar-e-Taiba on 26 November 2008, which killed 163 people, India was unable to respond with conventional military strikes. Any attack by India might either destabilise the Pakistani Government, or escalate the conflict to nuclear exchange. In the event of state disintegration, Pakistani nuclear weapons could fall into the hands of militant elements who would attempt to use those weapons against India or the West.

Unfortunately, there is no easy path to stabilising reform within Pakistan. Pakistan essentially has a feudal political establishment, run by a civilian aristocracy of wealthy agricultural landowners and industrialists, and the Army. The civilian political parties primarily function as patronage networks, without deep-seated ideological differences, and merely struggle to control state resources. As a key aim of the agricultural and industrial élites is to avoiding paying income taxes, the Pakistani Government is also chronically in debt. The Army is seen by most Pakistanis as the primary defender of the nation and the ultimate guarantor of domestic stability. The ever-present threat of India is used to justify the Army's disproportionate share of national resources, and the Army itself also owns and manages a large agricultural and industrial empire. Domestically, the Army is the ultimate power-broker between the political parties, and has acted on several occasions to remove the party in power. As successive governments have received bailouts from international financial institutions, neither the civilian political élites nor the Army have felt any real incentive to institute fundamental change.

For the time-being, the Army is objectively the most stable and responsible force to control the country. The Pakistani military is the only state institution that works effectively, and without it Pakistan would probably have disintegrated long ago. The dire alternatives are representatives of the rising wave of radical Islam who arose from the madrassas under the patronage of General Zia ul-Haq, and gained their training in the US-backed *mujahedeen* struggle against the Soviet occupation of Afghanistan. These elements, and more recent jihadist recruits, are currently involved in Kashmiri terrorist organisations like Jaysh-e-Mohammad, and Lashkar-e-Taiba, as well as in the Afghani and Pakistani Taliban which occupy Pakistan's border provinces. While the Pakistani Army and intelligence services are often unwilling to directly challenge these forces (and, indeed, currently cultivate relations with the Kashmiri groups and the Afghani Taliban), and external (and, particularly, American) attempts to move forces into Pakistani territory would almost certainly make things worse, this unstable situation is likely to continue.

As India's power increases, so will its ability to strategically encircle Pakistan, through relations with Iran and Afghanistan, and via naval power. At the same time, India's patience for Pakistan's continuing terrorist provocations will probably lessen. Nevertheless, Pakistan's deterrent capabilities remain, as attacks on the Pakistani state – either unsuccessful or successful – are likely to result in either nuclear exchange or widespread chaos and bloodshed. If India continues restraint, however, and reaches out to more moderate elements within the military and civilian political parties, it could leverage its growing economic strength to gradually help a more moderate Pakistani state develop.

The Challenge of China

On a grander strategic level, relations between India and China will be highly significant as India emerges as a great power. There is a growing interdependence between the two Asian giants, as China is now India's number-one trading partner, with more than

$52 billion in bilateral trade, and estimates are that China-India trade will surpass US-China trade by 2020. China's powerful manufacturing sector complements India's combination of a raw materials and cutting-edge technology economy. Strategically, a strong and influential India helps to create a more multipolar world, consistent with Chinese interests, although China increasingly regards India as its main Asian rival. China is thus involved in a complex game of encirclement with India. China has armed Pakistan with nuclear weapons and ballistic missile technology, and has built 'strong military-to-military ties with Burma, Pakistan, Nepal, Bangladesh, and Sri Lanka as part of what Indians see as a strategy to tie India down, Gulliver-like, in its region.' China is also developing deep-water ports throughout the Indian Ocean to support its projected blue-water naval capacity.

Meanwhile, on the border, China continues to press its claims to vast tracts of Indian territory. Over the past years, increased friction in the border area between India and China has led to incursions by Chinese troops, the wounding of several Indian border police, and a build-up of military forces on both sides, as Beijing has been uncharacteristically assertive in its claims to sections of India's Arunachal Pradesh state. The Indians responded by moving 30,000 troops and their latest warplanes into the area, leading some analysts to predict a China-India war within five years.

China rejects the McMahon Line that forms the border, and places the traditional Sino-Indian border at the base of the Himalayan foothills. Stratfor's George Friedman argues that, for China, control of Tibet is of vital strategic importance, providing a barrier against its populous and economically and militarily-advancing neighbour. The high mountain passes of Tibet provide virtually impenetrable terrain which is easy to protect militarily. Along the frontier directly south of this border, in India, is one of the largest population concentrations in the world. If China were to withdraw, Beijing fears that this population could migrate into Tibet, and Tibet could gradually turn into a beachhead for Indian power that would directly abut Sichuan and Yunnan provinces. The Chinese thus see control of Tibet as a matter of fundamental national security. They also see the 1959 decision by Indian Prime Minister Jawaharlal Nehru to give asylum to the Dalai Lama, and the continuing support for the Tibetan government-in-exile, as perpetuating this threat. Thus, 'Beijing's price for a border settlement and for normalisation of ties with India, appears to be that India dismantle the Tibetan settlement in Dharamshala and request the Dalai Lama take up residence in another country.'

On a broader front, 80 per cent of China's oil and gas supplies transit the Indian Ocean and South China Sea, so the Chinese navy is increasingly making its presence felt in the area in order to secure its lines of supply. For China, like India, the steady flow of imported resources is not just an issue of economic growth, but also of the longevity of the Chinese Communist Party. Chinese leaders increasingly fear that adversaries could blockade sea lanes and strategic bottlenecks such as the Strait of Malacca, and are thus moving to an offshore defence policy that will include "distant ocean defence". China's actions, however, may impinge upon India's interests and destabilise relations.

Jason Blazevic argues that, following "defensive realist" strategies, each nation will attempt to gain power for self-preservation and other nations will see this move as a strategic threat, thus decreasing collective security. As part of this competition, China has been developing a so-called "string-of-pearls" strategy, expanding influence into ports in Burma, Sri Lanka and Pakistan. According to a report by US defence contractor Booz Allen Hamilton, 'China is building strategic relationships along the sea lanes from the Middle East to the South China Sea in a way that suggests defensive and offensive positioning to protect China's energy interests.' China emerged as the biggest military spender in the Asia-Pacific in 2006, and now has the fourth-largest defence expenditure in the world. Its navy is also considered the third-largest in the world behind only the US and Russia, and is superior to the Indian Navy. In this context, India perceives Chinese actions as power maximisation, and fears that China's forward-basing strategy will be used to contain India and rapidly achieve hegemony in the Indian Ocean.

Meanwhile, China and India have adopted nuclear "assured retaliation" postures (what they sometimes refer to as "credible minimum deterrence"), which rely on a small but secure and survivable nuclear force that assures a retaliatory strike against a primary opponent. In many ways, this seems like the most stable aspect of the competition between India and China, though it is yet to be seen what reaction a new generation of *Surya* missiles might provoke in China. Meanwhile, analysts like Stephen Walt expect that China will follow a consistent but non-provocative build-up of its military capabilities and diplomatic alliances over the long-term, aiming to gradually edge the United States out of a hegemonic position. India is likely to mirror this build-up and thus tension, and possible low-level confrontation, may result on the India-China border and in the Indian Ocean region.

INDIA AND THE GLOBAL POWER SHIFT

The international security environment is witnessing a power shift from the developed Western states to Asia led by the rise of China and India. This power shift will have a significant impact on global geopolitics. Although a unipolar global order has been in place for a decade and a half, a non-polar world (as against a multipolar world) is in the making. Political, economic and demographic trends have made it inevitable.

As Richard Haass has noted, "In contrast to multipolarity — which involves several distinct poles or concentrations of power — a nonpolar international system is characterized by numerous centers with meaningful power. " He adds that while "the United States is and will long remain the largest single aggregation of power... power and influence are less and less linked in an era of nonpolarity. " According to Haass, "today's nonpolar world is not simply a result of the rise of other states and organizations or of the failures and follies of U. S. policy. It is also an inevitable consequence of globalization. "

Analysts assess that despite its pre-eminence in military, scientific and economic fields, the US remains a country in relative decline. Even if that decline is unlikely to make a difference in the near future, the certainty of new powers rising to be global players augurs for a new global power balance. Explosive rates of population and economic growth in Asian states are indicators of a new world order in which power will be more dispersed. The critical question is, if this multipolar world will have a benign or malign form. There are two likely possibilities on this. The world could fragment into competing blocs that attempt to resolve their differences through power politics as nation states did in the 19th and 20th centuries. Robert Kagan has talked of an 'axis of democracy', including the US, EU, India and Japan, counterbalancing a 'club of autocrats', including Russia, China and Iran. 2 The other possibility is of existing and rising powers choosing to manage their relations through mutual interdependence, as has been attempted successfully in Europe over the second half of the last century.

Global shifts happen rarely and are even less often peaceful. The transfer of power from west to east will dramatically change the context of dealing with international challenges. In the early 20th century the imperial order and the aspiring states of Germany and Japan failed to adjust to each other. That led to wars which devastated the better part of the world. The coming shift in power will have a greater impact globally and will require assimilation of diverse political and cultural systems. Today's rising powers seek redress of past grievances, are proudly nationalistic and want to claim their rightful place in the comity of nations. Asian rise in economic terms will translate into greater political and military power, thus increasing the potential damage from conflicts. Former British Prime Minister Tony Blair has noted that "In the next two decades China and India will undergo industrialisation four times the size of the United States and at five times the speed. . . For the first time in many centuries, power is moving East. " Blair added that

"In this new world, we must clear a path to partnership, not stand off against each other competing for power. The world…cannot afford a return to the 20th century struggles for hegemony. "

It is also clear that military power, however strong, is in itself insufficient to obtain the political objectives of a war. The capacity of weaker opponents to impose high costs through asymmetric or 4th Generation War fighting is enough to make even the strongest military power think carefully before embarking on a military option.

The costs of managing Iraq after an easy military victory offer a clear indication of a fundamental shift in military affairs. As Fareed Zakaria has written, "On every dimension other than military power — industrial, financial, social, cultural — the distribution of power is shifting, moving away from U. S. dominance. That does not mean we are entering an anti-American world. But we are moving into a post-American world, one defined and directed from many places and by many people.

Recent studies on managing the consequences of the waning US hegemony have in turn led to the need to choose between two policy approaches. One reflects a desire to use US military capacity in 'full spectrum dominance' and its global reach to contain rising powers.

The other looks at the evolving global power shift as an opportunity to build a new basis for global order, which would be predicated on cooperation and equity. According to Kishore Mahbubani, "The application of the three western principles of democracy, rule of law and social justice will go a long way towards creating a more stable world order.

But the West will not be able to apply them on its own. . . Hitherto the most successful partnerships have been West-West, for example the Trans-Atlantic Alliance. Equally strong East-West partnerships must be created. But in working with partners from other cultures and civilizations the West will have to curtail its ideological impulses and learn to be more pragmatic."

Bill Emmott has noted that "both the US and the EU should, as a matter of urgency, scrap or reform all the top organizations of global governance in which China, India and Japan are not properly and fully represented."

This would include the G8 and the UNSC. He also recommends that "the US should support the EAS (East Asia Summit) as Asia's principal political and economic forum and state that it sees Asian integration and intra-regional cooperation as desirable.

"Recent US policies in the wake of 9/11, clearly demonstrated the former approach. Its consequences in Iraq and the anti-American mood in the Islamic world have raised doubts on the viability of such a policy. What strategy initiatives will emerge from the principal determinant of the global order, i.e. the US, remains to be seen.

US Seeks to Maintain Primacy

The US has sought to maintain its position as the pre-eminent power by following a policy of defence transformation, which leverages its technological superiority. As the US National Security Strategy states, "Innovation within the armed forces will rest on experimentation with new approaches to warfare, strengthening joint operations, exploiting US intelligence advantages, and taking full advantage of science and technology. "7 Transformation is designed to help address not only the traditional threats but also the emerging asymmetric threats from both state and non-state actors.

According to the US Quadrennial Defence Review, "although the U. S. military maintains considerable advantages in traditional forms of warfare, this realm is not the only, or even the most likely, one in which adversaries will challenge the United States during the period immediately ahead. Enemies are more likely to pose asymmetric threats, including irregular, catastrophic and disruptive challenges. " The National Security Strategy notes that the US is "pursuing a future force that will provide tailored deterrence of both state and non-state threats...while assuring allies and dissuading potential competitors. "

Thus the US simultaneously has to prepare against threats from state as well as non-state actors, which have acquired greater significance post 9/11. With respect to non-state actors, the primary threat comes from Al Qaeda and associated groups against whom the US is in the midst of fighting the so-called Global War against Terror, which it admits is going to be a 'Long War'.

The Global War against Terror includes overseas fronts like Iraq and Afghanistan and also homeland defence against future terrorist attacks on US soil.

The US recognizes the asymmetric nature of the threat from China, which is unable to match US military capabilities and is hence seeking to negate US superiority by targeting its technological dependence. The Chinese anti-satellite test in January 2007 is an example of the new kind of asymmetric threat posed by China. Since the US depends heavily on space-based assets, this has led to fears of a new arms race in space. According to the US National Space Policy of 2006, "The United States considers space capabilities — including the ground and space segments and supporting links — vital to its national interests. Consistent with this policy, the United States will: preserve its rights, capabilities, and freedom of action in space; dissuade or deter others from either impeding those rights or developing capabilities intended to do so; take those actions necessary to protect its space capabilities; respond to interference; and deny, if necessary, adversaries the use of space capabilities hostile to U. S. national interests."

With respect to state actors, the Quadrennial Defence Review suggests that the primary threat comes from China. As it notes, "Of the major and emerging powers, China has the greatest potential to compete militarily with the United States and field disruptive military technologies that could over time off set traditional U. S. military advantages absent U. S. counter strategies."

The US is strengthening its alliances in the Asia-Pacific with Japan, South Korea and Australia as well as building bridges with emerging powers like India. This quest for building up its alliances and partnerships is primarily designed to hedge against the possibility that the rise of China may place it on a collision course with the US. Although an outright war is unlikely, the possibility that tensions in the Taiwan Straits could escalate into military action, drawing in the US cannot be ruled out.

China's Emergence as a Peer Competitor

Pentagon's 2005 report to Congress on China's military power acknowledges that its goal of modernizing national defence is proceeding well: "China does not now face a direct threat from another nation. Yet, it continues to invest heavily in its military, particularly in programs designed to improve power projection.

The pace and scope of China's military build-up are, already, such as to put regional military balances at risk. Current trends in China's military modernization could provide China with a force capable of prosecuting a range of military operations in Asia – well beyond Taiwan – potentially posing a credible threat to modern militaries operating in the region. "

The US recognizes the asymmetric nature of the threat from China, which is unable to match US military capabilities and is hence seeking to negate US superiority by targeting its technological dependence. The Chinese anti-satellite test in January 2007 is an example of the new kind of asymmetric threat posed by China. Although China continues to call for an arms control regime in space, Ashley Tellis has pointed out that China's counterspace programs give it an asymmetric capability to overcome US military superiority that is heavily dependent on space-based assets.

China has gone to great lengths to assure its neighbours that its path to development will be peaceful. A White Paper published in 2005 called China's Peaceful Development Road notes that, "China's road of peaceful development is a brand-new one for mankind in pursuit of civilization and progress, the inevitable way for China to achieve modernization, and a serious choice and solemn promise made by the Chinese government and the Chinese people, " adding that "China's development will never pose a threat to anyone. "

The Quadrennial Defence Review states that "shaping the choices of major and emerging powers requires a balanced approach, one that seeks cooperation but also creates prudent hedges against the possibility that cooperative approaches by themselves may fail to preclude future conflict. "

According to the US National Security Strategy of 2006, "as China becomes a global player, it must act as a responsible stakeholder that fulfills its obligations and works with the United States and others to advance the international system that has enabled its success: enforcing the international rules that have helped China lift itself out of a century of economic deprivation, embracing the economic and political standards that go along with that system of rules, and contributing to international stability and security by working with the United States and other major powers." The NSS adds that "our strategy seeks to encourage China to make the right strategic choices for its people, while we hedge against other possibilities."

China's military modernization is a function of its phenomenal economic growth, which has averaged 9. 5% for more than two decades. The dependence of China on foreign trade and investment for its economic modernization means that any disruption of the regional security environment in Asia will have adverse consequences for its objective of development which is still a long way away.

China's rising dependency on energy imports is leading it into an aggressive pursuit of overseas energy assets, which could lead to confrontation with the US over its links with regimes that are opposed to the US.

US policies towards Japan and India can be seen in the light of its stated desire to hedge against the possibility of the emergence of China as a revisionist power. However the US will have to be careful not to make the latter possibility self-fulfilling through its actions. For its part China would like to prevent a balancing coalition against it that could constrain its ability to prevent Taiwan breaking away to independence. China is aware that in its quest to achieve a moderately well-off society during the next two decades, it will remain vulnerable to external pressures.

Other Powers in the Region

Russia, the successor state of the erstwhile Soviet Union, is yet to play an international role in line with its size and military power, but its huge resources of energy underline its claim as a major player. Russia's relationship with the West remains tense in the light of Western efforts to bring democracy to countries in Russia's sphere of influence and US attempts to build missile defence sites in Eastern Europe. While Russia is wary of becoming a junior partner to China, its current friction with the West has led it towards a tactical embrace of China. The two countries held unprecedented joint military exercises in 2005 and have also joined hands to keep the US out of Central Asia, which they view as their backyard.

Ever since the end of World War II, Japan's status as a close ally of the US under the US-Japan Mutual Security Treaty has remained unchanged. The end of the Cold War did not have an immediate fallout on the division of labour within the US-Japan alliance, with the US continuing to bear the bulk of the responsibility for Japan's security. However Japan's inability to provide any military support towards the first Gulf War in 1991 came in for criticism and it responded by passing legislation that enabled the SDF to take part in UN peacekeeping operations. As the 1990s progressed, developments in the East Asian strategic neighbourhood gradually caused Japan to reassess its defence posture. The Taiwan Straits incident of the mid-1990s was an eye opener to Japan of China's military capabilities and intentions, while North Korea's withdrawal from the NPT and its missile tests had a direct bearing on Japan's security.

With frequent calls also coming from the US for Japan to take on an equal share of responsibility and to contribute towards collective security, Japan revised its defence doctrine and the guidelines of its defence cooperation with the US to provide logistical support for US military operations within the region. After 9/11, the nationalist government of Prime Minister Koizumi passed special legislation that allowed for Japanese forces to be sent to the Indian Ocean to provide logistical support for the US operation in Afghanistan. In 2003 Japan even approved a contingent of ground troops for the Iraq war although their mandate was to participate in humanitarian operations in a non-combat role, which restricted their effectiveness. These were the first signs that Japan was finally on the road to becoming a normal nation. In 2004, the New Defence Policy Outline institutionalized these changes in the realm of policy by making it part of Japan's defence doctrine to undertake a role outside East Asia in association with the international community and its alliance partner, the US.

Australia is a major regional power which has contributed to security in the region by maintaining peace and promoting state building in East Timor, Fiji and the Solomon Islands. Under Prime Minister Rudd, Australia is following a multilateral approach while preserving its traditional ties with the US. Although Australia invoked the ANZUS treaty for the first time after 9/11, it has indicated that this does not extend to a US-China conflict over Taiwan, apparently influenced by the benefits it could derive from China's economic growth. China is going ahead to improve ties with Australia as the agreement on the sale of Australian uranium to China showed. The US, Japan, Australia and India had initiated a quadrilateral dialogue in 2007 on the sidelines of the ARF summit in Manila. This had caused concern in China, which went to the extent of serving a demarche on all four countries seeking an explanation for the meeting.

However under the new Rudd government, Australia has decided to pull out of the quadrilateral. Although Australia is also a member of the East Asia Community, Prime Minister Rudd has recently proposed a new regional institution for the Asia-Pacific. During a visit to Japan, he also proposed a new international body to work for nuclear disarmament called the Nuclear Non-Proliferations and Disarmament Commission

8

Management of Security Chellenges for Super Power

INDIA'S SECURITY CHALLENGES - A FUTURISTIC PERSPECTIVE

"If you know your enemies and know yourself, you will not be imperilled in a hundred battles; if you do not know your enemies but do know yourself, you will win one and lose one; if you do not know your enemies nor yourself, you will be imperilled in every single battle".

The Art of War, Sun Tzu (6th Century BC), Chinese general and military strategist: India is widely believed to have arrived on the global stage. In fact, if one goes by the popular press both domestic and foreign, it is very difficult to not get swayed by the euphony being generated about India and her inevitable ascendance to rightful place in the comity of nations. Nonetheless this essay attempts to desist from merely joining the self-congratulatory chorus and instead objectively analyses the security threats - external, internal, covert and overt, state and non-state - posed to our country. Therefore at the outset, it must be emphasized though I am a strong believer in the idea of India, her resilience and ability to resurrect from every conceivable threat she has faced in the last two millennia; the essay tries to adopt a pragmatic strategist's approach in the analysis of country's security environment.

As most of the armies of the world adopt, the paper bases the quantum of threat posed by a security threat through its capability and interest and not by purported intention. We will explicitly list all security threats as well as economic, social, political and technological factors that can give rise to an increased security threat level. We will first analyse external and then internal security threats before evaluating which of the two, if at all, be more threatening to India in the coming decades.

INDIA'S SECURITY CHALLENGES: PERSPECTIVES AND PROSPECTS

The profound changes in the world wrought about by the end of the Cold War have made for a fundamental restructuring of international relations. The end of ideological rivalry provided an objective opportunity for evolving a better security environment. However, there is a great deal of uncertainty and fluidity all around, as the new global equilibrium gets in place. Two or three factors would deserve attention in this regard.

The Cold War bipolar structure has been replaced by a "polycentric" world with the United States, Japan, China, the European Union and Russia emerging as the main partners in power.

Technology and economic power has moved to the forefront of international relations, emerging as a crucial factor in global realignments in the new setting.

The near symmetry in power capabilities and global reach between the two superpowers in a tightly bipolar world has given way to a certain disaggregation in the levels of power and capabilities among the new centres of power, given their uneven spread of techno-economic power, military capabilities and political influence. Even the United States, the most powerful nation today, has neither the will nor the capability to play a global role of the earlier order and magnitude. China, Japan, the European Union and Russia are in a process of defining their role in the new world order. Relationships between and among these centres of power are increasingly marked by elements of both engagement and containment.

Notwithstanding a broad shift from confrontation to conciliation at the global and regional levels, new points of pressures are unfolding themselves even as some old conflicts remain unresolved. For the developing countries, there is also evidence of new concerted pressures in economic, security and nuclear fields.

It is clear that there are manifold pressures emanating from the international environment which make for a complex and multilayered set of challenges and opportunities for India in the changed world order. India would have to respond to, if not anticipate, the new challenges and maximise its strategic political options, drawing essentially from its own power potential and bargaining leverages. This would at the least call for proactive strategies in terms of both restructuring old ties and forging new relationships at the regional and global levels.

India's security perspectives would inevitably be governed by the interplay of its domestic imperatives, regional balance of forces and the global challenges which impinge on its role and capabilities. India with its size, resource potential and strategic location is being increasingly seen as a regional influential poised on the threshold of emerging as a centre of power in the new international order. This is as much a recognition of its credible democratic functioning as the potential of its vast economic resources and political clout. India is a large multiplural society which has been able to successfully manage the challenges emanating from regional, linguistic and religious diversities without damaging its national cohesiveness. The remarkable resilience of its democratic functioning in a secular federal framework, despite some distortions, has continued to bely the scepticism of its worst critics. India's democracy remains fundamentally secure, underpinned as it is by an active judiciary, free media and a functioning and vigilant Opposition. India's economic development has also remained steady over the years. In the last couple of years, the Indian economy has registered an impressive growth rate of 7 per cent. The expansion and diversification of its industrial capacity have made important strides. Currently India ranks among the topmost industrialised nations of the world. It has the distinction of having the third largest pool of trained and scientific manpower in the world. Agricultural production has also shown substantial growth resulting in not only self-sufficiency in food grains but also reserves of impressive buffer stocks. Today with its burgeoning middle class, huge untapped markets for trade and industry, and large scale foreign investments, India has emerged as an economic power of some significance on the global scene. India has also built an impressive level defence capability. It has the fourth largest Army in the world with an impeccable professional record. It has a credible and self-reliant defence structure which has been built assiduously over the past three decades. India's missile development programme has also grown apace underlining its indigenous technological capabilities.

It is clear that India is slated to play an increasingly larger role in the coming decades. Its future as a credible power would, however, depend as much on its ability to manage the present stage of transition as on the projection of its strategic perspectives and policy options for the future. Two or three points deserve mention in this regard. First, India's status and power projections remain essentially contingent on its national security in terms of political stability, economic development and military strength. Second, although the asymmetrical power structure in South Asia ensures India's centrality, its regional power and influence tends to get circumscribed by the neighbouring countries' sustained pressure to counter its pre-eminence. In particular, Pakistan's unceasing search for parity with India makes for a deep-rooted strategic dissonance in the region which effectively reduces its capacity to shape or influence events in its neighbourhood. Third, continued involvement of external powers in the region remains an integral part of South Asian geo-political realities. The end of the Cold War has weakened the inevitable link up between regional conflict and Great Power rivalry. However, the inability of the states of the region to evolve a credible bilateral and regional framework for cooperation would continue to play an important role in reinforcing the pattern of external involvement—primarily in pursuance of their own stategic interests—in the region. This is bound to impinge on India's security perspectives, both short-term and long-term.

An overarching framework of India's national security has to take cognisance of military and non-military dimensions in terms of both external threats and internal challenges to its territorial integrity and national unity. Threats to a nation emanate as much from external aggression as from internal strife but at times internal factors can erode national security more critically than any external danger. National power based on political stability, societal cohesion and economic development would thus remain central to the future of India's national security.

India is passing though a crucial period of its post-independence history. Successively fragile coalition governments at both the central and state levels are affecting India's political, social and economic stability at a time when it is facing major challenges to its unity and integrity as a nation. The Indian political system is being subjected to manifold pressures from the progressive collapse of political and public institutions; incipient erosion of democratic norms; social unrest and corruption underlining a growing malaise in Indian polity. Increasing demands for power by more and more socio-economic groups, on the one hand, and limited resources and capabilities for redistribution of wealth, on the other, make for growing political and social turmoil. Widening economic disparities and growing rate of unemployment pose a major challenge for India's economic development notwithstanding a credible economic performance. It is estimated that by the year 2000, the total number of people living below the poverty line will more than the entire Indian population at the time of independence.

India's growing inability to manage political and economic challenges on the domestic front is a cause of deep concern. Although India's national integrity remains fundamentally secure, pressures from fissiparous cleavages in growing challenges of communalism and religious fanaticism have acquired disturbing dimensions. Political manipulation of religious sentiments for narrow political ends has long-term implications for the future of India's secular federal framework. The incipient threats to Indian federal polity in many parts of the country are putting growing strains on the political structure. Although India has been so far able to manage these challenges with a certain skill and patience, there is growing anxiety about the pressures getting intensified at a time when there is a steady erosion in the state's role in resolving conflict and bringing about social transformation. This is accompanied by a decline in the mediating role of the governing elite and party system. Decline in the state's order and authority has led to greater violence outside the established political channels, compounding the general law and order situation.

Continuing civil strife and incipient secessionism poses a major problem for India's national security. The northeast continues to be characterised by an uneasy peace. Although there is no full scale armed insurrection for secessionism as resorted to by the Nagas and Mizos in the Sixties, the problem of insurgency in Tripura, Manipur and Nagaland continues. Assam which had settled to a period of normal political functioning after the volatile agitation on the influx of foreign nationals in the early Eighties, is once again going although the fire of violence perpetrated by the United Liberation Front of Assam (ULFA) which is committed to armed struggle for the formation of a sovereign "ASOM". Punjab went through the unfortunate agony of sustained armed violence for over a decade before normal political processes were restored after heavy-handed crushing of Khalistan terrorists. The people of the state have, however, paid a heavy price for the then government's short-sighted policies for narrow political ends which changed what was essentially a party agitation to a Sikh movement encompassing divergent orientation and rationales. This has important lessons for the future of Indian federal polity which can only be ignored at one's own peril.

The situation in Kashmir remains a cause for deep and continuing concern. Mishandling of a brewing political crisis brought about by the state government's dismal performance, marked by rampant corruption and inefficiency, led to an explosive situation in the sensitive valley. The eruption of violence in 1990 served to underline the appalling failure of the intelligence agencies and the complete isolation of the political and administrative machinery from the ground realities. In the event, alienation of large sections of the civil population and their growing sympathy for the militants left little meeting ground between the people and the government. The recent restoration of political processes in the state following Parliamentary and Assembly elections and the increased weariness of the people with economic dislocation and high-handed intrusion of outside militants is leading to a slow change in the equation of forces on the ground. But the overall situation remains precarious. The process of rebuilding the sundered economic and political fabric in the state and winning over the confidence of its people for any worthwhile and lasting solution continues to remain in uphill task. There is no gainsaying that the problems facing Indian polity are enormous as evidenced by the persistence of insurgency and slow entrenchment of terrorism in several parts of the country. If left unresolved, these could critically jeopardise India's national sovereignty and territorial integrity from within.

It is self-evident that the foremost task for India is to overcome the challenge to its nation building and national security. India's real autonomy in working out its destiny as an independent centre of power would lie in its internal strength and cohesion. There is no getting away from the urgent task of upholding its unity and integrity as a nation state through a credible framework of secular federal democracy. The need for reinvigorating its democratic functioning and strengthening the role and efficiency of the state remains imperative in this regard. India would also have make sustained efforts to vitalise its economy through optimisation of its vast resources, manpower and technical know-how. The need for redefining the role of the state in terms of eradication of poverty and greater economic equity remains self-evident. At the same time, India would have to raise itself to a new level of efficiency and competitiveness to acquire necessary leverages to stand up to growing global pressures and to hold its own in a friendly competitive world.

India can also not afford to drop its guard on building an adequate defence capability to counter any vulnerabilities which can be manipulated by external forces. There is some concern regarding growing deficiencies in India's conventional capability due to reduced defence expenditure in recent years. The need for adequate defence expenditure and defence allocation, constant modernisation and updating of its defence acquisitions for its defence preparedness remains imperative in this regard. A credible defence capability would provide an effective guarantee for maintaining its territorial integrity in the face of both external aggression and also externally engineered internal subversion that has emerged as a primary threat in recent years.

In the final analysis, it is only a politically stable, economically prosperous and militarily strong India which can seek to play its legitimate role in the world community, commensurate with its size and vast power potential.

Issues of regional peace and stability continue to loom large on India's strategic horizon. South Asia is today on the threshold of a new era of democratisation as the process of evolving democratic structure is under way in almost all the countries of the region. The peaceful electoral transfer of power in Pakistan four times in a brief span of nine years reflects a growing commitment to democratic norms in that country. Bangladesh is firmly back on the track of democratic functioning after a long paralytic spell of negative agitational politics. Notwithstanding ups and downs, Nepal also continues to manage its democratic experiment credibly. At the same time, there are vested and deeply entrenched authoritarian interests in all these states, particularly the ones which have been under military rule for long years. For instance, the continued dominance of bureaucratic military oligarchy in the political set-up in Pakistan makes for a fundamental dysjunctive in its policy. Given the fragile democratic institutions in all these countries, the democratic process itself is releasing new pressures. It is thus that the domestic environment in South Asia continues to remain generally characterised by political unrest and regime instability.

Pressures from ethno-sectarian conflicts and religious fundamentalism are also rising in all countries of South Asia. Pakistan is sitting atop an ethnic cauldron as pressures simmer, threatening to tear apart the fabric of Islamic identity from below. The challenge in Sindh underscores the disturbing dimensions of large scale violence between ethnic groups. The continued Punjabi domination in the power structure spells a certain uncertainty for the future of Pakistani federal polity. Running feuds between

Shias and Sunnis in various parts of Pakistan have become a common feature on the Pakistani scene. Sri Lanka remains mired in prolonged ethnic conflict as the continued intransigence of the Liberation Tigers of Tamil Eelam (LTTE) makes for a virtual civil war in the strife-torn island. Sinhalese resistance to grant of effective and substantive devolution power to the Tamils only queers the pitch of ethnic politics in the multi-ethnic society of Sri Lanka. Even Bangladesh which has a relatively homogeneous society is facing problems in overcoming difficulties in integrating its small tribal minority. The likelihood of the region remaining in a state of crisis due to rising scale of political and social discontent is thus going to be a part of South Asian realities for quite some time. This not only poses a threat to state structures within these countries but also has an adverse impact on the matrix of inter-state relationships in the region.

The overlap of a large number of ethnic, linguistic and religious groups across essentially porous borders in South Asia makes for a cross-border spill-over movement of refugees, guns and drugs which generates inter-state tensions. The steady movement of refugees, following prolonged domestic conflict in the countries of origin, has emerged as a multi-dimensional problem which affects regional security. Refugees who tend to settle down in the host countries, given the intractable nature of ethnic conflict, put an intolerable burden on the demographic, financial and social sectors which has long-term implications for national security of the host country. Pakistan is still reeling under the impact of 3.5 million Afghan refugees who sought refuge following the Afghanistan crisis in the Eighties. Thousands of refugees are living in camps in Nepal as a result of ethnic conflict in Bhutan. Bangladesh has also had to cope with the Rohingyyas fleeing from Myanmar.

For India particularly, which has been the host to the largest inflow of refugees with practically no outflow, the magnitude and frequency of refugee movement has been a vexing problem. This has particularly grave implications for the social, economic and political stability of the sensitive northeast. The presence of a large number of Chakmas in Tripura is intensifying tensions among the local inhabitants who are resenting encroachment on limited jobs and resources and scarce land. Thousands of Sri Lankans who sought refuge in Tamil Nadu in the Eighties are continuing to stay on, creating pressures with the attendant problem of anti-social and criminal activities. Induction of arms and anarchy with refugees is becoming a growing political liability. Internecine conflict among militant refugees groups and their continued links with trans-border militant groups intensifies social unrest and level of violence with grave implications for the future of civil society in these regions.

Growing linkages between drug trafficking and organised violence and the magnitude of the proliferation of small arms are also becoming major sources of instability in the region. In India there is growing concern regarding inter-state linkages between militant organisations, on the one hand, and between states and militant organisations on the other, adding to the complexity of secessionist movements. The crucial link-up between hostile external forces and domestic forces of political subversion poses a serious challenge to India's national security by giving impetus to secessionist forces. Terrorism in Kashmir since the Nineties, and earlier in Punjab in the Eighties, has acquired disturbing proportions with Pakistan's unabashed manipulation and support through planning and coordination, training of militants, and unlimited supply of arms and finances. The supply of sophisticated weaponry in particular—including rockets and explosive devices—has undeniably helped to raise the level of conflict to a new high.

By some accounts, the number of men lost in combatting the low intensity conflict in the sensitive state of Kashmir has outstripped the number of casualties in all the full scale Indo-Pak Wars put together. It may be mentioned here that internal political dynamics in Pakistan would continue to make for increasing domestic compulsions to keep the pot boiling in Kashmir, both in terms of diverting attention from pressing domestic problems as well as the inherent stakes of the military establishment in retaining the primacy of calling the shots in Pakistan.

In the strategic northeast ringed as it is by Myanmar, China and Bangladesh, incipient secessionism remains vulnerable to external manipulation. Although China which had offered arms and sanctuaries in the Sixties is no longer doing so, its unchanged stand on recognising the grant of statehood to Arunachal Pradesh and its military presence in Myanmar underscores its potential to foment trouble at a time of its own choosing. Bangladesh's involvement—albeit low key—is well-documented. Pakistan's Inter-Services Intelligence (ISI) is also carrying out anti-India activities from Nepal and Bangladesh adding to India's security concerns in view of persistently unsettled conditions in the northeast. Today the growing incidence of insurgency, fomented and abetted by hostile external forces has in some way emerged as a major problem for India's security establishment. The statement of the former Chief of Army, terming the low-intensity conflict as the foremost challenge for India's national security only serves to underline the growing intensity of the problem.

Proliferation of small arms in the region is yet another disturbing dimension of cross-border terrorism. The inflow of weapons is a direct fall-out of the Afghan conflict and the siphoning of major chunks of arms sent by the US, China and Saudi Arabia for onward transmission to the Afghan Mujahideen. It bears pointing out that "small" arms is a mere euphemism for progressively more sophisticated and lethal weapons. The weapons circulating in the region include automatic rifles, machine guns as also landmines, sophisticated explosive devices, and communication systems. Even more worrisome in the fact that these lethal devices are finding their way to non-state actors and terrorist groups. This has significantly altered the level of internal conflict in India's troubled regions, making for deep concern for the inevitably long-drawn and prolonged conflict in sensitive border states with major implications for the deployment and engagement of security forces.

Unwholesome linkages between the drug barons and arms dealers comprise yet another cause for concern. The enormous funds generated by drug sales are being increasingly used to finance purchase of sophisticated weaponry by terrorist groups in South Asia. South Asia is abutted by two of the largest drug producing areas on its western and eastern flanks.

The growth of narcotics trade has been exponential in Pakistan, with the presence of a reported 1.5 to 2 billion heroin addicts. Infiltration of drug money into the Pakistan economy and political system is now well documented. There are also growing reports of significant penetration by the narcotics network in Pakistan's law enforcement agencies and military intelligence.

The widespread Kalashnikov culture in Pakistan is a function of the mutually supportive phenomenon of drugs and weapons. Vast quantities of these arms have found their way to Punjab and Kashmir. These weapons have also been used to create internal unrest in urban centres as evident by the vicious bomb blasts in Bombay in 1993. India is also fast emerging as a transit route for the narcotics trade, given its strategic location between two major narcotics producing areas. Drugs from Pakistan and Myanmar are being transmited from India for onward transmission to European markets. It is no mere coincidence that the most critical challenges of insurgency in India are located in the sensitive border states in the northwest and northeast which adjoin the drug generating regions. More important, the growth of a flourishing criminal underworld underpinned by a nexus between illegal traders, drug peddlars, and gun dealers in tandem with internal security forces and law enforcement agencies is a cause for increasing concern. The enormous toll in human and economic terms as a consequence of mindless violence and narco-terrorism getting entrenched in civil society has implications which have yet to be comprehended fully.

The complexity of these transnational problems defies strictly national solutions. The urgency for building bilateral cooperative relationships and promoting a coordinated regional perspective on these critical developments which are cutting across the sanctity of national borders, remains, if anything, self-evident. The South Asian Association for Regional Cooperation (SAARC) Conventions on curbing drug trafficking and terrorism in the region are important steps forward in evolving suitable regional mechanisms to tackle the twin menace. The conventions, however, remain presently at odds with the ground realities. The political push to add substance to declarations of intent obviously awaits a qualitative improvement in the political climate in South Asia. Till such time, the challenges of narco-terrorism would call for sustained vigilance on India's part to counter the insidious threat to its national security.

South Asia has been generally characterised by a great deal of political and strategic complexity. To understand the complex South Asian phenomenon, one or two factors deserve special attention. First, India with its undeniably greater power potential and centrality looms large on the South Asian scene. Second, the legacy of common civilisational heritage has lent a sharper edge to neighbouring countries' sensitivities regarding their national identity in a clearly uneven setting. India with its looming presence and power potential is often projected as a core threat by these countries.

India's relations with practically all its neighbours have been strained over a whole range of issues be they of trade, or water sharing or migration or ethnic sensitivities. At the same time, there have been no even patterns of relationships in the region. India's relations with Bhutan and Maldives have been generally smooth and rancour-free. India's relations with Bangladesh, Nepal and Sri Lanka have witnessed significant ups and downs over the years but have never been allowed to dip to an unmanageable low. Indo-Bangladesh relations which had become extremely strained over the Farakka issue and the Tin Bigha controversy have witnessed a dramatic improvement with the signing of the historic agreement on sharing of Ganga waters. India and Nepal have also been able to put the unfortunate events of the Eighties behind them. Today they are set for a qualitatively improved relationship with closer economic ties and better political understanding. The signing of the Mahakali Treaty and grant of overland transit route for its trade with Bangladesh by India underlines the positive shift. The Indo-Sri Lankan relationship today is a far cry from the palpable antagonism of the Eighties.

However, the Indo-Pak relationship has been characterised by a virtually unbroken record of sustained hostility. Indo-Pak discord which to some extent has been rooted in the bitter legacy of partition became more sharp with the conflicting national interests and ideologies of the two states. Pakistan's inability to work out a viable form of nationalism and its eternal quest for achieving parity with its larger neighbour remains at the core of Pakistan's hostility towards India. The three Indo-Pak Wars—the only intra-regional wars in South Asia—were all motivated by Pakistan's desire to alter the status quo. Pakistan's military relationship with the United States in the Fifties was also directed to counter-balance India and erode its prominence in the region. This not only brought Cold War politics to the region, irretrievably puncturing the area of peace that Nehru had sought to build, but also considerably aggravated India's security concerns. Pakistan's continued overtures to external powers, particularly the United States and China, for diplomatic backing and augmentation of defence capabilities remains directed towards eroding India's pre-eminence and power. It is not necessary here to go into the details of unresolved issues between India and Pakistan except to mention that Indo-Pak relations have remained lockjammed over a wide range of issues—Kashmir, Siachin, the Afghanistan crisis and the nuclear issue. For the past five decades, Kashmir has, however, remained the central and overriding concern for Pakistan. Pakistan sees Kashmir as an unfinished agenda of partition which must be resolved on the basis of the UN Resolutions which have long been overtaken by the realities on the ground. India has made it clear that Kashmir is an integral part on which it can countenance no compromise. This is so not only for obvious strategic considerations but also because it would deal a blow to India's secular framework and open the floodgate to demands for separation. India, however, remains willing to discuss Kashmir and all other outstanding issues on the basis of the Simla Agreement which expressly enjoins bilateralism and non-recourse to force by both countries which is not what is on the Pakistani mind.

Meanwhile, Pakistan's continued support—money, training and sophisticated weaponry—to secessionists in Kashmir makes for grave tensions for India. This is not to underestimate the urgent need for India to take steps to put its own house in order but to point out that Pakistan's proxy war in Kashmir represents a direct and immediate threat to India's security. It is also important to bear in mind that Pakistan has never given up the option of going to war with India to get back Kashmir. This has its own implications for India's security planning notwithstanding a growing recognition in both countries that the realities of a crumbling economy and sustained international pressure would militate against a full-fledged war. The world opinion has also decisively veered towards a peaceful solution of the Kashmir problem, with both the United States and China recognising the inevitability of a bilateral negotiated settlement. There is also a section of opinion which considers nuclear deterrence itself as a stabilising factor in Indo-Pak relations. Nevertheless, Pakistan's declared nuclear capability makes for India's heightened security concern, given Pakistan's less than peaceful intentions towards India. There is no gainsaying that India is faced with Pakistan's nuclear challenges at a time when the absence of a credible Russian nuclear guarantee in the post-Cold War world makes it more vulnerable than at any time before.

This also aggravates the existing pressures emanating from Chinese nuclear might and United States' insidious nuclear presence in the region. Although India has made it abundantly clear that it has the capability to respond effectively to any nuclear misadventure by Pakistan, India's security perspectives would have to reckon with a nuclearised subcontinent in all its future calculations. It also needs to be borne in mind that while the Indo-Pak Agreement on not attacking each other's nuclear facilities is a positive step foward in confidence-building, this or any other such confidence-building measure would remain essentially meaningless unless simultaneous exploration is made of the ways and means to resolve the underlying problems between India and Pakistan.

It is thus that the recent resumption of Indo-Pak dialogue at the Foreign Secretary level, after a long period of tense silence, is a welcome development for the future of Indo-Pak relations. However, even as New Delhi's call for initiating a qualitatively new chapter of amity underlines its sincere desire for a more forward looking and constructive approach, Pakistan's usual style of blowing hot and cold and its recent efforts to militarily activate the ceasefire line do not at present give much cause for optimism for Pakistan's similar response. There is, however, no denying that it is in India's long-term interests to reduce hostility with its important South Asian neighbour. This would at the least call for proactive strategies to build greater trust and cooperation with Pakistan in a framework of mutual goodwill.

India's long-term security hinges perhaps in a larger measure on the future of Sino-Indian relations. It is, therefore, in India's abiding interest to work for peaceful and cooperative relations with its most powerful neighbour with whom it shares a long disputed border. A stalemate in Sino-Indian relations during the Sixties and Seventies only served to limit India's diplomatic manoeuvrability and potential role in the region.

Rajiv Gandhi's visit to China in 1988 marked a significant breakthrough in thawing the stalemate between the two countries. The agreement signed during the visit on maintaining peace and tranquillity on the Line of Actual Control (LAC), pending a final solution of the border dispute, was a momentous step forward in normalisation of ties between the two neighbours. Re-emphasis on Panchsheel and the decision to initiate confidence-building measures to reduce tensions on the borders underlined a new forward looking approach on the part of both countries. The formation of a joint Working Group at the level of Ministers to carry forward negotiations on the boundary question reflected the new political thrust at the highest level. The process of normalisation has been since carried foward by a number of steps. Agreements have been signed to re-establish the Consulate General in Shanghai and Bombay and to resume border trade across specified points along the Tibet border. A set of confidence-building measures have been set in motion: agreeing on joint verification of the LAC, meetings between the local commanders, mutually agreed pull-back of troops from forward areas and prevention of aerial violations. These measures have not only helped to effectively defuse tensions on the borders but have also considerably eased India's defence burdens. More important, for the first time since the Sixties, India does not have to reckon with the nightmarish prospects of a two-war front with China and Pakistan.

At the same time, India can ill afford to have a let up in its defence preparedness to meet the long-term Chinese challenge. Although China would be hard put to challenge India a la 1992 because of changed correlation of forces on the ground, there is no underestimating the challenge of China's emergence as a formidable power in conventional as well as nuclear capabilities which has resulted in a vast power gap between the two countries. China's defence modernisation is continuing to move apace. China also continues to be engaged in augmenting its nuclear arsenal as its launching of inter-continental ballistic missiles and underground nuclear tests amply underline. Notwithstanding China's foreswearing of "first use," India can hardly ignore the implications of a total nuclear asymmetry with China. China's major military build up in Tibet—reportedly deploying ballistic missiles of medium and intermediate range—makes for long-term strategic concerns for India's security.

It may be pertinent to note here that China's remarkably growing economy, which has received additional boost with the reversion of Hong Kong in July 1997 also gives it a definite leverage in international affairs as underlined by its manoeuvrability in its relations with the US. It has been in recent years showing greater willingness to assert its power in pursuance of its interests in the adjacent regions. China's flexing of muscles in the South China Sea and its increasing assertiveness vis-a-vis Taiwan illustrate this. Although at present China has great stakes in not upsetting its carefully structured political and economic equilibrium or aggravating tensions in its neighbourhood, given its growing economic and military power there would be continuing uncertainty regarding its future moves and projections.

In recent years, more than posing a direct military threat, China continues to represent a challenge to India's role in South Asia. China has, of course, visibly refrained from engaging in anti-Indian rhetoric in terms of its relations with its neighbours. It has also apparently softened its stand on Kashmir, urging Pakistan to virtually shelve the issue while working for improvement of relations with India in other areas. At the same time, it has remained committed to strengthening its political relations with all of India's neighbours. It continues to sell arms to Bangladesh, Pakistan, Sri Lanka and Burma which tends to hem India in a subtle way. In particular, its politico-strategic collaboration with Pakistan shows no appreciable change. China's help to Pakistan in developing its nuclear weapon capability is well-documented. Its recent supply of ring magnets and M-11 missiles has disturbing implications for India, seeking to threaten as it does the present balance of power in the region. China's supply of arms worth 1.6 billion dollars to Burma and its help in construction of naval and electronics facilities, and modernisation of its naval bases are also of concern to India in its strategic northeast and the adjacent seas.

China has, of course, come a long way since the Sixties in its national perspectives and world view, engaged as it is in consolidating its economic development, promoting regional peace and establishing a "just" new world order. This has led to a growing convergence of views with India which remains committed to world peace and a just and equitable world order. They have mutually shared perceptions on the need to preserve national territorial integrity and combatting challenges of fundamentalism, ethnic separatism and cross-border terrorism. There is also a broad understanding between the two countries on global trade issues and the pressures emanating from the industrialised world on human rights and good governance. All this augurs well for a more relaxed and cooperative relationship between India and China. It would, however, need to be clearly borne in mind for India's long-term projections that relations between the two Asian giants are bound to be marked by undercurrents of competition and contest, inherent in the logic of geo-political proximity and national rivalry. It also needs to be borne in mind that the border question has been shelved but not resolved. India has vital stakes in consolidating the process of normalisation with China but as long as the dynamics of military competition remains unchanged, a durable framework of Sino-Indian friendship would have to be underpinned by an overall balance of strength and a clear recognition of their mutual power status and stakes in the region.

It is clear from the foregoing that India has an abiding stake in peace and stability in its neighbourhood for its long-term security.

India is going through a phase of rapid economic transformation and is poised to play a significant role in the global stage in the coming century. There is no gainsaying that India's projection on the world scene would depend in no small measure on its effective and constructive neighbourhood diplomacy. This would at the least call for evolving a framework of cooperative security in its neighbourhood. This would essentially mean striving to reduce tensions with China and Pakistan, its two powerful neighbours, without compromising on its core national strategic interests. This is so not only because they separately and together constitute a long-term threat to its security but also because stable peace in this region hinges on India's friendly ties with these two countries. India's recent agreement with China offers ground for finding a viable basis of confidence on which to build cooperative relationships. India's offer of several confidence-building measures to Pakistan is also a step in the same direction. These include the agreement on prohibition of nuclear attack on population centres and economic targets; the agreement on "no first use" of nuclear weapons; and upgrading of communication links between DGMO of both sides. In some ways, the Simla Agreement itself provides for an effective mechanism for confidence-building between the two nations to build durable peace in the subcontinent. Sustained efforts to initiate new confidence-building measures and strengthen the existing mechanisms would remain imperative for building a credible framework of cooperative security in the region.

India would also need to take a lead in setting the tone for a framework of relations with its smaller neighbours. New Delhi is today committed to evolve a fresh perspective on its relations with its neighbours in a framework of positive asymmetry. There is no doubt that in the short run, anti-Indian rhetoric would continue to be manipulated at will by these countries, depending on their domestic compulsions, but in the long run, deft handling of the neighbours with flexibility and sensitivity is bound to lead to a more relaxed political environment. This itself would lend a great credibility to India's role as a regional influential.

Peace and development in the region is in the long term a sine qua non for India's long-term security perspectives in South Asia which is facing staggering problems of poverty, illiteracy, malnutrition and under-development. The biggest challenge to regional peace and security emanates from its poverty and the under-utilisation of its vast resources to address the socio-economic needs of its teeming millions. Pressures of endemic poverty and population explosion are becoming critical in the region. South Asia has sunk to the bottom rung in terms of the number of its people living below the line of poverty. SAARC provides an effective regional institutional arrangement for South Asia to optimise its regional resources and capabilities to promote the welfare of its peoples and a cooperative framework for the socio-economic development of the entire region. India as the largest South Asian power has a special responsibility to give a visible push to SAARC and invest in policies which are informed by a larger and long-term vision of a cooperative and stable South Asia.

An important challenge to India's security lies in the unfolding security environment in its adjacent neighbourhood which has a vital bearing on its geo-political interests. The volatile situation in Afghanistan is of major concern to India. Afghanistan seems set to witness a fierce and long drawn struggle among the main contenders for power which, if unresolved, will lead to grave destabilisation in the trouble-torn country.

Although India does not share any borders with Afghanistan, it has fundamental geo-political stakes in the unfolding events there which can be detrimental to its own long-term security interests in the region. India, therefore, has a major stake in any outcome of the protracted Afghanistan crisis. India rightly views any fundamentalist regime in Afghanistan as an insidious threat to its own secularism as well as a potentially destabilising factor in the region. An important dimension of Indian policy is the inevitable antagonism of such a regime to India which has traditionally enjoyed close links with Afghanistan based on a shared perception of regional interests. The possible spillover of a Taliban style fundamentalist regime, in terms of impact of ideology, violence and narco-terrorism, into Kashmir makes for deep concern for India's internal security. India has, therefore, a stake in seeing the evolution of a broad based government in

Afghanistan which takes care of the legitimate interests of all major groups to enable it to emerge as a stable and non-fundamentalist nation. It is in this context that India is keeping contacts with major groups within Afghanistan and supporting all broad regional initiatives from outside to solve the problem. A growing understanding with Iran and other likeminded countries is emerging as an important dimension of India's policy not only towards Afghanistan but also the politically sensitive Central Asia.

Of late, Central Asia has emerged as an area of major concern for India in view of India's long-term interest in this strategic area. This is because the situation in the region which continues to be fluid because of political instability and challenges of Islamic fundamentalism has wider implications for India's own vicinity. Central Asia has also emerged as a major strategic region in view of its vast untapped reserves of oil, natural gas and other precious resources. This has made the region a focus of sharp interest and struggle among most major powers, notably the United States, Russia, China, Iran and Turkey, who want to exploit the tremendous economic potential of the area. Although India can do little to influence the interplay of Great Power rivalry in the region, it has a stake in deepening and broadening its own interaction with the region. This would call for a more energised policy in building upon existing economic and cultural ties with the Central Asian countries making for its reinforced presence in this vital area. India is already engaged in an exercise of exploring the avenues for extending support in the field of infrastructure and technology. India has to continue to take into account in its larger security perspectives the region's great strategic, economic and political importance in terms of its energy reserves, strategic location and emerging political dynamics that are attracting wide attention and will have major implications for this whole region.

India also has vital interests in the emerging political and strategic dynamics in the Indian Ocean region. This is so because of its vital need for uninterrupted energy supplies and maritime trade through its strategic waterways. India is vitally interested in keeping the major sea lanes of communication in the Indian Ocean free for the movement of substantial portion of its trade, particularly in terms of access to vital oil supplies. Its objections to superpower presence in the Indian Ocean in the Cold War days was also a function of its concerns over escalation of tensions in its vital strategic vicinity. India's positive role in the newly formed Indian Ocean Rim Community also underlines its desire to evolve a cooperative framework of relations among the littoral countries of the Indian Ocean without undue interference of outside powers.

India's demand for oil supplies is slated to grow very steeply in the coming decades. Till such time that Central Asian vast reserves are fully exploited, the Persian Gulf which is currently accounting for 60 per cent of world's energy resources, would hold the key to global energy security. The potential of the South China Sea remains as yet largely untapped. West Asia and the Persian Gulf in particular would thus continue to remain a region of great strategic concern for all major powers, including some of the erstwhile self-sufficient countries like Russia, China and Indonesia whose reserves are getting fast depleted. Given India's strategic location to the area, India's has abiding interests in long-term stability and peace in the area because any potential destabilisation or conflict would lead to insecurity in India's strategic neighbourhood.

Given the external powers' continued quest for power and influence in the South Asian region, the need for diversification of strategic political options remains imperative for India as there is also evidence of new pressures in economic, security and nuclear fields. This calls for both restructuring the old ties and forging new relationships. India's policy towards the United States, Russia and China would have to be thus increasingly informed by the changing needs of national security and economic development as also the logic of its own role in the region.

Strategic and geo-political considerations had been critical for Indo-Soviet ties in the Cold War period. But it was essentially the mutuality of interests that sustained those ties lending them a certain autonomous structure, irrespective of extraneous inputs. Mutual convergence between the two countries rested on the basic premise of Soviet endorsement of India's pre-eminence in the region.

The Soviet support was critical for India in coping with its problems with both Pakistan and China, singly and together. More important, it helped India to build a credible and self-sufficient defence structure at a time when there was visible reluctance from the West to do so. In the post-Cold War world, India and Russia have been able to credibly rework their relationship despite the initial hitches in the transitional phase in a qualitatively altered framework.

Although there has been some reduction in the volume of trade and economic interaction between the two countries, the question of repayment of loan and currency adjustment has been settled to mutual satisfaction. The new treaty of friendship and cooperation between the two countries is a reaffirmation of the abiding mutuality of the interests between them. India and Russia would continue to have a convergence of interests in the developments in their proximate regions—Afghanistan and Central Asia—where both have vital geo-political interests in promoting peace and stability.

There is also mutuality of interest on the need of averting internal destabilisation from ethnic conflict and trans-border terrorism in large multiplural societies. This has particular significance for India which faces a simmering problem in the sensitive state of Kashmir. India also has a continued stake in strengthened defence relations with Russia, given its large scale dependence for Russian modern military hardware—at reasonable prices—and advanced civilian technology in space and nuclear fields. India has been able to procure military equipment with provision for technology transfer, joint production and export to third countries. Recently, India and Russia have set up a joint working group to address the operative elements of a long-term military technological programme—the only such programme Russia has signed with any foreign country—which has been extended for another ten years beyond 2000. Russia has also offered to India the latest and advanced technology in all areas of the defence field.

At the same time, any talk of "strategic partnership" is still premature, given Russia's strategic alliance with China and its continued dependence on the West. There are also difficulties in the supply of sensitive technology—underlined by the problems in the cyrogenic deal and differences over nuclear disarmament, particularly after Russia's signing of the Comprehensive Test Ban Treaty (CTBT) and India's own position on it.

There is, of course, some satisfaction in India that Russia has now re-endorsed its stand on India's pre-eminence in South Asia and moved back from the projection of equidistance between India and Pakistan. Moscow has now reaffirmed its support for India's stand on Kashmir and its firm commitment not to supply arms to Pakistan. Indo-Russian relations, although qualitatively altered in the changed world context, would have continued relevance for India's long-term strategic perspectives.

In the post-Cold War world, maintaining friendly and close relations with the United States, the only superpower today, which is capable of shaping the regional environment, would need to receive the highest priority in India's larger strategic calculations.

Indo-US relations have remained generally lukewarm over the years essentially for the United States' non-recognition of India as a power of consequence in the region. There has been no effort by the US to develop an autonomous approach to South Asia except in relationship to its broader global objectives. Shared democratic values have failed to provide a firm basis for understanding between the two countries whose divergent security interests lay at the root of the indifferent state of relations. This has remained so notwithstanding India's need and desire for improved relations with the United States, albeit on its own terms and from its own long-term security perspectives. The United States is seen in India as displaying singular insensitivity and disregard for India's vital security concerns in the region.

An important Indian objection to US policy in South Asia has been its commitment to the parity syndrome between India and Pakistan—including equating Indian and Pakistani nuclear policy—which India sees as not only immeasurably intensifying its security problems but also eroding India's pre-eminence in the natural balance of power in South Asia. Notwithstanding an improved phase of relationship in recent years, the United States' continued reluctance to deliver sensitive technology to India only serves to underline its disregard for India's sensitivities to the qualitative alteration of the military balance of the region over the years.

There are today greater opportunities for developing understanding between the two countries on promoting peace and stability in both South Asia as also the neighbouring strategic regions of the Persian Gulf and the Indian Ocean. Although differences persist over a range of issues—nuclear proliferation, Kashmir, trade related issues and restructuring of the Security Council—all of which have a vital bearing on India's larger security concerns there are some positive indications of Indo-US relations acquiring greater depth with evidence of more intense economic interaction and the evolution of a strategic dialogue between the two countries.

The United States which has emerged as India's single largest trading partner and investor, has an abiding interest in India's vast economy and burgeoning markets. India, of course, would need the US capital, technology and markets which remain crucial to India's future economic development. India has welcomed the recent US declaration—although belated—formally designating the Pakistan-sponsored organisation Harkat-ul-Ansar, operating in Kashmir, as a terrorist outfit. There is also some satisfaction with the US' full-hearted endorsement of the current Indo-Pak dialogue and its reaffirmation that it has no desire to intervene in Indo-Pak problems. All these would underline a growing US desire to build an independent relationship with India, notwithstanding Pakistan's continued relevance to its broader regional objectives. At the same time, a qualitative improvement in Indo-US relations would, in the long run, continue to remain contingent on the United States' recognition of India's regional pre-eminence in the building up of an independent policy towards India.

Given the inevitability of India's search for its own place in the global community, in view of its large size and power potential, and the growing complexity of its security challenges, India's nuclear policy would continue to have primacy in its national security agenda in the new world order. While nuclear disarmament must needs be India's long-term security goal, its nuclear policy has to take into account the given realities of the nuclear weapons having come to stay as an important bargaining leverage in international relations.

There is a growing recognition in India that given the current international realities and the situation of nuclear asymmetry in the region, mere retention of the nuclear option may not hold unconditionally in the altered scenario. India would have to give more sustained and serious thought to the timing of the exercise or non-exercise of its option in the days ahead. Developing a full-fledged nuclear weapon capability while continuing to press for total elimination of nuclear weapons will, of course, be the foremost challenge for India's future security perspectives.

Three or four factors deserve attention in this regard. First, time remains of the essence for India as domestic costs grow and international pressures mount on India to abandon its nuclear option and missile programme at a time when the nuclear powers are engaged in updating and refining their capabilities. Second, India has to reckon with the prospects of undeniable pressures from the US, China and Russia, should it operationalise its nuclear option. It may also find itself under increased Chinese nuclear threat in view of its unquestioned nuclear might today. Third, exercise of the nuclear option would bring to the fore the classic dilemma of development versus defence at a time when India's developmental goals require the greatest attention for sustaining its economic growth. Fourth, the goals of national security, short-term, as well as India's own aspirations, in the long-term, to play a global role of some significance, remain compelling for India's strategic perspectives. Last, can India afford to remain locked in continued confrontation with the nuclear powers—in the post-CTBT phase—and pay the inevitably high costs—economic, technological and political—without having actually exercised its nuclear option?

It is clear that the whole range of possibilities—retaining the present ambiguity, opting for recessed nuclear deterrence and operationalising its nuclear option—would hold the centre-stage of the national security agenda demanding a well coordinated and well thought out nuclear strategy that would sustain India's long-term security projections.

It is clear from the foregoing that India has to resolutely address itself to the emerging set of challenges and opportunities in the changed world order in a coordinated and comprehensive framework of paramount importance would be its ability to project its (long-term strategic perspectives and interests in responding to the interplay of domestic imperatives, regional balance of forces and global dynamics in the coming decades.

The overarching reality of India as a large independent nation which is destined to play an important role on the global stage would undoubtedly prevail over the present difficulties and obstacles.

The need for India to come to grips with the complexities of the rapidly changing configuration of forces at the domestic, regional and global levels, however, remains self-evident. India's long-term strategic perspectives would have to show greater dynamism and flexibility in responding to the increasingly complex demands of national security, regional aspirations and global commitments. This would at the least call for clearly defining India's security interests and evolving a coherent and multi-layered framework of its security policy and perspectives. In the final analysis, India's own strengths and capabilities—political, economic and military—would alone add substance to India's future projections as a power of some consequence in the emerging global order.

INTERNAL SECURITY THREATS TO INDIA

India's internal security challenges can be categorized under two heads – insurgency and extremism. We will explore the internal security threats to India in these lines.

Insurgency

India faces huge challenges in dousing the insurgency fires in many parts of the country – from the dense forests of Central India covering Chattisgarh, Jharkhand, few districts in Uttar Pradesh, West Bengal, few parts of Andhra Pradesh (so called Red Corridor) to North-East India. We all know the Pakistani sponsored and mooted terrorist activities in the state of J&K since 1989. Besides there are dozens of militant groups in ethnically diverse North Eastern part of the country. Indian strategy so far has been to first let a state handle its law and order situation and intervene only in cases of extreme urgency. This strategy needs a rethink because of signs of consolidation among many of the freedom-seekers e.g. there are indications that Maoists have tried to forge ties with Kashmiri separatists and ULFA to synergize their activities. Furthermore as Left-Wing Extremism (LWE) in India stretches has their proximity to important cities and both north-south and east west lines of communication - termed as "potentially dangerous" by the Indian Army. Therefore for successfully tackling the menace of LWE, two pronged strategy needs to be adopted – focus on socio-economic uplift of the affected areas as it is unfulfilled promise of the Indian state to her citizens (aka Directive Principles of the State) and secondly this is one of the root-causes of the rise of Naxal movement in the Indian hinterland. Sincere efforts must be taken to implement inclusive growth as an objective of public policy. On fighting the insurgency, inter-state cooperation is a must and jurisdictional issues should not be allowed to tackle a nation-wide insurgency. Failing which, it must be emphasized India will face sever governance crisis internally and might even descend into chaos.

Insurgency in NE part of the country goes till 1950s and has its genesis in the way those states were integrated into the Indian Union. Much water has since flown down the river Brahmaputra to reverse the flow of time. Inter-ethnic and inter-religious harmony should be maintained in the highly sensitive region through grass-root level participation of people. Besides illegal migration from Bangladesh rightly fuels resentment among the rightful Indian citizens and there should be no vote-bank politics with this critical development in Assam and other states. Otherwise changed demographics of these states can wreck havoc on the internal security of the country in the coming decades.

For tackling the issue of Jammu and Kashmir, numerous tomes have been written. But in a nutshell, the issue requires firm handling from the Centre. It is widely documented that Pakistani state fuels the seeds of alienation among the Kashmiri youth. Even within the state of J&K, Jammu and Ladakh have not shown secessionist movements and are well-integrated into the mainstream. It is only the Kashmir Valley which has seen such activities and adequate focus should be given towards job creation in this region.

Extremism

Religious extremism is other main internal security threat to the country. Without establishing cause-and-effect for this phenomenon as do most of the Right and Left wing intellectuals, there is urgency to tackle this issue. Fair and transparent law enforcement and quick, efficient judicial apparatus are required to stem the tide of religious extremism in the country – both minority as well as majority. Recent rhetorical statements from the politicians of certain political spectrum to milk this challenge for their advantage are indeed unfortunate.

Other challenges to internal security are astoundingly high level of corruption, political factionalism and caste wars – all of which require seasoned and firm political vision.

GREATER THREAT - INTERNAL OR EXTERNAL

It is indeed a complex task to determine which of the two threats will be greater for India. In fact, in highly dynamic external security situation and rapidly evolving internal socio-economic developments, the relative strengths of these challenges cannot be determined with certainty. But one can say that an internally weak nation cannot fight an external adversary successfully. So tackling internal insurgency successfully is a greater and immediate challenge than fighting wars abroad. Continued insurgency can provide a fillip to external aggression from our adversaries sensing internal weakness.

For example, left wing ultras can cripple rail and road infrastructure in the event of war and our enemies can very well factor this into their calculations. Similarly insurgencies in India are abetted and supported by our adversaries and the impact of the two challenges cannot be isolated per se.

Conclusion

As has been argued throughout this chapter, in area as humongous as national security it is difficult to ascertain which of the two threats – external or internal – will pose greater security threat to the country going forward. But if we take nation as an organism, to fight an external adversary internal strength is prerequisite. Internal cohesion and external defense preparedness is what gives a nation lethal power to deter a potential aggressor and preserve freedom. Indian history has shown throughout millennia, we have lost our freedom and riches by neglecting our frontiers or through internal factionalism. Any nation which is getting rich without paying adequate focus on defense invites aggression. Are our policymakers ready for the challenge to steward safely an ascendant India of the 21st Century?

INTERNAL SECURITY CHALLENGES

India was partitioned in the backdrop of large-scale communal riots, but the partition of the country on religious lines, without taking into consideration its multiple identities, instead of bringing the communal tensions down, in fact, worsened the situation. The two-nation theory created Pakistan, and it still survives on this theory. Pakistan finds it difficult to accept the reality that India continues to be a democratic, plural, multireligious society and that India today has more Muslim citizens than Pakistan. The Government of Pakistan has taken upon itself the responsibility of not only protecting its own citizens, but also the Indian Muslims. The power structure in theocratic Pakistan, dominated by the army, the feudal landlords, the bureaucracy and the religious leaders has been able to retain its hold over the levers of power by playing the anti- India and Islamic cards. Pakistan plays the Islamic card in its foreign policy also. It misses no opportunity to club India as an anti-Islamic country where Muslims are not safe. The continuing tensions between India and Pakistan have a direct bearing on the internal situation in India. They have further complicated the internal security situation.

The management of internal security, therefore, assumes great importance. If the internal security issues are tackled effectively, subversion by the external forces to that extent becomes more difficult. Unfortunately, the rise of contentious politics based on sectarian, ethnic, linguistic or other divisive criteria, is primarily responsible for the many communal and secessionist movements flourishing in India. The presence of hostile neighbours enables the internal conflicts to get external support, which includes money, arms and sanctuaries. The vested interests exploit these conditions to pursue their own agenda.

In a well-established political system and a developed economy, conflicts between the various group identities are kept under check as in due course they get assimilated into the national identity. But that has not happened in India as yet, where the wounds of the partition and the colonial rule have still not fully healed. Moreover, the dependence on the government by a large section of our people for their very survival sharpens these conflicts among them. The democratic institutions and the state structures are still not strong enough to fully harmonise these conflicts in a peaceful manner. Violence erupts when conflicting interests cannot be consensually reconciled. The hostile external forces, taking advantage of this situation through subversive propaganda, further accentuate these conflicts. They give material and ideological support to aggravate this sense of grievance to such an extent that a small minority are willing to become tools in their hands to subvert the stability and security of the country.

In addition, a number of secessionist and the so-called revolutionary movements are operating in India today. Their goal could be to overthrow the government and bring about revolutionary changes in the structure and functioning of the state, or even secession from the Indian Union. Ever since independence, India has been facing all types of violent conflicts based on religion, caste, language, ethnicity and regional loyalties. Political insecurity further compounds the problem. Preoccupied with the problem of survival, the governments in some of the most affected states are not looking at the problem from a long-term perspective. They have bought temporary peace by compromising with the subversive forces. Such shortsighted policies can have disastrous consequences in the long run. Instead of effectively dealing with them in the initial stages when the problem is manageable, they have allowed these anti-national forces to take roots and spread their tentacles far and wide. When a state government is unable to effectively deal with them, instead of strengthening the state police machinery, it rushes to the Centre to hand over its responsibility at the first sign of any serious trouble. It is not surprising that in these states some sections of the police have actually joined hands with the subversive forces against the central forces. "If you cannot fight them, join them". Finding themselves at the mercy of these subversive forces, the people tend to change sides and start supporting them instead of supporting the security forces. It would be wrong to assume that all those supporting, directly or indirectly, these forces are sympathetic to their ideology. Far from it! For most of them, preoccupied with the daily battle of survival, this is the obvious choice, because the police are unable to protect them. Polarisation on caste and religious lines can further reduce the credibility of the police in the minds of the people.

The police-politician-criminal nexus can embolden the criminal elements. Their activities can create an environment of lawlessness, where influential and rich people violate the law with impunity. The police is not the only component of the criminal justice system that has suffered because of this nexus. In fact, the entire criminal justice system is under strain. Not all crimes are being registered and those registered are not being properly investigated; and even out of those charge-sheeted, very few are ending in conviction. The conviction rate in case of heinous crimes is steadily falling. In some North-Eastern states it has reached almost zero level, where the police have stopped even submitting the charge sheets in the insurgency-related cases. When the fear of legal punishment disappears, organised crime finds it convenient to spread its tentacles. The crime syndicates are finding the new communication and information technology very useful. Extortion and payment of the so-called 'protection money' is more widespread than we would like to believe. According to some reports, direct extortion from the government funds runs into hundreds of crores of rupees. Many of the insurgent and militant groups are not driven by ideology, but by sheer greed. Money power is a bigger motivating factor than ideology. Vested interests have developed around these groups with active connivance of corrupt politicians, police officers and civil servants. Some politicians even take their assistance during election times. They have to return their favours when they come to power. This mutually beneficial relationship has seriously damaged the quality of governance in the interior areas. The real losers are the people. The development process gets seriously hampered in a violent environment. When large development funds are siphoned out by this unholy alliance between the criminal and corrupt forces, even the delivery of the most basic services like water, power, healthcare, education and communications becomes a stupendous task.

A vicious circle starts. The deprived and the marginalised sections of the society, unable to survive in the present system, get alienated. The militant and extremist forces thrive in this environment. The rise of Left extremism is more due to these compulsions than on ideological grounds. There are media reports about the carving out of a corridor by the Left extremist forces from Nepal to Tamil Nadu. Even if there is no truth in these reports, the involvement of hostile external forces in support of the Left extremist forces to destabilise the country cannot be ruled out.

The mushrooming of armed 'Senas' on caste and ethnic lines in some parts of the country is a direct consequence of the polarisation of the society. This phenomenon has also affected the police and the administration in general. Loss of public confidence in the capacity of the state to protect their life and property is the primary cause of this dangerous development. Far from controlling them, a politicised and partisan police actually encourages this development. The tensions in some parts of the country, especially in the tribal areas, due to a perceived threat to their identity is not new, but the rise of so many violent movements is a relatively recent development. In the border states these movements become secessionist because of the support they receive from the hostile neighbouring states.

The rise of fundamentalist forces is posing the most serious threat to India's security. Fired with religious zeal these forces have created an entirely new situation. The intelligence agencies in our neighbourhood and the organisations, like Al Qaida, and Jaish-e-Mohammad, are encouraging the so-called 'Jehadis' to enter India from outside. After first targeting the border states they have now spread deep inside the country. These bands of fanatics are not only indulging in subversive activities, but are spreading the virus of fundamentalism among the Indian Muslims. The break-up of the Indian Union continues to be the main goal of Pakistan's domestic and foreign policy. Easy availability of deadly weapons with the subversive groups operating in India has created new dangers for India's security.

With the 'Golden Crescent', and the 'Golden Triangle' in India's neighbourhood, drug trafficking poses yet another threat to our security. Drug syndicates are generating huge funds, a part of which is being used to give financial support to some of these subversive groups. The intelligence agencies like the ISI are recruiting a number of 'carriers' in drug trafficking as their agents. These agencies provide legal immunity for their criminal activities in their own country in addition to giving them financial and logistical support. Internal security challenges are not confined to any one area, but the North-East, Jammu and Kashmir, and the areas afflicted by Left extremism deserve special mention.

JAMMU & KASHMIR SECURITY CHALLENGES

The problem has been with us since independence even though Pakistan has no legal case. The ruler of this erstwhile princely state decided to accede to India. According to the Independence Act it was for the rulers of the princely states to decide to join India or Pakistan. Pakistan has been disputing the legality of the accession signed by the then J&K ruler, Maharaja Hari Singh. The initial hesitation of the Maharaja to accede to either India or Pakistan and the unilateral Indian offer to find out the wishes of the people of the state has given Pakistan an excuse to challenge the legality of the accession. It has been doing everything for the last 56 years to grab this state. It has not been able to achieve its objective through wars with India. So, it has started a proxy war since 1989. Waging of a proxy war fits into the Pakistani designs of bleeding India. Unfortunately, the weaknesses of the state and of the administrative systems have provided Pakistan with opportunities to fish in troubled waters. More interested in perpetuating their rule than governing the state, its rulers have been exploiting regional and religious differences. Anti-national forces thrived in this environment and Pakistan has missed no opportunity to support and encourage them. Over the years it has succeeded in building a pro- Pakistan base in the state. Frustrated in their efforts to gain power through democratic means, some politicians joined the anti-India front, more to put pressure on the Indian government than on ideological grounds. In a state, where the overwhelming population was against communal politics at the time of partition, the fundamentalist forces have managed to penetrate into the secular polity. The many serious problems of the people have to be addressed. It is not a coincidence that Pakistan's efforts to destabilise the situation in the state received some success only when our own political mismanagement provided it with an opportunity to intervene, as in 1965 and again in 1989. One of Pakistan's main aims is to divide the polity on communal lines.

The attitude of the Pakistani military government is unlikely to change in the near future. But that does not mean that Pakistan should be allowed to set the Kashmir agenda. Moves will have to be made on all fronts to regain the initiative on both political and diplomatic fronts. The proposals made in the announcements by the Cabinet Committee on Security on October 22 are steps in the right direction, but the ground situation does not justify over-optimism. There are likely to be many ups and downs on this long torturous road to peace in Jammu and Kashmir.

Left Extremism

Making a beginning in Naxalbari in West Bengal and Telengana in Andhra Pradesh in the 1970s, the movement has since spread to many states: Bihar, Jharkhand, Madhya Pradesh, Chhattisgarh and Orissa. The root cause for the rise in Left extremism is the inability of the states to address the many genuine grievances of the people. The gap between the unrealistic expectations, fuelled by populist rhetoric, and their actual fulfilment has increased and not decreased over the years. The younger generation is no longer willing to put up passively with injustice and humiliation without a fight. The bitterness of the angry young man against the prevailing unjust socio-economic system is spilling over. The older generation is not unsympathetic to them. An educational system which produces unemployable young boys and girls has not helped. Pressure on land has made the task of survival on agriculture more difficult. A callous district administration, especially in the rural areas, a clogged judicial system and feudal attitudes have compounded the problem. The land disputes have multiplied, but the land records and the judicial system to settle them is in disarray. There is a sense of frustration and anger.

The most prominent among the groups, that have mushroomed in the recent years, are the People's War Group (PWG) and the Marxist Communist Centre (MCC). But it is not ideology and revolutionary zeal that is driving them. For many, joining these groups is the only way to survive. Their main activity is extortion. Huge funds amounting to hundreds of crores of rupees are being extorted by them. What they cannot get through legitimate means they obtain through arms and explosives. Their tactics are no different from the insurgents and terrorists. Create terror and extort money. They are, however, not secessionists. Their aim is to overthrow what they call an unjust socio-economic system. But they are in no hurry to achieve their ideological aims as long as they can extort enough money. Corrupt politicians, policemen and civil servants have made their own adjustments with these groups. A live-and-let live attitude is mutually beneficial to all of them. Who knows how much money goes to the extremists and how much goes to the others. The real sufferers are the very people for whom the extremists are waging this war against the state.

In public perception a government that is unable to discharge all its responsibilities is more likely to respond when the demand is loud, organised and backed by acts of violence. The many progressive, well intentioned legislations are not being implemented effectively and sometimes have done more harm than good by creating more bitterness and frustration, e.g., the Minimum Wages Act. The marginal and deprived sections of the society are the worst hit.

Social and economic factors are important, but even more important are religion and identity. The secessionist movement in

J&K is politically motivated, but its ideological base is built around religious fundamentalism. Fired by religious fervour, the young recruits have no hesitation in attacking ruthlessly what they consider the decayed political and moral order, which they perceive as hedonistic. Once the instruments of governance are discredited, it is not too difficult to justify their destruction as in J&K, the North-East or in the states afflicted by Left extremism. In another sense, however, the aim of all these movements is no different from the aim of legitimate political movements. They too seek to acquire power, measured in terms of exercising influence or control over the people and acquisition of wealth for them is the source of all power. Extortion, therefore, becomes an essential part of their strategy. Their goal and strategy could change during the course of the movement. In the initial stages some of them may only demand economic and political justice or more autonomy in the existing political system, like the Bodos in Assam, but they can take a more extremist stand and demand secession in the later stages.

Effective steps to reduce ethnic and social inequalities, disparities in educational and employment opportunities, and for creating an effective machinery for the redressal of public grievance, are absolutely essential to improve the environment in which extremist violence flourishes. Steps to reduce economic deprivation and improve the delivery of essential services can erode the base of public support on which the extremist movements survive. It is relatively easier to find solutions to seemingly intractable political problems, like in J&K, in an environment where people are by and large satisfied with the functioning of the government agencies and are not deprived of essential services. More than anything else, it is the economic policies that would ultimately determine the future of these movements. A thriving economy, which gives hope and opportunity to the people, is more likely to defeat all types of extremist movements than any other strategy.

The need for a well co-ordinated security apparatus can hardly be overemphasised. It should include the police, the paramilitary forces, the army and the intelligence agencies. A composite force on the lines of the National Security Guards (NSG) should be organised in all the states, even in those states where the internal security situation is not so serious. It is easier to deal with the problems at the initial stages, than later, when the state police is no longer able to cope with them.

But in the states where the situation has gone beyond their control, the Centre, as laid down in the Constitution, is duty-bound to intervene, notwithstanding the fact that law and order is under the State List. The Union government is charged with the responsibility of protecting the states from internal disturbances under Article 353 of the Constitution, even though law and order comes under List-II, the State List. The Union government can issue directions to the state under Articles 257-258. Action for non-compliance of the directions from the Union government can be taken under Article 365. A state government can be dismissed under Article 356, if a situation arises in which the administration of the state cannot be carried on in accordance with the provisions of the Constitution. A national emergency can be declared under Article 352.

But, even if the Centre decides to intervene, the state's role cannot be minimised. The primary responsibility to deal with the security challenges must rest with the state governments. A situation should not be allowed to develop where the state government washes its hands off, or its forces instead of cooperating with the central forces, actually work against them. The many internal security challenges can be met effectively only with full cooperation between the central and the state governments. The police, the paramilitary forces, the army and all the intelligence agencies must act in close co-ordination. The hostile foreign forces can and will take advantage of the internal situation to destabilise the country in pursuit of their own agenda. All serious internal security problems: communal and sectarian violence, organised crime, drug-trafficking, labour and students' unrest, political violence and even economic crimes, if not checked effectively can develop an external dimension. There is an urgent need to make the police and the paramilitary forces more professional. The emphasis has to shift from 'more numbers' to 'more professionally trained forces'.

The internal security problems should not be treated as merely law and order problems. They have to be dealt with comprehensively in all their dimensions and at all levels — political, economic and social. They are all interlinked. At times, the required measures will conflict with each other. Going too far in one direction could be counter-productive. The security requirements have to be met, but that does not mean giving the security agencies a free hand. Striking the right balance is the key to success in meeting these challenges effectively. We need a comprehensive security policy that will be implemented effectively at all levels.

NORTH-EAST SECURITY CHALLENGES

The Naga leadership under Z.A. Phizo had challenged their integration into the Indian Union even before India became independent in 1947. The Naga insurgency started way back in the early 1950s. Since then the insurgencies in this region have multiplied and spread to many new areas. In this extremely diverse and strategically sensitive region, there are different reasons for the ethnic upsurges and insurgencies in different states. Some seek secession from the Indian Union, some others seek separate states and yet others greater autonomy within the existing state. The number of such insurgent groups could reach three-digit figures. In Manipur alone, more than twenty-five groups are operating. Thousands have died in the insurgency-related violence. Insurgencies have seriously affected the economic life of the region. The whole developmental process is seriously hampered because of this unending violence. One can imagine the plight of the people who are already living on the margin. What to talk of getting a share of the fruits of development, they are deprived even of the most basic services. Unfortunately, unlike Jammu & Kashmir, these violent movements do not stir much response in national consciousness. Even serious incidents of violence hardly find any mention in the so-called mainstream media. The geo-strategic importance of the North-East is not sufficiently appreciated even in the security establishment. All the states in the North-East share an international border with other countries and the seven North-Eastern states are linked to the rest of the country only by a narrow strip of land. The lack of physical, cultural and emotional links has encouraged a feeling of alienation, which is being exploited by the nottoo- friendly neighbours to pursue their own agenda. They are giving support and sanctuaries to many of these groups to use them as leverage against a much bigger and more powerful neighbour.

The roots of these many insurgencies in the North-East lie deep in its history and its geography. But, it would be wrong to treat it as one homogeneous region with common problems, or social systems and customs. Even physiographically, the region can be divided into three broad areas — hills, plateaus, and plains. The many ethnic groups, speaking many different languages and dialects, who inhabit this remote part of the country consider themselves as separate people with little in common with the people in the rest of the country. The lack of physical, cultural and emotional links has encouraged this feeling of separation.

The partition of the country seriously dislocated the old system of communications with serious demographic consequences. At the heart of the problem, however, is the new political consciousness and an urge for asserting their identity, especially among the fiercely independent tribal communities. The partition left the entire region land-locked, and even the old road, railway and river-waterway links with the rest of the country were severed, because they all passed through East Pakistan (now Bangladesh). The new rail link via North Bengal is circuitous and too long and expensive for easy access to the region. The air link is not only expensive, but also unreliable due to climatic conditions. The people have to bear enormous additional transport cost for all their supplies. Another intractable problem is created by the influx of migrants from East Pakistan and now continuing from Bangladesh. In the beginning it was confined to the Hindus leaving East Pakistan due to insecure conditions, but later, because of intense population pressure even Muslims started migrating. The fear that immigrant population will one day dominate them is keeping many of the insurgent and secessionist movements alive.

The terrain in this region is eminently suitable for insurgency. The hilly terrain and dense forests provide convenient hiding places to mount ambushes on the moving convoys of the security forces. Large parts of the interior areas have little or no police presence. The insurgent groups virtually control the administration in these areas. After attacking the security force they can easily disappear into the local population. Because of deprivation and alienation, a large section of the people tend to be sympathetic to the members of these groups. It is the alienation of the people that has sustained insurgency all these years, though logistic support and sanctuaries provided by the neighbouring states play a vital role in sustaining them. The dispersion of ethnic groups across the international boundaries has profoundly influenced the nature of political conflicts. However, it needs to be emphasised that internal-external linkages originate with the failure of the domestic political and administrative system in coping with the internal conflicts.

Secessionist leaders often adopt alternative strategies to achieve their goal. They keep on changing their tactics and demands according to the ground situation. The intensity of the conflict depends very much on how strong the public support is. Ethnicity can become an important dimension of internal conflict when it becomes intertwined with other social, political and economic issues. As conflicting groups go from one crisis to the next, they learn by experience to raise their demands to increase their bargaining power. Political changes that offer new opportunities for personal gain and extending their influence can spark violent conflicts. Even though most of them are conscious of the fact that secession is not a viable option, they keep on raising this demand to bring together the various contending conflicts on one platform. Making common cause against the Indian state is how many of these groups with conflicting ideologies cooperate with each other in their fight against the Indian state. The United Liberation Front of Assam (ULFA) was born out of the demand to throw out the migrants from Bangladesh, and yet its top leaders are today finding sanctuary in that country.

The South Asian countries have more in common with India than with other countries in the region. They do not even have a common boundary with each other. But this reality has not made them friendlier towards India. History and geography have encouraged negative sentiments rather than positive sentiments about India in these countries. The big powers too have not hesitated to fish in troubled waters. Till the 1970s, China was directly supporting the insurgencies in the North-East. Strategically, politically and economically the North-East is the most sensitive part of the country and should receive the serious attention it deserves.

The ongoing dialogue between the government and the NSCN (IM) is a positive development, but it is going to take a long and torturous route. The NSCN (IM)'s claim on the Naga-inhabited areas in the neighbouring states has created serious complications. The riots in Manipur in 2001 following the extension of the ceasefire to the areas beyond the boundaries of Nagaland are a pointer to the difficult road ahead. The situation in Assam has shown some signs of improvement, but large-scale extortion by the ULFA and other groups is posing serious problems. The NLFT and the ATTF continue to be active in Tripura. They have sanctuaries in Bangladesh. Mizoram is quiet, but there are problems between the Mizos and the Chakmas, and the Mizos and the Reangs. Thousands of Reang refugees from Mizoram are staying in camps in Tripura. In spite of many rounds of negotiations between the Mizoram government and the representatives of the Reangs, so far no solution appears to be in sight. The unending internecine feud between the NSCN (IM) and the NSCN (K) has spilled over from Nagaland to the neighbouring states and even to Myanmar. A number of Meitie and Kuki groups have sanctuaries in the Chin Hills in Myanmar. The ULFA and the Bodo groups have sanctuaries in the forests of Bhutan. There are unconfirmed reports of some sort of tie-up between the ULFA and the LTTE. A number of groups have also come up in Meghalaya and Arunachal Pradesh. Many experts have called the Naga insurgencies as the mother of all insurgencies in the North-East. The level of violence, however, in this explosive region continues to be high in spite of the fact that the ceasefire agreement with the NSCN (IM) has been in place since 1997. This only goes to show how difficult the road to peace is going to be in this trouble-torn region.

It is truism to say that it is not only a law and order problem. It has many other dimensions. No strategy will succeed unless it strikes a right balance between political, economic and security measures. There is need for closer co-ordination among the policymakers. Ideally, there is need for a consensus among the major political parties. The pursuit of narrow political agenda can be exploited by the subversive groups. Many political leaders in this region indulge in double-speak. They mouth nationalist slogans in Delhi but have no hesitation in making strong anti-national statements and collaborating with the insurgent groups in the state. Nor do they have any reservation in changing parties. They frequently hop from one political party to another. In Manipur some politicians have changed sides as many as six times in a year. A chief minister changed his party three times in one month, and his coalition partners three times in 48 hours. A party label has very little meaning. Money and muscle power with active support of the insurgent groups play a key role in the elections.

Most of these states are not financially viable. They hardly collect any revenue and depend almost entirely on the Union government for financial support. This has caused lack of responsibility in incurring public expenditure. For example, Manipur has created a huge bureaucratic structure with a workforce of almost 100,000 on its pay roll. Over 80% of its total revenue (both Plan and non-Plan) is spent on payment of salaries and pensions. Extortion by the insurgent groups, the leakage's of huge funds through corrupt practices leave very little for development. And they conveniently put the blame on the Centre for not giving them adequate funds. Through years of neglect this potentially rich region is today the most backward, almost primitive, part of our country. In these appalling conditions an alienated population becomes an easy target for the secessionist propaganda.

COUNTER ISIS THREAT WITH STRONGER INTERNAL SECURITY, MINDSET CHANGE

There was a recent news that said the Islamic State of Iraq and Syria (ISIS) plans to take over large parts of the world, including almost the entire Indian subcontinent, within the next five years. The plan is detailed in a book entitled Empire of Fear: Inside the Islamic State by Andrew Hoksen. It has a map, which throws light on the ISIS plans to establish its authority over the Middle East, North Africa and most of the Indian subcontinent and parts of Europe by 2020. According to another news item, a recruitment document purportedly written by ISIS terrorists and obtained by the American media outlines a strategy to draw the US into an all-out war by attacking India. Bruce Riedel, a senior fellow with the Brookings Institution, said that "attacking India is the Holy Grail of South Asian jihadis".

How serious is the threat? Opinions would differ, but it would be an invitation to disaster if India did not prepare for the contingency of an ISIS onslaught. We have to remember that the ISIS continues to expand its area of influence notwithstanding aerial strikes by US-led coalition forces. It is estimated that since September 2014, the coalition has flown 6,000 sorties and killed no less than 15,000 ISIS fighters, yet the caliphate's strength has grown from around 20,000-30,000 to as many as 70,000 soldiers. The figure includes 20,000 foreigners described as 'the largest convergence of Islamist terrorists in the history of the world'—larger than what we saw in Afghanistan!

The ISIS is no longer a distant phenomenon. It has reached our neighbourhood. The Pakistan Taliban has declared its allegiance to the ISIS. In Bangladesh, there have been arrests of individuals engaged in recruiting Bangladeshis for the ISIS. According to an analyst, the growing influence of the ISIS in Bangladesh "potentially signals more trouble ahead". In Maldives, entire families have left the country to participate in the battles being waged by the ISIS. Actually, the ISIS has made its presence felt in India already, particularly in Jammu and Kashmir, where its flags are displayed by Kashmiri youths now and then.

The government of India is unfortunately living in a state of denial. The official view is that very few Indians have gone to join the ISIS. True, but as stated in the US Country Report on Terrorism for 2014, 'given India's large Muslim population, potential socio-religious marginalisation and active ISIL online propaganda efforts, there remains a risk of increased ISIL recruitment of Indian nationals". What should worry our policy makers is that if and when the ISIS targets India directly, it would have full support of transnational terrorist groups like the Lashkar-e-Toiba, Hizbul Mujahideen and Jaish-e-Muhammad as also the indigenous outfits like the Indian Mujahideen and Students Islamic Movement of India.

There is enough evidence to suggest that the Indian Muslims are gradually getting radicalised. This was demonstrated in the response to the January 7 terror attack on Charlie Hebdo. Tufail Ahmad, a former journalist with the BBC who carried out a review of Facebook comments made by Muslim youth on the Paris shooting, found that "the geography of this radicalisation in India is indeed very wide, fertile and raw". Comments celebrating the killings were made by Muslim youths living in cities across the country. Hasan Suroor has also said that "the nature of Indian Muslim radicalisation stands dramatically transformed with jihadi groups looking upon India as a fertile new ground for recruitment".

The government of India needs to draw a comprehensive strategy to deal with the developing threat. The only positive step, albeit belated, it has taken so far is to collect information about de-radicalisation programmes in other countries and examining their suitability in India's context. However, much more needs to be done. The battle has to be fought in the minds of the people. A counter-narrative must be developed. The Grand Imam of Egypt's Al Azhar mosque has said that extremism is the result of "bad interpretations of the Koran and the Sunnah". The moderate Muslims of India should be encouraged to speak. The madarsah system of education will have to be mainstreamed. And, above all, India's internal security architecture will need to be reinforced.

ISIS ATTACK THREAT: WHY INDIA SHOULD BE AFRAID

A recent document titled, "A Brief History of the Islamic State Caliphate (ISC): The Caliphate According to the Prophet" was recently found in Pakistan. The 32-page document, translated by a Harvard researcher, suggested that the next big Islamic State (ISIS) target in the region would be India. It suggested that the objective of the group was not merely to undertake an occasional terrorist strike in the country, but to wage a full-fledged attack against India, by uniting all jihadi groups in the region, under its leadership. This raises some pertinent questions regarding the nature, probability and intensity of the challenge at hand.

According to Bruce Riedel, a senior fellow at Brookings and a former Central Intelligence Agency (CIA) hand with over 30 years of experience, "striking India would magnify the Islamic State's stature" and it is the "Holy Grail of South Asian jihadists". Riedel's assessment is true in terms of India's value as a target. However, there are distinct differentiating factors which must be borne in mind before taking this threat at its face value. First, the Iraq and Syrian examples clearly suggest that the ISIS achieved unparalleled success, which eventually led to its control over large areas in both countries.

This was facilitated by support from the Sunni minority in Iraq, which felt dispossessed of power, prestige and influence within the governing structure of the country. It led to support from important Sunni leaders and members of former Iraq president Saddam Hussein's army. This gave the ISIS local support, money and professional military leadership to wage its war. Second, the control over vast territories, especially the oil rich region of the country, provided steady funding, making the ISIS the richest terrorist group in the world. Third, its spectacular rise became a rallying point for all fundamentalist and radical elements, who saw the ISIS as the true inheritor of the Islamic Caliphate. Fourth, the group mastered the art of exploiting social media and the internet and employed simple, yet powerful messages to attract fighters and supporters from across the world. This has reinforced the ISIS as the sole representative of believers the world over. And fifth, it succeeded in strife-torn states, which were unstable and failing. This allowed the ISIS to fill the power vacuum in specific regions of countries like Iraq, Syria and of late, some areas of Afghanistan.

If one were to relate these factors with the intended attack on India, it becomes apparent that India does not suffer from any of the vulnerabilities that the ISIS has exploited elsewhere. However, this does not suggest that the group cannot sustain a terror campaign, which unlike their modus operandi in Iraq, need not focus at seizing and controlling territory. Its strategy against India could be based on a different set of principles. First, the ISIS can become the fulcrum of terrorism against India, thereby focussing the combined energy of different groups under its umbrella. Second, it can be supported by Pakistan's Inter-Services Intelligence (ISI), thereby providing it a well-established intelligence and logistic network, in a symbiotic relationship. Third, the social media campaign by the ISIS is ideally placed to exploit alienated members of the society. This has already been witnessed to a lesser degree, in which a small number of people have volunteered to fight for the terrorist group in Iraq. This can potentially achieve sharper focus if it is brought to bear on Indian targets, especially in the immediate aftermath of communally surcharged incidents. Fourth, while India may be amongst the most challenging targets for a radical organisation like the ISIS, given the strong roots of liberalism, democracy and secularism in the country, from the perspective of the ISIS, this is a prize which could well tip the balance in its favour, not only in the region but also beyond. This could imply that the resources and energy likely to be employed against India will make the terrorist group amongst the most serious challenge faced by the country so far. Fifth, the ISIS has foreseen the possibility of the US and its allies standing alongside India. However, past experience suggests limited cooperation by the US against terrorist threats specifically aimed at the country. It is more likely that it will be India's fight for its safety and security on the basis of its resilience and capacity.

If this is the possible nature and magnitude of the threat posed, here is the logical query that begs an answer: is India prepared for the challenge? A fair assessment suggests both a "yes" and a "no". While India has a long experience in fighting different forms of insurgency and terrorism, this by no means suggest that we are ready for the next wave, especially because this could come with renewed intensity. Here are five areas of focus that could substantially raise the level of preparedness of India against the ISIS threat. First, it is important for realisation to seep into the national consciousness that alienation leads to radicalism, which in turn, provides fertile ground for recruitment of terrorists. Any action that fuels this cycle of hatred must become a cognisable offence and be dealt with severely, irrespective of its short-term impact.

Second, a large part of the preparatory work in the fight against terrorism is done by research analysts and intelligence agents, well before kinetic measures are applied. This must receive the necessary impetus through cross platform recruitment of specialists dealing with social media, big data analysis, terrorism finance and technical intelligence, to name a few. Third, the Gurdaspur terrorist strike has yet again reinforced the importance of decentralised and specialist counterterrorism capabilities. There are lessons, both positive and negative that the experience has thrown up in terms of reaction time, weapon and equipment profile, tactical capacities and perception management.

This must be brainstormed and its benefits shared with all states which could well become the target of the next strike. Fourth, a large section of the society is blissfully unaware of the ISIS as a threat. It is very important to take on its challenge through a simple and appealing counter-narrative, which highlights and challenges the threat it represents.

This remains conspicuous by its absence at present. Fifth, the government realises the threat of radical ideology and its adverse impact. However, it must also understand the limited ability of the state to fight the contagion. This can best be done by social groups, NGOs and student bodies, which can reach out easily to the population at large, as compared to state institutions. I have often realised that my children connect easily with their peers and each other when it comes to some of the troubling issues faced by them. Similarly, student groups are better placed to fight radicalism, rather than straight-jacketed thoughts coming from official pronouncements and press notes.

The ISIS may not be a serious threat at present. However, it certainly has the potential to destabilise the social fabric and rule of law in the country. We have often been found wanting in the face of internal security challenges. If the writing is on the wall with respect to the ISIS, this is one instance in which we might as well get our act in order, in order to neutralise the threat well before it gains disturbing proportions.

PROCLAMATION OF CALIPHATE BY ISIS CHALLENGES FOR INDIA

On June 29, 2014 at the beginning of the Holy month of Ramzan (Ramadan), a group called the Islamic State in Iraq and Levant (ISIL) (also known as ISIS), declared the establishment of an Islamic 'Caliphate' in the areas controlled by it in Iraq and Syria. The Caliphate was subsequently rechristened 'Islamic State (IS)' and their leader Abu Bakr al-Baghdadi proclaimed 'Caliph'. The group's spokesman Abu Muhammad al-Adnani said in a statement, 'He is the Imam and Khalifah (Caliph) for the Muslims everywhere,' and asked all Muslim groups around the world to pay allegiance to him. 'It is incumbent upon all Muslims to pledge allegiance to (him) and support him...The legality of all emirates, groups, states, and organizations, becomes null by the expansion of the Khalifah's authority and arrival of its troops to their areas,' the statement added. Earlier in June, in a lightening advance, ISIS had captured areas in western and northern Iraq and amalgamated them with areas of northern and eastern Syria that had been under their control for nearly two years.

Charles Lister, Visiting Fellow at the Brookings Doha Centre, considers the announcement of the restoration of the caliphate as the most significant development in international jihadism since 9/11. The rise of ISIS and the proclamation has raised serious concerns not only in the Middle East but also around the globe.

Nostalgia of caliphate and international jihad

The idea of caliphate evokes a deep nostalgia for Islam's glory and power in the minds of Muslims around the world, Indian Muslims being no exception. This coupled with the present state of the Muslim Ummah characterised by political instability, economic and technological backwardness and perceived domination of Muslim regimes by the west, fuel a desire to 'revert' to the 'golden' age of the caliphate amongst many Muslims. Many Salafist theoreticians, prominent amongst them being Maulana Maududi and Syed Qutb in their writings have proclaimed the establishment of the caliphate as divinely ordained. They also lay down the 'divine' plan for the establishment of the caliphate.

These Salafists divide history into two parts, the period of 'jahiliyyah' (ignorance) and the period of 'Islam'. The present world is the world of 'jahiliyyah' which will be followed by the world of Islam. To achieve the world of Islam, 'jihad' has to be carried out in three stages, the first being the strengthening of one's faith (adherence to Salafist Islam), the second 'hijrat' (moving from 'infidel' communities to 'faithful' communities) and third 'jihad'. It is not surprising then that the ISIS has been using social media and YouTube as propaganda tools that show Muslims from around the world congregating in the areas controlled by it, burning their passports (hijrat), pledging allegiance to the caliphate (IS), and eulogizing jihad. The video posted shows these jihadis from foreign countries threatening their country of origin with jihad once they return.

The virus of international jihad has not affected Indian Muslims much to the chagrin of international jihadist organizations like the Al-Qaeda. Al-Qaeda has generally failed to win recruits in India; so much so that an Urdu video posted onAs-Shabab (media wing of Al-Qaeda) featuring the militant cleric Maulana Aasim Umar, in June 2013 asked the Indian Muslims in frustration, 'Why is there no storm in your ocean?' As per a newspaper report ('Al-Qaeda's Indian dilemma', Tufail Ahmed, 27 June 2013, New Indian Express), 'in the years after 9/11 only three Indians reportedly got entangled in international jihadi networks: Kafeel Ahmed, a Bangalore-born Muslim who was raised in Saudi Arabia, died carrying out a car bombing at the Glasgow airport; Dhiren Barot aka Abu Musa al-Hindi, a Vadodara-born Hindu who got radicalized in Britain, converted to Islam and is imprisoned over his role in jihad; Mohammad Niaz, who was arrested in Paris and is believed to have ties to the Students Islamic Movement of India. These cases of jihadi radicalization occurred abroad (not in India).' However, the situation may have changed recently with some Indian nationals having joined the Al-Qaeda. Indians have been seen training with other Al-Qaeda terrorists in the propaganda videos released by As-Shabab. Following the arrest of alleged Indian Mujahideen operative Yasin Bhatkal last August, investigators found evidence of two youths from Azamgarh in UP having gone to Afghanistan to join al-Qaeda and 'fighting in Afghanistan-Pakistan border'.

The aim of the IS caliphate is to establish Islamic world domination of which India forms a part. The map released by the IS shows India under the 'Islamic State of Khorasan' which comprises areas of Iran, the Central Asian republics, Afghanistan and Pakistan. It would be worthwhile to mention here that the region of 'Khorasan' holds a very important place in the idea of Jihad and is rooted in 'faith'. It is said that Prophet Muhammad (PBUH) prophesized that ancient Khorasan would be the initial theatre of war for the 'End of Times' battles. This initial battle ground also incorporates 'Ghazwa-e-Hind', or the battle of India. Syed Saleem Shahzad in his book 'Inside the Al-Qaeda and the Taliban' argues that it is because of this belief that Al-Qaeda, despite being an Arab organization chose South Asia and Afghanistan as the areas to start its jihadist struggle. He writes, 'It is part of Islamic faith that the Prophet's predictions will come to pass, and once the Muslim armies have won the battle ofKhorasan and India, they will march to the Middle East to join forces with the promised Mahdi (the ultimate reformer), and do battle against the Antichrist and its Western allies for the liberation of Palestine.'

Radicalization of Muslim youth

The establishment of IS has raised genuine concerns in the Indian security establishment about the radicalization of Indian Muslim youth. The New Indian Express (Intelligence fears Iraq conflict tremors in India, 6 July 2014), quoting intelligence sources reported that 'Indian agencies have also warned of Al-Qaeda al-Hind (AQAH) penetration and alleged tie up with SIMI and Indian Mujahadeen (IM) to carry out terror activities in India. An offshoot of Al-Qaeda, AQAH is said to be involved in recruiting terror cells in IM's fertile ground in Bihar, UP and Rajasthan to carry out Jihad in Syria and Iraq.'

There have been reports of Indian nationals fighting with the ISIS in Syria and Iraq. A Tamil Nadu born Singapore resident,Haji Fakkurudin Usman Ali was reported to be fighting for the ISIS in Syria. Ali is believed to have been radicalised by another man from

Tamil Nadu called Gul Mohammad Maraikar, who was deported to India recently. The Times of India (June 9, 2014) reported that Indian agencies were monitoring the activities of 18 Indian youth currently based in Iraq and Syria over their suspected involvement in sectarian violence in these countries. Similarly Indian Express (July 14, 2014), reported that four youths from Mumbai had joined the IS to wage jihad. Though the figures may not be large the government is wary that these youths, on their return may unleash violence in India.

As an on and off reader of Urdu newspapers, I find the attitude of the Urdu press to the IS generally ambivalent if not 'favourable'. They have generally projected the IS in a favourable light. The comment by one of the nurses who returned to India wherein she said that they were treated well by their captors was given prominent front page coverage. However, reportage on the excesses of the IS, like killings of the Shias, destruction of their mosques and atrocities committed on minorities were generally muted and found limited news space. Such articles and op-eds may end up giving further legitimacy to the IS in the eyes of the Indian Muslims especially of the majority Sunni sect.

Jihad in Kashmir and cross border terrorism

The rise of IS may give a fillip to the jihadi forces in Kashmir and cross border terrorism. There are historical linkages between ISIS and Pakistani terrorist organisations. ISIS traces its origins to Jama'at al-Tawhid wal-Jihad (JTJ) and later Al-Qaeda in Iraq (AQI), founded by Abu Musab-al Zarqawi. Zarqawi is said to have moved to Pakistan at the age of 23 to participate in the Afghan Jihad and lived in Hayatabad area of Peshawar. He was hosted by Lashkar-e-Janghvi (LeJ)and is said to have trained their cadres in his training camp on the Pakistan-Afghanistan border. It was in Pakistan that he came in touch with Al-Qaeda leaders and also adopted the fundamentalist Salafist Islam. Later he developed differences with the top Al Qaeda leadership of Zawahiri and Bin Laden. They disowned him for the indiscriminate killings of Muslims in Iraq. During his stay in Pakistan (till 1999), is said to have deeply influenced the cadres of Lashkar-e-Taiba (LeT) and Lashkar-e-Janghvi (LeJ). No wonder on his death by drone strike (7 June

2006), Jamat-ud-Dawa (renamed LeT) held a funeral meeting for him in absentia. (10 June 2007). The current leader if IS, Abu-Bakr al Baghdadi, is a disciple of Al-Zarqawi.

A study of the social media feeds of radical Sunni organisations like the Sipah-e-Sahaba and Lashkar-e-Janghvi of Pakistan reveal that they are supportive of the IS. A splinter group of Taliban, Tehrik-e-Khilafat of Pakistan has already pledged allegiance to the IS and has promised to raise the Islamic flag in South Asia andKhorasan. The Chairman of the United Jihad Council (UJC), Syed Salahuddin has sought help from Al- Qaeda and other transnational jihadi organisations in their struggle to liberate Kashmir. 'If Al-Qaeda, Taliban or any other organisation extends a helping hand to the Kashmiris, we will welcome it', he said, accusing the Indian army of running a 'reign of terror' in Kashmir. Though the IS was not overtly mentioned, reading between the lines and the timing of the statement makes it clear that the exhortation was as much to the Al Qaeda/Taliban as to the IS.

Sectarianism and Shia Sunni conflict

The ISIS is a rabidly sectarian Sunni organisation. Post the takeover of major towns in western and northern Iraq, ISIS spokesperson Abu Muhammad al-Adnani pledged to transform Iraq into a living hell for 'the Shia and other heretics' and called upon the destruction of Shia holy sites of Najaf and Karbala. In response Ayatollah Sistani; Iraq's highest ranking Shia cleric gave a call to arms to all able bodied Shias to protect these holy sites. This qualifies as his most radical fatwa to date. Ayatollah Sistani had urged restraint to his followers even during the US occupation of Iraq, his commitment unwavering even during the attack on Al-Asqari mosque in the Shia holy city of Samara.

Intelligence agencies fear that the ripples of this sectarian conflict may soon be felt in India. On June 19, 2014, Shia and Sunni youths clashed in the Sadatgunj and Talkatora areas of Old Lucknow over the activities of ISIS in Iraq. Uttar Pradesh Local Intelligence Unit (LIU) reported that Shia organisations in several districts in UP were trying to persuade young boys to fight in Iraq by offering them monetary benefits. Times of India reported (June 26, 2014) that 'an organization called Anjuman-e-Haideri has started recruiting volunteers pledging to protect Shia holy shrines in Iraq. Hasan Haider, an executive member of the group claims that more than 20,000 people have registered so far from all over India and, if granted visas, will go and serve in Iraq.' Such sectarian conflicts do not augur well for peace in India.

Impact on Indian economy

Middle East is extremely important for India geo strategically; its stability in India's core national interest. India depends on the Middle East for much of its energy requirements and any increase in global oil prices may put a severe strain on India's current account deficit and lead to inflationary pressure. India also has a large diaspora in the Middle East which remits nearly 30 billion dollars. Any instability in this region does not augur well for India. So far, much to the relief of Indian policymakers the conflict remains confined to the Iraqi theatre. However the situation could change. There are disturbing reports of ISIS participating in the current Israeli Palestinian conflict in Gaza. If the theatre of conflict expands and other countries drawn into conflict, Indian economy may be impacted negatively.

In conclusion it can thus be said that the rise of the IS poses major challenge to India's internal security and economic interests. Indian security agencies need to adopt a proactive approach in responding to these security challenges. To check radicalization of the Musim youth, authorities have to initiate a dialogue with every sections/sects of the Muslim society. The Ulemas and elders of the Muslim community have a responsibility to check the growth of these radical tendencies. Thankfully, none of the Muslim leadership /Ulemas in India has supported the announcement of Caliphate by IS. India also needs to diversify its crude basket and remain engaged with the governments of the Middle East so that its energy supplies are not disrupted and the Indian diaspora remains safe.

9

Modi Make India a Global Superpower

PRIME MINISTER NARENDRA MODI has moved on a number of fronts during his first year in office and has achieved some success. While the focus has understandably been on what his measures mean for India, the fact is that they have global implications of the first order. Developing countries around the world are comparing India and China, trying to decide which model is best for achieving rapid economic growth.

India is the world's largest democracy, and China is an authoritarian regime where political activity is proscribed. Obstacles that routinely frustrate growth in India can be bulldozed away in China. There are no problems with obtaining land for factories or putting up offices and apartments in China. Infrastructure, from power plants to modern highways and bullet trains, sprouts up everywhere. China's economic growth has been on an unprecedented scale in human history: A 17-fold increase per capita since 1980 compared with 4.5 in India.

India must demonstrate that democracy doesn't equate with sluggishness and inefficiency and that free people are capable of internal regeneration and reform.

Indians are proud that this year their country's economic growth may exceed China's. But this should be a routine performance.

There's no reason that India shouldn't achieve real double-digit annual growth rates for the next 20 years. After all, India can combine the best of two worlds: harvesting the immense expansion that comes from catching up with developed countries and enjoying the growth, particularly in exports, that comes from its high-tech prowess. Doing this would not only enormously improve India's living standards but also mean a more humane, democratic and richer world. People around the globe would look to India for inspiration on how they should be governed, on how free people can achieve more progress and enjoy happier lives than those living under dictatorships.

MODI AT FIFA 2014: A GOLDEN BRICS OPPORTUNITY

Brazilian President Dilma Rousseff's invitation for Prime Minister Narendra Modi to attend the final of FIFA World Cup 2014 on the sidelines of attending the BRICS summit may prove a golden opportunity for Modi to share the dais with world leaders and give a boost to his newly-elected Government's strategic ambitions.

The Prime Minister, if he accepts the invite, would be included in the long list of high-profile guests heading towards Brazil to attend the final of the planet's most popular game. Brazil also happens to be among the most football crazy of nations where love for the game is unparalleled.

This summit, scheduled to be hosted by the Brazilian city of Fortaleza, would also be Narendra Modi's first multilateral visit. All BRICS leaders such asChinese President Xi Jinping, Russian President Vladimir Putin and South African President Jacob Zuma have already confirmed their attendance to the biggest sporting extravaganza, where teams from more than 30 nations are playing for the title. Tour to Brazil would give Narendra Modi an opportunity to discuss ways to improve economic relations.

Earlier last week, the Prime Minister had released commemorative postage stamps on the 2014 FIFA World Cup and hoped that the international event becomes a 'bridge for connecting nations'.

While releasing the stamps at his official residence, Modi had said, "Sports bring about a spirit of amity and belonging among nations of the world. May the FIFA World Cup become a bridge for connecting nations together!"

Even RSS Sahsarkaryavah, Dattatreya Hosabale, in his recent article, called the FIFA World Cup a 'unifying sport' which connects people of different strata of the society in almost every part of the world. With its global reach, FIFA World Cup has brought all of humankind close to each other. The game of football is symbolic of youth, its power and its tremendous potential for development in any country.

If the Prime Minister agrees to go, all eyes would be on Narendra Modi's first meet with China's Xi Jinping, who is giving clear signals of wanting to better relations with India ever since Modi came to office. China is expected to leave no stones unturned to woo the Indian PM and boost trade ties as Modi would, at that point of time, have recently returned from Japan's tour.

Modi will be on a tour of Japan between July 4 and 5. The two countries might pledge to work closely towards further development of the Japan-India Strategic and Global Partnership. Thus, Jinping would try to make the most of this occasion and bring the dialogue between New Delhi and Beijing to rest on a more positive note. India-China talks were put on a backburner during the Manmohan Singh regime in New Delhi. Even, the recent visit of Chinese Foreign Minister Wang Yi was a significant move towards the same.

Narendra Modi's meeting with Russian President Vladimir Putin would be the next most important thing to be looked at. India has had very good relations with Moscow and discussions over technology and defence cooperation would top the agenda during the meet between the two. Russia has been India's largest supplier of defence equipment and would definitely want to win Modi's heart.

With Brazil, which is another developing economy like India, Modi could try to boost trade ties as the two have witnessed an upswing in the recent years. Also, from Brazil Modi, known for keenly observing development works, might take some guidelines for developing football-like sports culture back home. It is a known fact that the popularity of soccer is limited to only certain parts of India like Bengal and the North-East. The Prime Minister who once was the chairperson of Gujarat Cricket Association and might take lessons from five-time FIFA champion Brazil's success story in football. India at present ranks 154th in FIFA world ranking. Modi can take points from Brazil to help improve India's performance by increasing the popularity of the sport in other parts of India.

During his electioneering in North East, where football is followed like crazy, Modi batted for developing the region as sports hub. The PM may take some lessons from Brazil for improving sports infrastructure in North East to give the sports a boost. Also, India for the first time will be hosting Under-17 FIFA World Cup in 2017, and PM's visit to the bigger format of the event would only prove beneficiary. This might help India actually dream about hosting sporting events as vast as FIFA World Cup.

Apart from enjoying the World Cup final, Modi, might make the best of the situation by inviting several top leaders to New Delhi for the purpose of enhancing trade ties with other global leaders. Apart from meeting BRICS leaders, the Prime Minister will also get a chance to interact with leaders of other Latin American and European countries.

FOR NARENDRA MODI, FIRST BRICS TRIP A SUCCESS

Prime Minister Narendra Modi wrapped up his first major multilateral visit to a *foreign*country on Wednesday, having separately met China President Xi Jinping, Russia President Vladimir Putin, Brazil President Dilma Rousseff and South African President Jacob Zuma over the last two days in Fortaleza and Brasilia.

In a breakthrough at the Sixth BRICS Summit, *India* got the presidency of the NewDevelopment Bank — the name that Modi endorsed in his departure statement in Delhi— that was launched with an initial capital of $50 billion on Tuesday after the leaders signed the Fortaleza Declaration. While China walked away with the bank's headquarters, which will be located in Shanghai, New Delhi got Beijing to agree on equal shareholding rights for all members. As she headed into last minute negotiations on Tuesday, Minister of State for FinanceNirmala Sitharaman told The Indian Express that India was particular that BRICS countries should have equal shareholding rights in the new bank. India pitched hard for the presidency, and deft negotiations ensured South Africa and Brazil backed India's bid.

Sources said Modi's body language was confident. "His handshakes are firm," said a government official. After his bilateral meeting with Putin, which was immediately followed by the signing of the Fortaleza Declaration, a beaming Modi walked out of the convention centre, seeming satisfied at the outcome of the Summit.

Many of his ideas, like the one on a BRICS University, found mention in the declaration. The declaration specifically mentioned that China and Russia reiterated the importance they attach to Brazil, India and South Africa's status and role in international affairs and support their aspirations to play a greater role in the UN. During his meeting with Putin, Modi appreciated the clarity with which the Russian President spoke on UN reforms. Putin is expected in Delhi for the annual summit in December. Modi has asked him to extend his stay so that he can visit some nuclear construction site also. Meanwhile, in a surprise gesture, Rousseff received Modi with full military honours at the Presidential Palace before their breakfast meeting on Wednesday. "This is a specialgesture since this was not a bilateral visit," said a government official. Modi thanked Rousseff for arranging a meeting of BRICS leaders with their South Americancounterparts, and praised her for the historic summit, given its outcomes.

Sources said Modi prepared well for every meeting. Ahead of his bilateral meeting with the Chinese President, he read up on Xi's experiences before he took the high office. "Such preparation helps break the ice," said an official. With Putin, the PM referred to his visit to Ahmedabad's sister city Astrakhan in Russia earlier.

MODI LEAVES FOR BRAZIL TO ATTEND BRICS SUMMIT

Prime Minister Narendra Modi today left for Brazil to attend a summit meeting of the BRICS nations that will address regional crises and security threats to restore a climate of peace while advancing global economic stability. Modi left Berlin this morning for Fortaleza, Brazil after an overnight stopover.

Usually, Indian Prime Ministers transit through Frankfurt for further journeys across the Atlantic.

Berlin was preferred to Frankfurt for a transit halt on Germany's request for a possible bilateral meeting with Chancellor Angela Merkel but she flew to Brazil to watch the FIFA World Cup final between Germany and Argentina. In a departure statement in New Delhi, Modi said that India looks forward to the BRICS initiative for setting up the New Development Bank and Contingent Reserve Arrangement.

Modi is visiting Brazil at the invitation of Brazilian President Dilma Rousseff to attend the Sixth BRICS Summit being held in Fortaleza and Brasilia on 15-16 July. The Prime Minister is accompanied by a high-level delegation that includes Minister of State for Finance Nirmala Sitharaman, National Security Adviser A K Doval, Foreign Secretary Sujatha Singh and Finance Secretary Arvind Mayaram.

The other priority for India are about the presidency of the bank and the name to be given for it. Apparently, India would like it to be called the New Development Bank, an expression used by Modi in his departure statement yesterday. "I also look forward to our discussions to further advance intra-BRICS economic cooperation and our collective efforts to advance global economic stability and prosperity. In particular, I look forward to the successful conclusion of major BRICS initiatives like the New Development Bank and the Contingent Reserve Arrangement, which have seen significant progress since their launch in New Delhi in 2012," Modi said in the statement. "These initiatives will support growth and stability in BRICS and also benefit other developing countries," he said.

India wants the modalities for the establishment of the bank through a simple route and not a complicated one. It wants to avoid the pitfalls of the Bretton Woods institution of one who pays more calls the tune. During his meetings with Chinese and Russian presidents, bilateral issues may also come up but no big ticket items are likely to be decided since it would be a get to know meeting.

Both Xi and Putin are likely to visit India in September and November-December respectively this year. While with Xi it will be Modi's first meeting, he has already met Putin on earlier occasions. With China, Modi may discuss the need for maintaining peace and tranquility along the border so that bilateral problems can be resolved in an amicable manner. Bilateral trade will also come up for discussion with the Chinese leader and India is keen that the present imbalance in trade should be resolved. Modi is also keen on Chinese investment in India.

It's a long journey ahead, but the dream is as big as big can be. Whether Modi can achieve it depends on a billion-plus fellow Indians and our friends in BRICS nations who constitute 40% of the world's population. The US and Europe watch with certain fear and sufficient, and perhaps justified, cynicism at this 'ragtag group' which right now looks like a heap of bricks rather than the fortress that BRICS nations hope to finally build. Prime minister Modi heads a nation known for a syncretic approach to world powers. President Xi Jinping's China holds the US economy by the scruff of its neck and the US can do little about the lopsided balance of trade. Russian President Vladimir Putin has been the US and Europe's pet hate for years. Jacob Zuma, president of South Africa, hopes to lead Africa in the new power equation. Will the US, the lone superpower in the world, allow these 'upstarts' to 'blitzkrieg' the economic system. Do these BRICS have the guts to challenge the present world system? Neither is possible or desirable right now. What is needed is a 'more just system'. Read more

In the meeting with Russian leader, the continuance of good relations between the two countries be maintained. Russia would like India to continue the good trend in ties that was set up by earlier governments. Russia is also keen to provide technology and is looking for a new site in India for setting up a civil nuclear plant because Haripur in West Bengal is not working out.

Already the nuclear liability issues over Kudankulam plant 3 and 4 units have been resolved. The BRICS summit theme,

"Inclusive Growth; Sustainable Development", will enable India to shape the post-2015 Development Agenda being discussed in the United Nations.

The Prime Minister is accompanied by a high-level delegation that includes Minister of State for Finance Nirmala Sitharaman, National Security Adviser A K Doval, Foreign Secretary Sujatha Singh and Finance Secretary Arvind Mayaram.

PRIME MINISTER TO LAUNCH 'MAKE IN INDIA' INITIATIVE

Prime Minister Shri Narendra Modi will launch "Make in India" initiative on 25th September 2014 from Vigyan Bhawan in New Delhi. The launch will be at both national level, state level and in Missions abroad. The 'Make in India' initiative has its origin in the Prime Minister's Independence Day speech where he gave a clarion call to 'Make in India' and 'Zero Defect; Zero Effect' policy. State Governments, Business Chambers, Indian Missions aboard are playing an active role in the launch of the initiative.

The Government is committed to chart out a new path wherein business entities are extended red carpet welcome in a spirit of active cooperation. Invest India will act as the first reference point for guiding foreign investors on all aspects of regulatory and policy issues and to assist them in obtaining regulatory clearances. The Government is closely looking into all regulatory processes with a view to making them simple and reducing the burden of compliance on investors.

A dedicated cell has been created to answer queries from business entities through a newly created web portal . While an exhaustive set of FAQs on this portal will help the investor find instant answers to their general queries, the back-end support team of the cell would be answering specific queries within 72 hours.

A pro-active approach will be deployed to track visitors for their geographical location, interest and real time user behaviour. Subsequent visits will be customised for the visitor based on the information collected. Visitors registered on the website or raising queries will be followed up with relevant information and newsletter. Investor facilitation cell will provide assistance to the foreign investors from the time of their arrival in the country to the time of their departure. The initiative will also target top companies across sectors in identified countries.

The 'Make in India' initiative also aims at identifying select domestic companies having leadership in innovation and new technology for turning them into global champions. The focus will be on promoting green and advanced manufacturing and helping these companies to become an important part of the global value chain.

The Government has identified 25 key sectors in which our country has the potential of becoming a world leader. The Prime Minister will be releasing separate brochures for these sectors along with a general brochure. The brochures covering sectors like automobiles, chemicals, IT, pharmaceuticals, textiles, ports, aviation, leather, tourism and hospitality, wellness, railways among others will provide details of growth drivers, investment opportunities, sector specific FDI and other policies and related agencies.

Since the new Government took over, a series of initiatives have been taken to revitalise the industrial sector in general and manufacturing sector in particular. To mention a few:

-The process of applying for Industrial License and Industrial Entrepreneur Memorandum has been made online on the e-Biz website 24*7;

-A vast number of Defence items have been de-licensed;

-The validity of Industrial license has been extended to three years;

-With a view to providing flexibility in working hours and increased intake of apprentices for on the job training, the Government has decided to amend a number of labour laws;

-An advisory has been sent to all Departments/ State Governments to simplify and rationalize regulatory environment which includes:

– on-line filing of all returns in a unified form;

– no inspection without the approval of the Head of the Department, etc.

Recently the Foreign Direct Investment policy has been liberalized. 100% FDI under automatic route has been permitted in construction, operation and maintenance in specified Rail Infrastructure projects; FDI in Defence liberalized from 26% to 49%. In cases of modernization of state-of-art proposals, FDI can go up to 100%; the norms for FDI in the Construction Development sector are being eased.

The government is committed to improving the physical infrastructure. Development of dedicated freight corridors and investment in improving our ports and airports are underway. These corridors would house Industrial agglomerations along with smart cities. The private sector would be playing a significant role in these developmental works.

For the manufacturing sector to take advantage of the improved physical infrastructure, the need for having a strong human capital is recognized. Government's effort would be to equip the working age population with the right kinds of skill so that the manufacturing sector finds them employable. One of the first decisions that the new Government has taken is to set up a separate Department of Skill Development and Entrepreneurship.

Various prominent National and International industry leaders are likely to attend the programme to launch the campaign along with Ministers, senior officials, Ambassadors and opinion leaders.

INDIA'S ECONOMIC INITIATIVES: A MAGNET FOR INVESTMENTS

The Bharatiya Janata Party (BJP)-led National Democratic Alliance (NDA) government has introduced a multitude of economic programs since 2014. Make in India remains the flagship initiative; all other development programs seek to complement it. Each new program addresses specific electoral campaign promises, and is followed by a promotional-blitz wherein catchy slogans highlight fundamental aims. The latest one, announced just last week, is Start Up India.

Make in India, Digital India, Smart Cities, Skill India, Housing for All and Start Up India are the government's top priority economic projects. They collectively envision India as a high-functioning economy focused on industry, innovation and entrepreneurship; the promotion of investor confidence; job creation; the development of infrastructure; and achieving total digital connectivity. The effectiveness of these programs, some barely few months old, cannot be fully assessed until they mature over the next several years. However, preliminary assessments can be made on the basis of industry projections, the level of collaboration between central and state governments, the commitment of private sector participants, and FDI flows.

Make in India

India's manufacturing sector is stagnant in comparison its flourishing services sector. Make in India thus aims to boost investment and industrial production to increase the GDP share of manufacturing from the current 16 percent to 25 percent. To achieve this, the government has identified 25 focus sectors for development. 100 percent FDI is allowed in all sectors except Space (74 percent), Defense (49 percent) and News Media (26 percent). A key emphasis of this campaign is improving the ease of doing business in these sectors – faster clearances, transparency for permits and financing, as well as efficient e-governance mechanisms.

Since the launch of Make in India in September 2014, FDI into the country has witnessed a 48 percent jump in the seven-month period between October 2014 and April 2015, and a 31 percent increase, valued at US $9.50 billion, between April and June 2015. It is still early days, and critical infrastructural developments are needed to convert investment into manufacturing gains. Nevertheless, Make in India affirms that India is open for business.

Digital India

India currently exhibits a pronounced digital divide. While it has the second-largest online population in the world after China, more than a billion Indians still lack access to internet facilities. The government is trying to fix this imbalance through its Digital India initiative, which has three core areas – the creation of digital infrastructure, delivery of e-governance and digital services, and spreading digital literacy. Slated for completion by 2019 on the basis of a selective public-private-partnership (PPP) model, Digital India aims to connect 250,000 gram panchayats (village councils) in three years, build a national information infrastructure by March 2017 (at a cost of about US $2.3 billion), and establish public Wi-Fi hotspots among other plans.

The development of this infrastructure will help boost investment in the immediate term. Thus far, US $74.07 billion in investment has been announced for the Digital India mission, along with the generation of employment for 1.8 million people. Indian companies such as Reliance Industries, the Aditya Birla Group, Bharati Airtel and the Tata Group have all pledged investments, while foreign companies such as Google, Facebook and Microsoft are also contributing. Once this digital infrastructure is established, foreign investors will be able to exploit a rise in digital innovation, efficiency and productivity across India's economy and government.

Smart Cities

A huge obstacle in the way of India's development is its problematic infrastructure. The Smart Cities initiative aims to create cities where basic infrastructure is built on a sustainable model. Under the initiative, smart cities should also benefit from assured water and electricity supply, sanitation and solid waste management, urban mobility and efficient public transport, IT connectivity, e-governance and citizen participation and the safety and security of citizens. The Ministry of Urban Development has selected 100 cities and towns as future smart cities – every Indian state has at least one such city. The Smart Cities Council India has been formed and will be part of the U.S.-based Smart Cities Council – a collective of smart city experts and organizations operating in over 140 countries.

The Indian government has set aside US $7.2 billion for the Smart Cities mission, and the money will be released to local urban bodies over five years. This funding will translate into job creation and sectoral growth, raising the profile of respective Indian states as ideal business and investment destinations. In order to succeed, the Smart Cities mission will require complete center-state cooperation, financial accountability by state and local governments, bureaucratic efficiency, effective public-private-partnerships and investment flows.

Skill India

India has a unique demographic dividend. The country has a high proportion of working age population, while accelerated economic growth has increased the demand for skilled manpower. At the same time, India is also a very difficult country to source skilled labor. The Skill India campaign was launched this July to prepare graduates and workers alike for the skills needed by industry. The goal of the program is to train 400 million people by 2022 over the next seven years through the National Skill Development Corporation. The flagship scheme under the Skill India mission is the US $226 million Pradhan Mantri Kaushal Vikas Yojana (PMKVY) that will train 2.4 million youth and certify them through a portable "skill card", which can be scanned by prospective employers. Under another programme, the Skill Loan scheme, loans will be offered to 3.4 million youths to attend skill development programs over the next five years. Additionally, the National Policy for Skill Development and Entrepreneurship 2015 has been formulated, and is India's first integrated national policy for developing skills and promoting entrepreneurship on a large scale.

While Skill India goals will take time to bear fruit, it must be noted that labor reforms and the organization of the informal sector are also necessary. These reforms will further boost the scale and productivity of Indian labor, and allow India's workforce to genuinely benefit from programs like Skill India.

Housing for All

An estimated 1.77 million people live without housing in India, according to the 2011 census. Moreover, 65 million people live in slums – a figure that could rise to 104 million in 2017, by some estimates. Overcoming this housing challenge is the target of Housing for All. Under this mission, the central government is set to build 20 million homes for the urban poor by 2022, which will coincide with the 75th year of India's independence. This will require investments of up to US $181 billion – the state exchequer has already committed US $45 billion. Housing for All will be rolled out in three phases. Altogether, it will rehabilitate slum dwellers and provide affordable housing to the poor through credit-linked subsidy as well as via a public-private-partnership (PPP) model. As of August 2015, the government has identified 305 cities and towns across nine of the 15 states that have signed Memoranda of Agreement (MoA) with the Ministry of Housing and Urban Poverty Alleviation for the program.

The project is bound to boost the economy as the construction sector typically has a huge multiplier effect. But achieving the mission's goal will be no easy task – it necessitates the transformation of existing urban infrastructure, and improving basic municipal service provision for water, electricity and sanitation. It will also depend on city-state relations – bureaucratic approval processes will need to be fast tracked, while authorities will need to ensure that programs actually benefit intended beneficiaries.

Start Up India

In his Independence Day address on August 15, Modi announced the government's latest initiative "Start Up India, Stand up India". The program is designed to promote financing for start-ups and incentives to boost entrepreneurship. Start-ups had already been a part of the government's campaign to promote job creation through entrepreneurship, and it is included in the objectives of the Skill India and Digital India initiatives.

The Start Up India campaign will, however, see another form of assistance to people who want to start new ventures and businesses, particularly those from demographic groups that have experienced discrimination.

Towards this end, Modi has urged banks to provide loans to dalit, tribal and women entrepreneurs. He has also launched the Bharat Fund at the Startup Konnect program held during his visit to the U.S. this week, which will provide seed funding to Indian entrepreneurs in the health, agriculture, financial inclusion, renewable energy, biotechnology and technology sectors. Despite being only a month since its announcement, Modi's recent speeches and talking points during the U.S. trip clearly reflect that Start Up India is a key priority for the government – it will promote institutions supporting entrepreneurs in the country.

MAKE IN INDIA: WILL MANUFACTURERS RIDE THE RED CARPET IN 2016?

2015 will undoubtedly be known as the year that the Union Government pulled out all stops to drive manufacturing growth in the country through Make in India. The big-bang campaign was promoted through world-class visuals and aggressively marketed by none other than our globe-trotting Prime Minister, who has become the country's biggest brand ambassador.

On 12 December, MakeInIndia tweeted,

The confidence, especially against the backdrop of a sluggish global economy, is backed by figures that appear to signal an inflection point for Indian manufacturing. In the past 14 months, the government has received proposals ofRs1.20 lakh crore from companies who have expressed an interest in manufacturing electronics in India. Already, smartphones made in India rose to 24.8 percent of total handset sales in April-June 2015, from 19.9 percent in the prior quarter.

In January this year, Spice Group signed an MoU with the UP government to setup a mobile phone manufacturing unit in the state. Smartphone heavyweight Samsung followed up in February, announcing that the Samsung Z1 would be made at itsNoida plant. Huawei opened a new research and development (R&D) campus in Bengaluru later in the year. Other handset makers such as Xiaomi, Wistron Corp., and Vivo mobile, among others, have set up or announced the setting up of manufacturing facilities in India. Networking major Cisco recently has unveiled three new products that have been conceptualized and made in India.

Homegrown phone manufacturing major Micromax announced it had begun shifting production from China to India. The company is setting up manufacturing facilities in Uttarakhand, Andhra Pradesh, Rajasthan, Madhya Pradesh and Telanganain a bid ramp up domestic production and reduce its dependence on imports from China.

Micromax has been one of the front-runners of the Make in India initiative, by assembling the products locally and quickly ramping up and building complete manufacturing capacity in close partnership with the Government.We are focusing on making India a manufacturing hub and plan to export products from India to other markets. As of today, we are localizing to the extent of 7-8% of our total devices and targetreaching 10% by March 2016."

A Yen to Make in India

While telecom and electronics are the front-runners, the government has also allowed up to 49% foreign direct investment (FDI) in the lucrative defence sector and 100% in railways infrastructure. Alstom and GE have signed agreements with Indian Railways to set up locomotive manufacturing facilities in the country. The government also announced its plan to invest $10 billion in two semiconductor plants to boost electronic manufacturing sector.Foxconn has committed to investing $5 billion over five years in a high-tech semiconductor manufacturing facility in Maharashtra.

In a move that could change India's mass transportation landscape, Modi wrapped up a deal with his Japanese counterpart, Shinzo Abe, to bring in the Shikansen high-speed "Bullet" trains to India with transfer of technology and a Make in India component.

Addressing the India-Japan Business Leaders Forum in New Delhi earlier this month, the Prime Minister said, "Today, there is a Make in India movement in Japan. I have been told that $11-12 billion in funds have been earmarked for it. This clearly indicates how both countries can move forward." Modi added that Japan had committed an investment of $35 billion. Abe too has stated that Japanese companies would get ¥1.5 trillion to support their participation in the Make in India initiative.

And in what can only be described as coming full circle, Japanese car maker Suzuki will import 20,000-30,000 cars manufactured byits Indian arm, Maruti Suzuki, under the Make in India initiative. Amitabh Kant, Secretary,Department of Industrial Policy & Promotion, GOI, tweeted recently, Maruti will be exporting Baleno cars made in India to Japan. We have come a long way! Now need 2 accelerate!" and followed it up with,

"Japanese companies rank India as No 1 most promising investment destination in the medium term."

Schemes for startups

The Prime Minister has also announced the government's Startup India Initiative, which will encourage entrepreneurship among Indian youth at the grassroots level. The action plan for this will be unveiled on 16 January. The scheme is widely expected to get tax breaks at the next Union Budget. WhenModi made the announcement on Independence Day 2015, he said that each of the 1.25 lakh bank branches in the country should encourage at least one Dalit or Adivasi entrepreneur, and at least one woman entrepreneur. Since then, several government bodies and associations launched a number of schemes and initiatives to promote the needs of startups and entrepreneurs. In September, the National Research Development Corporation (NRDC) urged the centre to grant Rs250 crore in seed funding to 500 manufacturing startups.

Dr H Purushotham, Chairman and MD, NRDC said the proposal is being examined by the Ministry of Science and Technology, following which the NRDC would constitute an investment committee and decide the parameters on which investments will be made. NRDC provides value-added services to manufacturing startups under the Programme for Inspiring Inventors & Innovators (PIII) and the Programme for Development of Technologies for Commercialization (PDTC).

NRDC's new-year resolution is to empower at least one manufacturing startup a day so that our contribution adds to the government's Make in India and Startup India initiatives of Government of India," Purushotham told YourStory.

Startups in India can also avail loans under the Pradhan Mantri MUDRA Yojana (PMMY).

'MAKE IN INDIA' CAMPAIGN LAUNCHED TO MAKE INDIA A GLOBAL MANUFACTURING DESTINATION

India's Prime Minister, Narendra Modi, launched the 'Make in India' campaign to tell the world that things are changing in

India: doing business is going to get easier, efficient and transparent. In his Independence Day speech on 15 August, the PM invited businesses from across the world saying, "Come, make in India! Come, manufacture in India! Sell in any country of the world but manufacture here."

Consequently, 'Make in India' is a programme for making India's environment conducive to business. The Government aims to eliminate unnecessary laws and regulations and shorten bureaucratic processes, upgrade physical infrastructure to support growth, open up more sectors to foreign direct investment (FDI), and most importantly, be seen as a true business partner instead of a mere 'permit-issuing authority'.

Manufacturing accounts for only 15% of India's GDP, which is dismal compared to other developing South East Asian nations. The Indian Government wants to raise that share to 25% by 2022 and is committed to transforming India into a global manufacturing destination, while ensuring that goods are manufactured with 'zero defect' and with 'zero effect' on the environment.

The Government has identified 25 sectors that India could become a world leader in and listed growth drivers, investment opportunities, the FDI policy, sectoral policies and specific reasons to invest in each sector. These sectors include automobiles, aviation, biotechnology, chemicals, construction, defence manufacturing, electronics, information technology and Business Process Management, pharmaceuticals, renewable energy, textiles, ports, tourism and hospitality, wellness, etc.

Pro-business initiatives: red carpet, not red tape for investors

India is laying out the proverbial red carpet for foreign investors where Invest India, the Government's official agency, will act as the first reference point for guiding foreign investors with all regulatory and policy issues and assist them in obtaining regulatory clearances.

Measures have been taken to reduce red tape and have an efficient system with online applications for industrial licenses, whose validity has also been extended to three years. The eBiz website, a convenient, single-window IT platform for all Government-to-business services, will work as a catalyst in the investment process.

FDI norms are being liberalised

India's high-value industrial sectors – defence, construction and railways – are now open to global participation with liberalised foreign investment norms. The FDI cap for defence has been raised from 26% to 49% with up to 100% being allowed on a case-to-case basis and foreign portfolio investment will be permitted up to 24% under the automatic route. Up to 100% FDI through the automatic route is now permitted in areas related to railway infrastructure and FDI in construction is also being liberalised to support increasing urbanisation and provide affordable housing for all. Modi also urged Indian business leaders to look at FDI as 'First Develop India' and then as Foreign Direct Investment.

Impetus to infrastructure

The Indian Government is committed to improving manufacturing infrastructure by developing industrial corridors, industrial clusters and smart cities across the country. It has also signed several agreements with foreign governments to assist in the process. With the focus on building a Digital India, the PM also spoke of the importance of 'i-ways' (digital information highways) besides highways.

10

India: The Next Solar Superpower

India grabbed the headlines recently when it announced its GDP growth in the fourth quarter of 2015 at 7.3%. For the fiscal year ending March 2016, India should report growth of 7.6%.

Nonetheless, India is still an emerging economy, suffering plenty of growing pains. Among them is the lack of power throughout the country. Roughly 400 million Indians lack access to basic electricity. Many of the rest suffer through all-too-common power outages.

However, Prime Minister Narendra Modi has pledged to provide 24-hour electricity to all of India's 1.3 billion citizens by the end of his term in 2019. An ambitious target, to say the least.

India Goes Green

The Indian government is targeting an investment of $250 billion into power generation and transmission by the end of the decade. Of that amount, $100 billion would be invested into renewable energies – led by solar power.

Tim Buckley of the Institute for Energy Economics and Financial Analysis has said, "India is executing one of the most radical energy sector transformations ever undertaken."

Luckily, as Buckley said, "The flow of finance is matching the ambition." Over $100 billion in financing has been announced over the past 12 months. India certainly needs it. India's electric grid presently has a capacity of less than 300 gigawatts. It can reliably handle roughly 272 gigawatts, less than 30 gigawatts of which is from renewable energy sources.

Going Big in Solar

Modi has targeted 100 gigawatts of solar power installations by 2022 – a goal which seems unreachable – especially if one considers that the goal is more than twice the current capacity of the two leaders in solar power, China and Germany. But India is forging ahead. Solar projects with nine gigawatts of capacity are already underway. Many of these projects will be online later this year.

The push toward solar energy will make India the fourth-largest market for solar panels over the next two years, according to many estimates. The good news for India is that the country gets a lot of sun. So it's logical that solar players from all over the world are moving in. Solar-related investments in India have soared by 80% in 2015.

Abundant sunlight is translating into the ability of future providers of solar power to charge less for electricity than coal-fired power generators in India. In December, SB Energy won an auction for a 25-year, 350 megawatt solar project in the Indian state of Andhra Pradesh at 4.63 rupees (7 cents) per kilowatt hour.

SB Energy is a joint venture between the large Indian conglomerate Bharti Enterprises, Taiwan tech giant Foxconn, and Japan'sSoftbank Group Corp. (SFTBY). In fact, Softbank has pledged roughly $20 billion to install 20 gigawatts of solar power in India. Other players are also jostling for position in India's solar power market. Local firms include India's Azure Power and Bharat Light & Power. Among the global players entering the Indian market are China's China Group and Sany Group Co. Ltd., along withSunEdison Inc. (SUNE). The latter also recently won a contract in the same state for a 500 megawatt project at the same 4.63 rupee per kilowatt hour rate.

HOW INDIA CAN BECOME A SOLAR SUPER POWER

There is a "Green Energy Revolution" underway in India that can increase prosperity for millions of poor families by harnessing the abundant and clean energy of the sun. With the right policies in place India can easily become a world leader in solar energy. This solar endeavor could also help address acute power shortages, and make a real difference in slowing the pace of climate change. Since being elected in May 2014, Prime Minister Narendra Modi has outlined his vision for increasing India's renewable energy capacity five-fold from 30 GW to 175 GW, including a boost in solar power generation from 20 GW to 100 GW. The plan is to achieve these targets by 2022. But to do so, India needs a National Energy Policy, Regulatory Programs and innovative financing mechanisms that encourage the development of distributed energy, particularly, applications that combine solar generation with energy storage.

India has already taken positive steps by announcing very aggressive goals to meet 40 percent of its energy needs through renewables by 2030. I firmly believe that, with favorable policies and strategic economic investments, India could meet all of its energy needs through renewables by 2050.

Solar Power Potential in India

India is endowed with abundant free solar energy. Using the country's deserts and farm land and taking advantage of 300 to 330 sunny days a year, India could easily generate 5,000 trillion kWh of solar energy. In other words, India could easily install around 1,000 GW of solar generation — equivalent to four times the current peak power demand (about 250 GW) — using just 0.5 percent of its land. In addition, India can produce over 200 GW from wind power. As economist and activist Jeremy Rifkin said, while speaking in New Delhi in January 2012: "India is the Saudi Arabia of renewable energy sources and, if properly utilized, India can realize its place in the world as a great power — but political will is required for the eventual shift from fossil fuels to renewable energy."

India is both densely populated and has high solar insolation, providing ideal conditions for the exponential growth of solar power as a future energy source. With GDP growing at about 8 percent, solar PV is the only renewable energy resource that can bridge the 'gap' between supply and demand. Solar energy can transform India and help to bring about decentralized distribution of energy, thereby empowering people at the grassroots level and eliminating the need for costly expansion of transmission and distribution systems.

How Can India Achieve Its Economic, Environmental and Energy Goals?

For India, a combination of solar power and energy storage is the answer to true energy independence. For its part, the Indian government has taken several measurable steps toward improving infrastructure and power reliability but, more needs to be done — and fast. Along with expediting the adoption of solar and other renewable energy resources, to secure its energy future India urgently needs to implement innovative policies and financing mechanisms (such as capital and interest subsidies, viability gap funding, concessional finance, etc.) to promote increased use of abundant, sustainable, solar energy.

In addition, micro-grids have the potential to change the way communities generate and use energy, can reduce costs, increase reliability and improve environmental performance. Micro-grids can be used to take substantial electrical load off the existing power grid and so reduce the need for building new or expanding existing transmission and distribution systems.

By implementing the following 10 strategies, India can begin to become a "Solar Super Power":

- Develop National Renewable Energy (RE) Policy - Enact and deploy a comprehensive new energy roadmap or innovative RE policies (e.g., PPAs, Net Metering, FIT, etc.) without delay. In addition, set National Renewable Energy Standards/Policy such as 20 percent by 2020, 40 percent by 2030 and 100 percent by 2050 — to create demand, new industries and innovation, and a new wave of green jobs.
- Invite International Developers to meet the revised JSNM targets of 100 GW of Solar and 75 MW of Wind by 2022 and beyond.
- Electrifying Transportation - Expedite a move to electrify transportation by encouraging expanded use of Electric

Vehicles (EV) and plug-in hybrids, and deployment of solar-powered EV charging stations around the country. Develop and implement time-of-day pricing to encourage charging of vehicles at night and other times when peak demand is low. In addition, launch the public transportation system of the future with zero-emission battery-powered Electric Buses in all major cities to reduce air pollution and reverse climate change.

- Energy Efficiency - Make Energy Efficiency a high priority by expediting the development and implementation of cost-effective energy efficiency standards. To reduce the long term demand for energy, engage states, industrial companies, utilities and other stakeholders to accelerate energy efficiency investments such as large scale nationwide use of LED lamps.
- Utility-Scale Projects - Phase out conventional energy subsidies, and develop a long term plan to replace fossil and nuclear plants with utility-scale renewable generation.
- Innovative Financing Solution - Provide innovative financing (including Tax-Free Solar Bonds or Green Infrastructure Bonds, accelerated depreciation mechanism, and access to credit at globally competitive rates, etc.) to instill more confidence from potential investors and decrease the cost of financing for renewable energy projects. Create and fund a national smart infrastructure bank for renewable energy.
- Develop large-scale "Solar Manufacturing Hubs" in India to facilitate mass production of PV, CSP and CPV equipment.
- Decentralized Energy – Avoid future fossil fuel investments in India and, instead, emphasize nationwide deployment of community scale solar projects (installing 100 million solar roofs, solar co-operatives, and solar cities, etc.) and micro-grids with storage. India's present 40GW solar target should be extended to include photovoltaic panels on the rooftop of every home in India, generating enough power to reduce the country's massive dependence on fossil fuels.

- Develop Energy Storage including thermal, grid battery storage (e.g., Tesla Powerwall home battery backup), compressed air/gas, vehicles-to-grid/home, pumped hydro, fuel cells or hydrogen (H2 - produced from renewable energy only), flywheels, superconducting magnets and super capacitors. Develop a "hydrogen economy" plan. If done successfully, hydrogen and electricity will eventually become society's primary energy carriers for the twenty-first century.
- Establish R&D facilities within academia, research institutions, industry, government and private entities to guide technology development in India.

India's clean energy targets are realistic, desirable and fully achievable. All that is needed now to make this concept a reality is political commitment and appropriate investments and funding for building many more solar power systems, solar farms, hybrid solar-natural gas plants, solar thermal storage and advanced battery-based grid energy storage systems. Excess energy generated from solar could be stored in various forms and then used during times of peak demand. Investment in those technologies would provide an economic stimulus of at least $1 trillion, and perhaps much more if all indirect effects are included. Given its abundant sunshine, India could even use solar power to produce "solar fuels" (e.g., using electrolysis to extract hydrogen from water), which could be exported to meet the voracious demand for clean energy from the big north Asian economies.

Solar energy provides a golden opportunity for India to move toward a 100 percent clean energy future while reducing poverty, ensuring energy security and combating climate change. Solar energy has the potential to propel India forward as a "Solar Super Power." However, for India to meet its future energy needs, it can no longer afford to delay deployment of solar energy.

THE FUTURE OF SOLAR IN INDIA

The real question is whether India – notorious for its bureaucracy – can achieve its lofty goals. Some smart people think it can. The International Energy Agency forecasts India will be *the* driver in solar energy for the next 25 years. BMI Research, part of the Fitch rating agency, thinks India will get to 45 gigawatts of added solar power capacity by 2024. That's short of the stated target, but a nine-fold increase nevertheless. Remember, India is trying to do what Germany did. But in half the time. That means India's ambitions will be a boon for power equipment supplies in general – and not just solar power panel makers. Power grid modernization, for example, should provide a boost for companies like Switzerland's ABB Ltd. (ABB), too. For now at least, India is providing a sunny outlook for the solar industry.

ENERGY SECURITY OF INDIA IN THE 21ST CENTURY

The Genesis

Energy sector has been one of the strategic sectors of the Indian economy since independence. However this sector has been receiving special significance in terms of policy and reforms only after the first oil crisis of 1973. India's energy production and consumption patterns have undergone substantial change over the last five and a half decade.

The policy initiatives taken and the fast technological adaptation have played a considerable role in enhancing the production of energy, whereas the economic growth of the economy which led to faster industrial growth is the factor behind the fast growth and changing pattern of energy consumption. The growth of the economy is directly related to the demand of the energy, more particularly the commercial usage of energy increases with economy moving ahead. This has led to the serious gap between the demand and supply of energy in India. Coal, petroleum and natural gas and power happen to be the important parts of energy sector. Therefore, the analysis of the same is attempted.

The Present Scenario

India accounted for 12.5 percent of total primary energy consumption in the Asia-Pacific region and 3 percent of the world primary energy consumption in 2000-01 . Per capita energy consumption remains low at 486 KGOF (Kilograms of Oil Equivalent) compared with a world average of 1659 KGOE in

1998. Inspite of the low consumption as compared to the global standards, there is an increasing oil and coal imports in recent years with net energy imports increasing from 8% in 1980 to 20% in 2001 which is an area of concern for the Indian energy sector.

Coal

The major consumer of coal in India is the power sector which consumes more than the two-third of the production. The other industries that depend on coal are steel, cement, fertilizers, chemicals, paper etc. India is comfortable with the reserves of this resource. Therefore, it has a dominant position in the economy even today. Three quarters of the total coal reserves in India are concentrated in the states of Bihar, Madhya Pradesh, and West Bengal.

Oil & Gas

Most of the demand of the Oil and Gas emerged from the transportation sector. The industries and agriculture also are the major consumers. However the domestic production is quite not enough to meet the growing domestic requirements. The import dependency reached 73.3% in the recent past. However, the effects of global slowdown were reflected in the Indian economy too and were manifested as postponement of several planned refinery capacity additions/pipelines, and work-in-progress of grassroots refineries. The recent success of the discovery of the Godavari basin in the Andhra Pradesh region has not only improved the energy security of the country by boosting possible gas production by 50%, but also raised the prospects of Indian sedimentary basins in the international arena.

Power

The power sector reforms need to strengthened and made deeper for meeting the rising domestic needs. The increasing demand supply gap, the obsolescence of the installed plants, frequent failures of the grids, rising losses faced by the electricity boards, loss in the distribution, relatively high cost of production are some of the major concerns in this sector. Too much reliance on the non-renewable sources to generate power is also unviable in the long run. India at present has an installed generating capacity of around 107 GW, which is classified further into 70% thermal, 25% hydro, 3% nuclear; and 2% wind & power. A major portion of this installed capacity is still under the government control and only a small portion is owned by private sector. However the situation was quite reverse before independence where the power sector was dominated by private sector presence. Later due to its strategic nature, all the segments of the power sector were nationalized. It is paradoxical that today again we would be seeking the help of private players to meet the demand supply gap. This model is already being followed in certain states of India such as Maharashtra, AP and Orissa.

Sectoral energy consumption by fuel (%)

Sector	*Coal*	*Natural gas Products*	*Petroleum*	*Power*	*Total*
Agriculture	0	1.3	9.5	89.2	100
Industry	73.1	2.4	13.6	10.9	100
Transport	0	0	98.5	1.5	100
Residential	0	1.1	71.3	27.6	100
Others	0	33.9	60.9	5.2	100

Future Trends

With the forecasts of faster growth of the economy in the near future, the demand for the energy will surely increase from all the sectors. The highest demand will for the coal as it forms the major source of energy all over the globe. The estimates show that coal imports will meet 22% of total coal consumption requirements in 2006. The shortfall has to be met by increased domestic production, lest it increases the pressure on the import bill. The demand for oil and power will also be high; this implies that the imports of oil might increase in the future if domestic sources are not exploited quickly. It is estimated that 75 percent of oil consumption needs will be met by imports in the near future. At present, India does not import any natural gas but demand is supply constrained and imports of gas is likely to arise in the coming years. This import dependence not only means huge foreign exchange outflow, but it implies the vulnerability of the country on external market. This results in frequent fluctuations in the domestic economy especially those sectors which are directly dependent on energy imports.

Solutions

India will continue to experience an energy supply shortfall through the forecast applied. The gap has been exacerbated since 1985, when the country became a net importer of coal. India has been unable to raise its oil production substantially in the 1990s. Rising oil demand of close to 10 percent per year has led to sizable oil import bills. In addition, the government subsidizes refined oil product prices, thus compounding the overall monetary loss to the government.

The demand growth at a projected annual rate of 4.6 percent is expected till 2010. This is the highest incremental energy demand rate of any major country. In the wake of depleting fossil fuel resources, renewable energy sources such as solar, wind, biomass, small hydro, etc. are emerging as alternative energy options.

The potential for expanding the use of RETs (Renewable Energy Technologies) for energy generation is vast in India and awaits exploitation. Chemical sources of energy such as hydrogen energy, alternative /biofuels for surface transportation, geothermal energy, and ocean energy are also being explored as an opportunity to harness energy in the long run.

Inspite of the slow growth there is a lot of potential in this sector. Though environmentally friendly, the high initial cost of RET has been a major deterrent in harnessing the renewable resources.Indian economy not only is highly import dependent but it also shows high level of geographic concentration in the import of the energy requirements. This calls for diversification of sources of oil imports.

Therefore, the Major Solutions and Strategy that should be followed can be summarized as follows:

1. Development of renewable sources as quickly as possible.
2. Finding substitutes for the energy sources and uses.
3. Development of new technology which will preserve the existing energy and also makes its usage efficient.

4. Try and find ways and means to impart awareness among the people towards effective consumption.
5. Allowing Domestic firms to explore opportunities abroad in exploration and refining so as to earn foreign exchange.
6. Allowing the Foreign Direct Investment in these sectors on a priority basis to enhance the capacity and also share the burden of creating productive infrastructure.
7. Increase the utilization of the domestic energy resources to give a boost to output.
8. Create new capacities to improve the energy infrastructure.
9. Allow more and more private sector participation and reduce the control of government in pricing.
10. Bring about more competition and competitiveness in these sectors.

Bibliography

Ahmad, Imtiaz: *State and Foreign Policy: India's Role in South Asia*, New Delhi, Vikas, 1993.

Anurag Gangal : *Contemporary Global Power : A Modi Perspective*, Jammu, Vinod, 1995.

Azad, Maulana Abul Kalam: *India Wins Freedom*, New Delhi, Orient Longman, 1959.

Behari, Madhuri: *Indian Trade since Independence: Chronology of Events*, Delhi, D.K. Publications, 1983.

Bhatia, Shyam: *India's Nuclear Bomb*, Ghaziabad: Vikas Publishing House, 1979.

Bradley, John. *Learning to Glow: A Nuclear Reader*. Tucson: University of Arizona Press, 2000.

Damrosch, L.F.: *Law and Force in the New International Order*, Boulder, Westview Press, 1991.

Duncan, Francis. *Rickover and the Nuclear Navy: The Discipline of Technology*. Annapolis: Naval Institute Press, 1990.

Freedman, Lawrence. *The Evolution of Nuclear Strategy*. Studies in International Security, #20. New York: St. Martin's Press, 1981.

Friedman, G.: *The Future of War: Power, Technology and American World Dominance in the 21st Century*, N.Y., Random House, 1996.

Ghosh, Arun : *Indian Industrialization: Structure and Policy Issues*. New York: Oxford University Press, 1992.

Heathcote, T. A.: *The Indian Army – The Garrison of British Imperial India, 1822–1922*. David & Charles. Newton Abbot, Devon. 1974.

Henken, Louis, *Foreign Affairs and the Constitution*, NY, 1972.

Jha, Prem Shankar: *India: A Political Economy of Stagnation*, Bombay, Oxford University Press, 1980.

Jones, W.H.: *The Government and Politics of Indian Army*, London, Hutchinson, 1971.

Leo Tansky, *US and USSR Aid to Developing Countries: A Comparative Study of India, Turkey, and the UAR*, New York, 1967.

Majumdar, R. C.: *An Advanced History of India*, New York, St. Martin's Press, 1967.

Mary, W.: *Asian Power and Politics: the Cultural Dimensions of Authority*, Cambridge, Belknap Press, 1985.

Mathur, Krishan D.: *Conduct of India's Foreign Policy.* New Delhi: South Asian Publishers, 1996.

Morris, W.H.: *The Government and Politics of India*, London, Hutchinson, 1971.

Narula, Sanjay : *Indian Politics*, New Delhi, Murari Lal and Sons, 2007.

Nininger, Robert D. *Minerals for Atomic Energy*. New York: D. Van Nostrand Company, Inc., 1954.

Noorani, A.G. : *Indian Political Trials : 1775-1947*, New Delhi, Oxford University Press, 2005.

Prasad, Lal Bahadur : *Indian Political System and Law*, New Delhi, Shree, 2005.

Roger, Alexander: *Battle Honours of the British Empire and Commonwealth Land Forces 1662–1991*. Crowood Press. Marlborough. 2003.

Vohra, Ranbir. *The Making of India: A Historical Survey.* Armonk, N.Y.: M. E. Sharp, 1997.

Yasin, Mohammad : *Indian Politics : Processes, Issues and Trends*, New Delhi, Kanishka, 2004.

Index

A

Asian Foreign Policy, 135.
Asian Super Power, 147.

B

Balance of Power, 21, 28, 31, 38, 52, 82, 108, 120, 125, 151, 224, 258, 271.
BRICS Opportunity, 264.
BRICS Summit, 134, 266, 267, 268.

D

Diplomacy, 24, 25, 28, 48, 50, 51, 130, 132, 134, 141, 150, 154, 228.

E

Economic Power, 33, 84, 151, 210, 212.
Economic Reforms, 3, 158, 161, 169, 173, 186.
Emerging Superpower, 1.
Energy Security, 27, 80, 155, 230, 287, 289.

F

Foreign Policy, 19, 20, 21, 29, 32, 34, 35, 37, 45, 46, 47, 48, 49, 50, 58, 96, 97, 99, 100, 101, 102, 103, 104, 105, 106, 123, 126, 127, 129, 130, 131, 132, 133, 134, 135, 136, 138, 144, 151, 152, 153, 154, 155, 238, 243.

G

Global Economy, 11, 25, 53, 135, 152, 153, 277.
Global Power, 34, 35, 86, 94, 95, 96, 97, 98, 104, 157, 158, 192, 223, 224.
Global Power Shift, 200.
Global Response, 34.
Global Superpower, 263.
Great Power, 19, 147, 149, 150, 193, 197, 284.
Growing Soft Power, 54.

I

Indian Economic Power, 156.
Indian Economic Reforms, 173.
Indian Force, 58.
Indian Infantry, 55, 57.
Industry Development, 73.
Internal Security, 57, 210, 220, 228, 235, 236, 237, 238, 242, 246, 247, 253, 256, 262.
Investments, 157, 171, 175, 186, 212, 272, 274, 275, 279, 283, 284, 286, 287.
ISIS Attack, 253.

M

Make in India, 144, 270, 272, 273, 277, 278, 279, 280.

Military Modernization, 44, 45, 63, 64, 65, 205, 206.
Military Super Power, 44.

N

Narendra Modi, 105, 106, 126, 130, 134, 135, 136, 264, 266, 267, 270, 279, 282, 284.
Nuclear Power, 14, 34, 35, 67, 68, 69, 70, 71, 72, 73, 74, 76, 77, 78, 79.

O

Opportunity, 19, 110, 112, 126, 134, 143, 150, 169, 171, 181, 182, 202, 210, 238, 243, 245, 264, 287, 291.

P

Power Growth, 67.
Power Plants, 69, 72, 74, 77, 263.

R

Rising Military, 44.

S

Security, 10, 17, 20, 22, 24, 25, 26, 27, 28, 31, 32, 33, 37, 39, 40, 41, 44, 45, 46, 50, 51, 57, 62, 80, 84, 97, 98, 99, 100, 102, 108, 112, 116, 121, 122, 123, 124, 126, 127, 128, 129, 130, 132, 133, 134, 136, 137, 138, 139, 140, 141, 142, 144, 147, 148, 149, 150, 151, 155, 158, 193, 199, 200, 203, 205, 212, 213, 214, 215, 217, 218, 219, 220, 221, 222, 228, 229, 230, 232, 233, 234, 235, 236, 237, 238, 239, 240, 241, 242, 243, 245, 246, 247, 249, 251, 253, 255, 256, 259, 262, 268, 270, 274, 287, 288, 289.
Soft Power, 46, 47, 48, 49, 55.
Solar Superpower, 282.

W

Weapons, 34, 36.

❑❑❑